ECONOMICS AND SOCIOLOGY OF INDUSTRY
A Realistic Analysis of Development

ECONOMICS
AND SOCIOLOGY
OF INDUSTRY

A Realistic Analysis of Development

REVISED EDITION

BY

P. SARGANT FLORENCE

BALTIMORE
THE JOHNS HOPKINS PRESS

Published in Great Britain by C. A. Watts & Co. Ltd.
Copyright © 1964, 1969 by P. Sargant Florence
Library of Congress Catalog Card No. 69-16037

Standard Book Number in U.S. 8018-1066-3

Printed in Great Britain

CONTENTS

1. Nine measurable trends—2. The trend away from agriculture toward industrial and service activity—3. Science applied to industry—4. The increase in staff—5. Widening of markets and supply sources—6. The persistent differentiation of manufacturing industries—7. Four further trends and causal relation between trends—8. The scope of future chapters

1. General economic mobilization: the recruitment of women—2. Changing economic structure and mobility between industries—3. A model for free mobility analysis—4. The economics and sociology of mobility—5. The conflicting forces in adapting to development: a summary

1. Relevance and measurement of industrial location—2. The trend toward industrial urbanization—3. Six propositions in modern urbanization—4. Correlates of industrial location—5. Location measurement as a tool for policy

1. Measures of the size of plant, the upward variegated trend—2. Measurement of the size of firms, the concentration of control—3. Correlates of size of plant and firm—4. Interpretation of the

facts, the law of increasing return—5. Factors limiting increasing returns in particular industries—6. Factors limiting increasing returns in general—7. Management as a limiting factor—8. Limits to labour cohesion—9. Incentives for productivity

1. The firm, its policy and risks in the market—2. The form of government of the firm—3. Economics and sociology of company government—4. The role of National or State Government and planning

1. Identification and contrast of countries developed and under-developed—2. Fitting industry to the resources of underdeveloped countries—3. Resources particular to certain countries—4. Resource patterns common to underdeveloped countries—5. The case of the tourist trade—6. Aid, trade, and planning

1. Conditions for economic success: the tripod for higher living standards—2. Sociological obstacles to growth of production—3. Inequality and limits to the stability and more equal distribution of income—4. The population explosion—5. Summary of fears and hopes for standards of living

1. The need for sociology in development—2. Types of social sciences required—3. Induction, isolation, and indication—4. Integration and interpretation—5. Practical development policy, virtuous and vicious circles

LIST OF TABLES

PREFACE TO THE SECOND EDITION

THOUGH such reprinting is fashionable today, this book is not an assemblage of the essays and articles that I have written in the past. It is, however, an attempt to review and bring up to date the realistic analysis of industry, which has over several years been undertaken by a number of British and United States economists, mostly working independently, though quite a proportion of the authors quoted in my bibliography have been pupils or colleagues at Birmingham. The bibliography includes a few classics, but otherwise is very much an integral part of my review, and its entries, placed in alphabetical order, are referred to in numbers inserted in the text instead of in repetitive footnotes. These references and the review presented in my text match up, I trust, with my title and subtitle.

By the *realistic analysis* of my subtitle I refer, as the phrase was used in the Tripos rubric at Cambridge, to an approach based on observation and records of the *real* facts, but proceeding beyond mere description and empiricism to comprehensive measurement and causal analysis and a hunt for some possible underlying logic.

My own hunting has found the type of work being done (including its technology, demand catered for, and sources of supply drawn from) as a main factor determining the characteristics of different industries—even their form of government.

In bringing out an edition with more United States illustrations added to the British, I am not just pointing out again the similarity of the location patterns, size-of-plant structure and ownership and control in the corresponding industries of the two economies as I did in my *Logic of British and American Industry*. I am taking these similarities a step further as evidence of the prevailing influence of the type of work done, and its input–output, supply and demand setting, over geographical, historical, national and political factors.

The pervasiveness of this "ergological" interpretation will, no doubt, be disputed. Be that as it may, the essence of realistic analysis can be brought into relief by contrast with an opposite practice, that of building elaborately upon unverifiable or unfalsifiable assumptions often taken over from "authoritative" writers. Galbraith has quite recently written (219) of the "varied interpretation" to which Marx (and Keynes too!) have lent themselves. "Marx is the only writer since biblical times for whom reinterpretation is not a scholarly pursuit but a profession." When I was a Cambridge undergraduate we learned to worry *not* about what X or Y said, but about the truth; and thanks to the labours of census-takers, registrars of companies, statistical divisions of ministries, and research institutions, the truth, and often the exactly measured truth, can now be obtained about industries and their characteristics. The U.S. classifies all manufactures conveniently and fairly logically into one of twenty "major groups". These comprehensive groups are ranked by certain measured characters in the final table (XIX) of this book. Beside measures of technique, such as capital intensity, and of markets and sources of supply, measures include the size, siting and scope of industries' plants, their merger, growth and fluctuation, and the concentration of control in their larger firms. Testing trends and possible correlations in these measures needs painstaking spade-work without the glamour and status of abstract and pure theory such as deductions from economic man. The economic motive is powerful and is far from ignored in this book, but it should be treated as a plausible hypothesis to be tested rather than assumed as an axiom, as do so many economists—Malthus in his population theory, honourably excepted.

"Painstaking" reads in many critical reviews almost as a term of contempt, but taking pains is not just a matter of observing and calculating accurately; realistic analysis includes being careful to use appropriate indicators of the point *really* at issue and not just some slick, easily handled average measure of the data, and it means, also, checking hypotheses exhaustively. Pain, indeed, comes with increasing cost when all relevant cases have to be comprehensively measured and accounted for, and not just (as "realistic" is often interpreted) some few actual cases cited as neat illustrations. In spite of contempt, this painstaking research has been the approach bringing success to the physical and biological sciences in contrast to the barren results of medieval scholasticism, however fascinating.

Increasing pain has, I suspect, deterred quite a galaxy of economists from realistic research. For one of the most remarkable phenomena is the continuous preaching of what I am preaching and, I hope, practising, by established economists and publicists with so little subsequent practice. Dr. Keynes (107, p. 17) pointed out that Mill, Cairnes, and Bagehot "all insist that the appeal to observation and experience must come in, before the hypothetical laws of the science can be applied to the interpretation and explanation of concrete industrial facts". He himself maintained (107, p. 172) "it is only by the unprejudiced combination of the two methods that any complete development of economics is possible". Unfortunately those able and willing to carry out induction are, here and now, comparatively scarce, nor is university training adequate for any large additional supplies of social researchers. If I may use the economist's own apparatus of thought, induction should have, at present, greater marginal utility than deduction. Analysis must solve not only statistical problems now being brilliantly tackled in social accounting and econometrics but the "peristatistical" problems involved in research design (71, pp. 205–9). Though some contemporary reviewers seem to think only statistical method and "intuition" to be involved, there is still a role for a combination of non-statistical and statistical reasoning in the realistic analysis of practical problems, such as (below, pp. 214–20) the effects of science upon industry, or the population explosion consequent upon successful public hygiene.

Modern industry with its complex structure and government ramifies in many directions and, if it is to be analysed realistically and fully, requires (so runs one of my themes) the co-operation and co-ordination of a number of social sciences besides economics—hence *sociology* in my title. Industrial economics has now to deal more and more with large organizations or institutions and realistic economists such as Farrell (214) and Gordon in his second edition preface (89) recognize as one of the main types of practical problem the effect of social structure, including process of government, upon economic behaviour; the effect, for instance, of control by salaried managers upon pricing or dividends. Recent investigators such as Barna (10) or Mackintosh (125) have brought out the importance of the attitude as well as the abilities of those in control of firms. Nowhere is this more evident than in the risks and uncertainty that have to be faced when planning capital investment, or exports, or when pricing generally, in relation to costs and the demand curve. The controversies still unresolved here might perhaps come nearer resolution if more attention were paid to the bodies and types of persons whose attitude is so important to the growth of the national economy. If the characteristics of an industry are, as suggested, largely ergological, those of the single firm within an industry are largely to be interpreted by sociology and social psychology. To quote Barna (10, p. 48): "Investigation . . . brought to light differences in the attitude of managements, underlying behaviour in basically similar situations. The speed and energy with which firms seized a given opportunity, and the efficiency with which they exploited it, varied enormously and appear to have been associated with the character of the firm."

My subtitle's *development* needs no introduction in these days of "dynamic economics". If institutions and social conventions are important in the developed countries, how much greater are their influence on development in the poor but populous underdeveloped portion of the world! Here the trend in development most urgently needing attention, apart from the population explosion that underlies it, is the rapid urbanization which I have particularly considered in Chapter III—an urbanization unfortunately not always supported by sufficient industrialization. It is in fact becoming a sociological rather than an economic trend due to the insufficiency of tribal or peasant agriculture to support the growth of the rural population rather than any positive industrial attraction. But city custom, breaking down tribal or peasant society, will certainly have its economic, as it is having its political, effect.

Much of the contents of the book was first given as the Charles Beard lectures at Ruskin College, Oxford, sponsored by the Rationalist Press Association; subsequently brought up to date for lectures at the Johns Hopkins University, Baltimore, in 1959 and the Leverhulme lectures at the Royal University of Malta in 1962 and, in 1963, for the first edition. The present edition, using more of the United States data, has involved large additions to Chapters I to V and has enabled me to present a more cogent Appendix. A summary outline of the argument has been added. Where the last dates that I cite are not up to the minute, the slow process of publication, official or otherwise, must be borne in mind; also the fact that many of the more relevant intensive inquiries are conducted only occasionally. But delay in publication is less serious when measuring, as in this book, the structural characteristics and long-term trends than when measuring short-term fluctuations. In fact, the text demonstrates repeatedly the relative stability of industrial structure.

I received much help in writing Chapter IV from Dr. Leslie Smyth of Keele University and in revising Chapters VI and VII from my colleague, Dr. David Wightman. I am deeply grateful, too, to Miss Irene Bowyer for proof reading, indexing and supervising the bibliography (pp. 270–78) which takes the place of footnotes. In preparing the second edition I received further help from Professor Joel B. Dirlam of Rhode Island University and Dr. John Blair, Senior Economist to the U.S. Senate Sub-committee for Anti-Trust and Monopoly, and I am most grateful to Mrs. Rita Lowe for her work on the revised index.

P. SARGANT FLORENCE

Birmingham 1968

SUMMARY OUTLINE OF THE BOOK'S ARGUMENT

FOUR themes run through this book. They are indicated by the words in the title and in the subtitle—*A Realistic Analysis of Development*—and are an attempt to add substance to the somewhat abstract assumptions upon which economists tend to build today.

1. The title *Economics and Sociology* indicates that social sciences other than economics will be used to explain industrial behaviour, particularly when knowledge is needed on the relative importance of ability and motivation, and when questions of organization are raised. A chapter (VIII) is devoted to the relationship between existing social sciences.

2. *Realistic* indicates that the study will be based on observation of facts rather than on deductions from assumptions untested by facts. Its approach is empirical and comparative as between countries and industries.

3. *Analysis* indicates that the facts will not just be catalogued but where possible counted and measured quantitatively, generalized more and more widely, and interpreted systematically in the light of some hypothesis. My main, "ergological", hypothesis is described in Chapter I and summarized below (page xvi). It stems from the wide quantitative differences in the traits of the various industries and determines the sequence of the central chapters.

4. Finally, *development* indicates that the emphasis will be "dynamic"—on changes, processes, and trends, rather than stages, particularly the trends by which an underdeveloped country becomes a developed country. For practical planning, the analysis of industry must look into processes that are circular, ending up as they began. Accepting that more affluent standards of living are desired, particular attention is directed

to "vicious" circles arising out of poverty and leading to a further round of poverty. This forms the basis of practical policies to avoid unemployment and lack of remunerative occupation generally.

I

Sections 1–5. The "development" of an economy is usually taken to mean a trend toward a structure and organization making for a higher standard of living of the population. The most available crude measure is the average income a head. Though still crude, an improved measure of a "standard" which would take account of the distribution of income is amplified later when discussing underdeveloped countries. It is the level above which all, or nearly all, the population lives. Observable with the final trend toward higher living standards are eight associated trends. Five of them can be described as technical or economic and are common to capitalist and communist economies—

(i) The trend away from agriculture toward manufacturing and service activity.

(ii) The application of science to industry resulting, particularly, in mechanization and automation and the more intensive use of capital.

(iii) The increase of staff compared to production workers.

(iv) Thanks mainly to cheaper transport and communication, the widening of markets and of sources of supply. Some countries now live as through-put economies.

(v) The persistent differentiation of manufacturing industries upon which rests my main hypothesis interpreting differences between industries in structure, organization and behaviour.

Section 6. Industries within the manufacturing sector as well as whole economic sectors are differentiated measurably in the Census by a high degree of specialization in their activities and the completeness of their coverage of these specialized activities; and this differentiation is found common to all developed economies. It is not, however, foreordained, but due to the logic

B

of events. Wide measurable differences (given in the Appendix) appear not only between the activities but also between the structure and organization of these various sectors and industries; my underlying hypothesis is that their organizational differences are the fairly logical consequence not only of technology, as stated often enough, but also of more fundamental circumstances or setting of their activities or work. Derived from *ergon*, the Greek for work, it will be referred to as an ergological interpretation. The circumstances include, on the supply or input side, the type of materials and resources to be used (heavy, perishable, uniform) and, on the demand or output side, the type of market to be served (consumer, producer, mass, batch, jobbing).

Sections 7 and 8. Three further measurable trends involve not merely the structure of economic activities, but the sociology of organic structures, namely (vi) the growth of towns, and (vii) of plants or firms and (viii) their government hierarchy. Detailed consideration is postponed till Chapters III, IV and V. Meanwhile sociological factors must be introduced in discussing the need and facts of industrial mobilization and mobility.

II

Sections 1 and 2. The first five measurable trends referring to the relation of individual men and jobs are mainly economic rather than sociological. Really to achieve a higher standard of living, they need, however, a certain total mobilization of human resources, and a deployment requiring a mobility of those resources between different economic activities. Though Engel's Law is firmly established on the facts, and can predict economic activities specializing less on needs and more on luxuries, changes in the composition of a nation's activities to meet new demands are often erratic. Neither mobilization nor mobility necessarily increases with development; neither can be traced in any particular order as definite linear trends. They are introduced in this second chapter, after the five mainly economic trends, because both mobilization and mobility involve sociology and prepare the ground for the three further, more sociological, trends.

Sections 3 and 4. To analyse ability, as well as incentives (affecting the will), to move and to adapt to the changing structure or composition of activities, sociology and especially social psychology must be included in any model of possible influence upon measurable tests of mobility such as labour turnover. Considerable research has established the effect of status and other social as well as economic factors such as earnings, in the role of attractives to move or to stay put for different types of workers.

Section 5. Sociological and economic forces affecting mobility, as other forms of industrial behaviour and performance, are often found in conflict. A summary of these conflicts can be drawn up systematically in the form of thesis, antithesis and synthesis.

III

Sections 1–3. The sixth measurable trend, and the first on the list to involve social as well as economic structure, is that of urbanization and the localization of industries in relation to the population. It is equally evident in capitalist and communist countries, and is partly the reverse side of the trend away from agriculture, but is, more positively, the consequence of the comparative efficiency of manufactures and of the higher wages they offer.

Particular cities tend to specialize in particular manufactures and to grow faster or slower in accordance with the growth and decline of these industries in the national composition; also certain services tend to localize in the largest city for a country or region, and a hierarchy of cities and towns can be observed from the largest metropolitan area to the small market town, each rank specializing in certain service activities. Where agriculture is still the chief industry of a region, the lower ranks of this hierarchy—the market towns and villages—can be observed regularly spaced out on the map.

Section 4. The location quotient and coefficient of localization have been devised for measuring respectively the incidence of particular industries in particular places, and the degree of their localization generally. Both show very wide differences between market- or material-oriented, footloose or swarming industries. These differences are correlated with the industry's sizes of plant. The general rule appearing from the facts is that in dispersed, unlocalized industries smaller plants prevail; in localized industries, larger plants. But two deviations occur from this rule. Dispersed industries are particularly likely to have no prevailing plant size; and in the core of the large cities, and where the materials for an early-stage manufacture are highly localized, there the localized industries have a small or medium plant structure. Thus a city may offer external economies to the several plants of an industry as a large factory offers internal economies in co-ordinating its several departments.

Section 5. To avoid the economic and social disadvantages of urban congestion and suburban commuting as well as unemployment, "unoccupation" and loss of population in particular regions, the location of industries has been planned nationally with the help of the quotients and coefficients.

IV

Section 1. The social structure of industry is a matter not only of site but of *size* and *scope* of activities of organizations such as plants or firms; the seventh trend is a *measurable enlargement of such industrial organizations.*

Four salient features have been observed in measuring the sizes of manufacturing plants: (i) a rise in their output and the power capacity of their equipment, but (ii) only a slow rise in the number of persons employed—in fact owing to the rapid substitution of machines for men U.S. plants appear since 1954 to have levelled off on average in the number each employs; (iii) a variety of plant sizes within each industry, but (iv), for most industries, a distinctly characteristic level of size round which the variety of size occurs so that the industry can be said to have some "prevailing" grade of plant size. In short there is a slow upward variegated trend in size.

Section 2. The sizes of firms show the same features still more markedly since most large firms own more than one plant and, in general, the larger the firm the larger its constituent plants.

The variety of firm sizes (feature (iii)) within an industry is particularly marked and in some industries ranges from no employees at all to over 100,000.

The firm is the unit of government and, though its absolute size is, like the size of a plant, important to questions of cost and efficiency, its size relative to other firms in the industry is still more important, because the question arises of monopoly or oligopoly power. If output is concentrated in the hands of a single firm or a few firms and the concentration ratio is therefore high, as it appears to be in many industries today, price and production may not really be settled by competition in the markets. The consumer may be in some industries no longer sovereign. Prices may be "administered" and the industry governed quasi-politically.

Section 3. Size of plant and of firm appear to correlate positively with mechanization and with high earnings of labour. Large firms show on balance greater stability of profits on capital than do smaller organizations.

Section 4. Interpreting the facts observed and measured, the increased sizes of plants and firms can probably be attributed, though indirectly (as explained later), to the law of increasing return involving the principles of bulk transactions, of massed reserves and of multiples. Certainly, large organization presents possibilities of the full use of more specialized machines and specialists.

Section 5. But the fact of differing prevalent sizes of plants and firms in different industries suggests "ergological" interpretation through their different technology and the different circumstances of the demand and supply for their work.

Section 6. The slowness of the increase in size of plant and firm for industry in general, together with the variety of sizes observed within each industry, points to the indirect relation between the law of increasing return (which properly applies to single lines of production) and the size of organizations which usually include many lines of production. Plants or firms in the same industry may be small because they operate only a few (possibly large) lines, or large because they integrate, diversify or mix a large number of lines, none, however, on a large scale with benefit of increasing return.

Section 7. The orthodox theory is that the inability of management to cope is the factor limiting the expansion of plants or firms to be expected from increasing return. Realistic observation indicates, however, that in some, particularly family, firms no motive to grow exists and that, in others, the top manager has been able to expand operations by delegating work without excessive cost of staff. Motives act through persons moved and results depend largely on the type of manager motivated, whether an owner-manager entrepreneur or a non-owning salaried manager. A model of probable economic, psychological and sociological motives that have made for and against expansion can be set up accordingly.

Sections 8 and 9. Large organizations such as are slowly emerging put a strain on the cohesive behaviour of their members. Measures of labour turnover, absenteeism and strikes disclose departures from cohesion (particularly where work is monotonous) such as Blue Monday absence, green-hand turnover, and restriction of output by whole groups. Measuring in large factories the results of planned incentives to productivity shows that on piece-wages workers produce considerably greater output; but feelings of unfairness in computing the piece-rates set and other psychological factors are likely to engender, on piece-rates, more grievances and strikes.

V

Section 1. The eighth measurable trend is the divorce within most large industrial firms of control from ownership, and the emergence in a Managerial Revolution of a governing hierarchy of salaried managers in place of the entrepreneur or the family business. Where much of the output is concentrated in a few firms, the government of these firms may be responsible, as suggested in the previous chapter, for the industry's price policy and other lines of behaviour, whether, for instance, to expand in the light of the risk of investment in an uncertain and fluctuating situation and, if so, how capital will be raised. All the more reason, therefore, for a realistic analysis of the organization that governs a large firm.

Section 2. The prevailing form of organization in manufacturing today is the "company" or "corporation" with a Board of

Directors nominally elected and controlled by the shareholders. In reality the directors usually co-opt one another and decide without reference to the owners on the major policies involving investment of capital and other large risks. The directors take the risks, the shareholders bear them.

In the management of the large corporations problems arise such as the separation of powers and the delegation of control which, being more familiar to them, political scientists should tackle rather than economists.

Section 3. Considerable research has been carried out on the membership, the distribution of voting shares, and the qualifications of directors in large companies or corporations and the behaviour and policies of these corporations according to their size and the nature of their work. Some revision is called for of accepted theory on profit motivation, sources of capital and distribution of dividend. The modern trend toward greater divorce of control from ownership, brings concentration of government into the hands of a few, often shareless, salaried directors with a growth motivation and a policy of static dividends and self-finance out of the residuary profits. The prices set by a single large firm may hold sway for a whole industry, but the possibilities are still limited "ergologically" by the nature of a firm's work.

Section 4. In the government of industry the State Government always plays some role though varying in strength from detailed planning in communist countries, to allegedly minimum interference in the United States. Midway comes the government role in underdeveloped countries and in the mixed economies of Western Europe with their nationalization of certain industries. Even in its minimum, United States, role we find Government not only protecting industries against foreign competition, but supplying information and auxiliary services to industry. To meet the later phase of industrial development Governments have been trying to cope with situations where the market mechanism for pricing and the allocation of resources is threatened by natural monopolies or by the emergence, which we have traced, of a few large firms concentrating control over much of an industry's whole output and possibly determining prices.

Government policy in the U.S. is to reintroduce competition

and thus restore market mechanism by banning restrictive agreements between firms or breaking up trusts or any firm judged too large; and even in some industries to enforce a certain plane of competition "fair" to all competitors and to consumers. If, as already shown, there is concentration in a few persons of government within corporations, it is doubly dangerous to have a few such large corporations concentrating control over a whole industry.

VI

Section 1. The underdeveloped countries are distinguished by their low average income-a-head but they have a syndrome of other characteristics such as the high proportion of workers in agriculture. Most of them are, in fact, at an early stage in all the measurable trends listed in Chapter I.

Section 2. For success in raising the standard of living of underdeveloped countries, industrialization cannot be adopted indiscriminately. Realistic analysis must measure the feasibility of particular industries and their "fit" to the country's particular resources.

Section 3. Many resources, such as oil, certain metals and favourable climates for cotton or sugar growing, are restricted to certain countries and these can specialize at least on the earlier processes of manufacture. Countries differ also in the size of their market but most underdeveloped countries have a low total income and must look to federation or a common market for a sufficient demand to justify large-plant industries.

Section 4. And most underdeveloped countries lack sufficient capital, skilled labour, management and the auxiliary services for business. The industries actually successful in underdeveloped countries conform to these constraints in human resources.

Section 5. The tourist trade as an example needs less capital and auxiliary services than most manufacturing industry and is exceptional among services in not being tied to the consumers' market.

Section 6. National plans have been adopted by most underdeveloped countries based on feasibility studies and the hope of foreign aid as well as trade. Targets are set for gross national product, total of employment, exports and capital investment. But, besides lack of capital, large economic obstacles to a "take-off" are the high cost of manufacturing with inexperienced staff and workers.

VII

Section 1. The sociological are, however, still stronger than the economic obstacles to the implementation of plans for under-developed countries. To raise the standard of living and indeed to prevent its falling, with consequent starvation, a "tripod" of policies is required: higher production, more equal distribution of income and restriction of population growth.

Section 2. A chief obstacle to production in economies that are largely agricultural is not failure to increase scientific knowledge but the failure to use existing knowledge where small-scale farming is the rule. Further social obstacles are feudal systems of land tenure and the caste system preventing mobility.

Section 3. Income distribution is more unequal in most under-developed than in developed countries and Government policies of redistribution through a welfare programme are made difficult by lack of taxable resources and by national govern-ments in the hands of a rich class.

Section 4. The population explosion in underdeveloped countries is due to spectacular falls in death-rates while high birth-rates are being maintained. The reduction in death-rates has been due to a few experts applying scientific knowledge in the prevention of disease. To reduce birth-rates action is needed by much greater numbers. Most sociologists have stressed the lack of motivation as the obstacle to birth control, but this neglects unduly the part played by ignorance and lack of clinical facilities.

Section 5. In most underdeveloped countries it is now rather doubtful whether the food supply can ever keep up with, let alone surpass, the present rate of increase in population and it is more realistic to speak, still, of "underdeveloped" rather than "developing" countries.

VIII

Section 1. Real development can be helped by the social sciences, since the practical problem is not more knowledge of the physical world but largely one of adaptation of the bulk of the population to the economic requirement of existing technology —use of machinery, larger units of organization, training of management.

Section 2. The social sciences fall into two main types: studies of behaviour such as economics, and studies of the behaving groups and organizations such as sociology and much of political science. Industry with its large-scale monopolistic organizations now requires integration of both types of study for its understanding.

Sections 3 and 4. The processes by which the social sciences have reached and can reach conclusions based on facts may be summed up alliteratively as Induction, Isolation of Factors, Indication, Integration and Interpretation. The least familiar of these processes is the careful use of an "indicator" that is measurable to stand as a proxy for the real, but less measurable, matter at issue.

Section 5. For practical purposes it is essential to single out vicious circles which need to be broken at some point from virtuous circles, which can, thanks often to competition restoring equilibrium, be left alone. With changing technology, circles may change character. Motor transport, for instance, has broken the vicious grip of the old steam railway monopoly. Though the social sciences speak in the indicative, not the optative, mood, various specific aims can be accepted, such as higher standards of living, which under laissez faire often appear blocked by vicious circles. Here the social sciences must study methods of positive interference, by the State or otherwise, to break the circle.

CHAPTER I

ECONOMIC TRENDS IN INDUSTRIAL DEVELOPMENT

1. Nine Measurable Trends

The aim of this book as its subtitle implies is to analyse the important economic and sociological factors in the real world of industry. With a view to practical action, we may then discover the circumstances favouring and limiting industrial development in countries developed and underdeveloped.

Industry refers, as in common usage, to the manufacturing sector and excludes agriculture and mining and most services; but may, when so stated, include building and public utilities. Industrial development is important to all persons except the purely aesthetic or ascetic—keen, perhaps, on the "simple life"—because it appears to have brought with it higher standards of living and ultimately the relief of abject poverty. A realistic measured analysis of the conditions favouring industrialization and the consequential higher standards must begin, to put it alliteratively, by tracing the main *trends, traits* and *trains of events* appearing in the past and present development of the currently industrialized countries.

Development is a continuing dynamic process. The trend of events should be traced first, quantitatively if possible, before the traits or characteristics are laid down that are found at any one stage of the process. J. A. Hobson in his *Evolution of Capitalism* (96) was a pioneer in this quantitative tracing of trends, but since his day the greatly increased statistical data allow more certain and more exact conclusions to be established. When trends and traits are established, we are in a position to suggest and, again perhaps quantitatively, to test the causal train of events and the relationships between trait and trait, trend and trend, trait and trend.

In the historical development of modern economies nine

1

more or less independent industrial trends can be fairly reliably disentangled and measured—

1. The growing importance of industrial and service as against agricultural activities.

2. The application of science (such as in mechanization or chemical treatment) to agriculture, mining, transport, and industry itself, involving investment of capital.

3. The growing proportion of organizers, managers, and research, technical, and administrative staff compared to actual working operatives in industry.

4. Largely as a result of science applied to transport and communication, the widening of the market and sources of supply, especially for manufacturing industries, and the localizing of particular industries in various countries or regions within countries.

5. Partly as a consequence, the differentiation of certain manufacturing industries with distinct characteristics.

6. Urbanization: the growth of industrial cities and conurbations faster than the population generally.

7. Enlargement of the size of industrial organizations such as factories and firms.

8. Emergence of a governing hierarchy of top managers in industry who, even in a capitalist economy, do not necessarily own the capital.

9. Though subject to fluctuations, higher standards of living of the total population.

The nine trends fall into four classes. The first five trends can be studied without reference to any organization of persons. They state some changing relations between individual persons and their activities, occupations, techniques or markets, in short, some change in the "activity structure" of a society, and are mainly economic trends.

The sixth, seventh, and eighth trends, on the other hand, immediately involve bodies and organizations of people and are (in the sense discussed later) largely sociological. There is, however, a further distinction between the sixth and seventh trends, which refer to changes in the "organic" *structure* of industry (particularly the size of its firms, plants, and cities) and the eighth trend, which refers to changes in the *government* of industry, in, as it were, its physiological processes. As we shall see, the distinction is important because all developing countries, Communist as well as Western, follow a certain pattern in the anatomy of their industry in the sixth and seventh as they do for the first five trends, but their trend in the form of government follows no single pattern. A particular example of this is that, though control by management has emerged, the Russians have not, since their Revolution, developed the joint-stock company or corporation now so characteristic a form of Western industrial government.

The ninth trend, the rise in standards of living, is largely the consequence of the other eight. Like the eighth a class by itself, it is the aim of policy in developed and underdeveloped countries, and its achievement is thought of as "progress". Three significant features in this progress have been established by statistical measurement. The first is that the countries at present rich are in a sense *nouveaux riches* and have advanced rapidly in income-a-head during the course of the last half-century—a result that may give hope to the countries at present poor. In terms of constant prices (level of 1963) the U.S. national gross product a head examined during periods of years has shown a continuous and fast rise. From an annual average of $577 in the decade 1869–78, it rose by 90 per cent to $1,087 in 1899, by 60 per cent to $1,757 thirty years on in 1929, and by 75 per cent to $2,870 in a similar thirty years to 1959. In the sixty-five years 1899 to 1964 the annual per cent change in gross national product has been calculated as 1·6 per cent a head of population (217, p. 57).

In Britain (151) national income-a-head has risen in terms of constant prices (level of 1900) from an average of £25·7 in the five years 1870 to 1874 to £41·5 in 1900–4 (a rise of 61 per cent in the thirty years) and to £56·0 in 1934–8 (a rise of 34 per cent in the thirty-four years). Since then, till quite recently, the trend has accelerated again and the rise may be reckoned at almost 75 per cent for the last half-century.

The second feature in progress, statistically established, is that the year-to-year course of the trend was by no means smooth, and it is for this reason that five-year periods have just been compared. In the United States falls in product per head of 3 per cent occurred for the whole decade 1929 to 1939 and more recently a fall of 3·1 per cent in the one year 1957–8. In Britain, apart from the years of war, falls in income-a-head in any one year of over 2 per cent (associated with the slump phase of the trade cycle) occurred in 1879, 1892, 1903, 1908 and again in 1921. This instability exposed all persons engaged in industry to financial loss or to unemployment and is, possibly, a price to be paid for the rapid long-run trend due to the application of science. Economists differ as to the fact of this possible connexion or the reasons for it, but Schumpeter (172) has made out a strong case for attributing trade cycles under the capitalist system to a concentration of scientific innovations at certain times.

The third and, for us, most significant feature of the rise in living standards statistically measured is the tremendous distance the poorer underdeveloped countries have to travel before they reach the *present* level of the rich or, indeed, any of their very recent past levels. To be sure, national income-a-head is a less satisfactory indicator of differences *between* countries than it is between periods in *one* country, and the deficiencies of this measure are discussed later (VI, §1). It will be found far from worthless, however, and Table I gives the measurements published by the United Nations in 1949 and 1957 for the ten richest and poorest countries and five large countries in the middle. The same measures calculated by Rodan and brought up to 1964 by Higgins (223) are also given. The table is the key to much of this book, and its salient features must briefly be surveyed.

The difference between income-a-head a year in the United States and Burma, the highest and lowest given in the table, was, in 1957, as 100 to 2·3. In this scale Britain came seventh, with about 45 per cent, and India came near the bottom, with 3 per cent of the United States income-a-head. The significant fact is that differences between rich and poor countries seem not to have narrowed; and, certainly, hopes of a rapid rise from poverty have so far been disappointed.

Few countries have had the same amount of research devoted to them as the United States or Britain and when some of these poorer countries are being dealt with, it is not possible to measure rise or fall in income-a-head so exactly. The fourth column of Table I is thus only a rough index measuring the trend in each country between 1949 and 1957 compared with the "world" total for sixty-two countries where data were available in the two years. This world income-a-head rose between the two years mainly because of inflation, from $327·3 to $500·0 or by 1·53. The proportionate rise in each country's income-a-head is then expressed as a percentage of this ratio. Thus Burma's income-a-head rose from $36 to $48 or by 1·33. This is 87 per cent of 1·53. The advantage of these index numbers, given in column 4, is that, according as they stand below or above 100, they show at a glance whether the income-a-head of a country has fallen or has risen *relatively* to the world.

The 1964 data continue to show the widening gap between the richer and poorer nations. Burma, instead of the 2·3 per cent of the U.S. income-a-head in 1957, had in 1964 2·0 per cent. The (unweighted) average income-a-head of the ten highest-income countries was in 1957, $1,190; of the lowest-income countries $81·6, i.e. 6·8 per cent. In 1964 average income of the same ten higher-income countries was $1,788; of the same low-income countries $111·3, i.e. 6·3 per cent. The limited significance of their exact positions in this so-called league table of the underdeveloped countries will be discussed in Section 1 of Chapter VI, devoted to their industrialization.

The fifth column of Table I gives the percentage of the total occupied population that is engaged in agriculture. The close correlation of low income-a-head with high percentage in agriculture will be seen at a glance. None of the ten countries lowest in income-a-head has an agricultural percentage below the 54 per cent of Peru, and none of the ten countries highest in income-a-head has an agricultural percentage above Norway's 24 per cent. If all countries with sufficient data are included, the correlation of poverty with high agricultural occupation is extremely close.

The significance of the birth-rates and expectation of life in the last columns will be discussed later (in Chapter VII) when dealing with sociological limits to economic development.

Income-a-head by which countries are being compared is not the same as productivity-a-worker, particularly where productivity refers only to manufacture. Besides differences in productivity and the rate of change of productivity in different economic activities, divergence is also due to the proportion of

TABLE I

COMPARISON OF DEVELOPED AND UNDERDEVELOPED COUNTRIES
in respect of Income-a-head, Percentage in Agriculture, Birth-rates and Life Expectation

Countries	Income-a-head a year			Percentage Change Relative to World 1949–57	Percentage in Agriculture 1957 or nearest year	Birth-rate (crude) per 1,000 Population 1957 or nearest year	Male Expectation of Life, at 0 Life-table previous to 1957
	$ *1964	$ 1957	$ 1949				
		(1)	(2)	(3)	(4)	(5)	(6)
Ten with Lowest 1957 Income-a-head							
Burma	65	48	36	87	69	50·0	N.A.
Pakistan	73	52	51	67	70	43–46†	N.A.
India	80	62	57	71	69	39·1	32·4
Nigeria	84	69	67	67	N.A.	49·2	N.A.
Bolivia	104	69	55	82	N.A.	34·9	49·7
Congo	103	74	52	93	84*	38·1	37·6
Thailand	113	85	36	155	75	34·2	48·7
Egypt	150	112	100	73	73	37·8	35·6
Ceylon	130	116	67	113	57*	37·3	60·3
Peru	209	123	100	81	54	37·2	46·1
Average	111·1	81·6	62·1	88·3	65	41·9	44·3

All (5) Other Countries (with Population over 40 m.)							
Brazil	287	251	112	147	56	43·0	39·3
Japan	498	252	100	165	33	17·3	65·2
Italy	714	403	235	112	35	18·1	63·7
W. Germany	1,275	741	320	152	12	17·0	64·6
France	1,306	847	482	115	20	18·5	65·0
Ten with the Highest 1957 Income-a-head							
Denmark	1,360	869	689	83	19	16·8	69·9
Norway	1,306	914	587	102	24	18·0	71·1
Belgium	1,571	920	582	103	11	17·0	62·0
United Kingdom	1,371	954	773	81	4	16·5	67·6
Australia	1,755	1,074	679	103	17	22·9	67·1
New Zealand	1,611	1,166	856	88	20	26·2	68·3
Switzerland	1,799	1,223	849	94	20	17·7	66·4
Sweden	1,806	1,267	780	105	19	14·5	70·9
Canada	2,148	1,458	870	110	19	28·3	66·3
U.S.A.	3,242	2,101	1,453	95	12	25·0	66·4
Average	*1,788*	*1,190*	*812*	*96·0*	*16½*	*20·3*	*67·7*
THE WORLD	—	500	327·3	100	—	—	—

Sources: (1) and (2). Sixty-two countries are listed by Andic and Peacock, *see* Bibliography (4). The top and the bottom of this table gives the ten now independent countries with the highest and with the lowest income-a-head in 1957. In the middle of the table all other countries (5) with over 40 million population are listed. Countries in the Communist bloc and all with population below 2 million are omitted.

(3) The world change from 327·3 to 500 is an increase (mainly due to a fall in the purchasing power of the dollar) of 152·6 per cent. The column gives the change in each country as a percentage of the world change.

(4)–(6) *United Nations Demographic and Statistical Yearbooks*, 1957–9.

N.A.   Not Available

* Higgins, *Economic Development*, 1967, (223, pp. 851–4).

† Estimate for 1962 (183, 1966) Birth-rates not published for earlier years.

C

heads in a population which are those of workers. One country's working force may per worker be 10 per cent more productive than another's, but if 20 per cent less of its total head of population is at work, that country's standard of living—its average production *per head of population*—will be the lower. Increasing the proportion of the population at work is not one of the linear trends in development. Spreading education and raising the school-leaving age (an index of higher development) will, for instance, lower the proportion at work. This proportion and the factors in its determination will, therefore, be taken up in the next chapter as a question, largely sociological, of economic mobilization.

Anticipating this next chapter and the two chapters (VI and VII) devoted to the underdeveloped economies, it can be stated that the range of difference between the productivity-a-worker of different countries is narrower than the range of differences in income-a-head. In the underdeveloped countries the workers usually form a smaller proportion of the total population and more of them are in agriculture. If we confine attention to *manufacturing* productivity-a-worker, the range of difference is still narrower. The underdeveloped countries have a particularly low income-a-head because their rather lower manufacturing productivity-a-worker is diluted by a higher proportion of relatively low-value-producing agriculturists and further diluted by a higher proportion of their population being unoccupied. In short, the underdeveloped countries have only a small band of workers engaged in the high-value-producing manufacture, the rest doubly dilute the standard of living by working in low-producing agriculture or not working at all.

2. THE TREND AWAY FROM AGRICULTURE TOWARD INDUSTRIAL AND SERVICE ACTIVITY

The trend away from agriculture and into industrial occupations is so universally measurable that, exceptionally, Russia has been included. Table II traces the trend in England and Wales, the United States, and the U.S.S.R. and reveals that in England agricultural employment in 1960 had been reduced to as low a proportion as 4 per cent of the total employed. At

first there was a corresponding rise in the proportion in manufacture, but later a slowing down of this rise.

Mining and building occupied normally only a small percentage of the population and show little trend. The remaining
proportion of the occupied population—occupied in services—
is rising. These facts appear to support the "law of tertiary production" formulated by Fisher (52, pp. 25–31) and developed

TABLE II

PERCENTAGES OF OCCUPIED POPULATION ENGAGED IN
AGRICULTURE: PAST AND PRESENT IN DEVELOPED
COUNTRIES, PRESENT IN UNDERDEVELOPED
CONTINENTS

	England and Wales	U.S.A.	Russia	Underdeveloped continents or countries			
1821	34						
1841	22						
1861	18						
1880–1	12	49					
1900–1	8	37					
1920–1	7	27					
1930–1	6	21	(1928) 80				
1940–1	—	18	(1937) 56				
1949–51	5	12	(1955) 43	Asia	70	S. America	60
				Africa	74	C. America	67
1965	4	6		India	70	Indonesia	66
				Pakistan	74	Egypt	55
				Mexico	52	Brazil	52

Sources
Col. 1. Robinson, E. A. G. (160).
Col. 2. *U.S. Statistical Abstract* (1966, p. 221).
Col. 3. U.S.S.R. Economy (190).
Col. 4. Burns, A. R. (29, p. 39) refers to 1949.
International Labour Office Yearbook of Labour Statistics.
U.N. (F.A.O.) Production Year Book 1967, pp. 18–19.

by Colin Clark (40, pp. 70–1), to the effect that, under full
development, employment in the "tertiary" service industries
increases fastest. How firm is this generalization? During the
1939–45 war and in the years just after, this trend toward employment in the service industries was reversed in Britain and
the United States. But in more recent years, apart from the
virtual disappearance of the domestic servant (a million strong
in England fifty years ago), the trend has been resumed again.

When underdeveloped are being compared with developed
countries, as in Table I, Column 5, the statistics are often

deceptive. Before the trend toward differentiation sets in, persons counted as agriculturists will be mainly pursuing a subsistence economy, but incidentally transporting and marketing some of their produce, making their own rough tools, supplies like soap, clothing, and houses. Thus, as Bauer and Yamey point out (11, pp. 40–2) the proportion statistically classified as agriculturists will cloak a certain amount of manufacturing, building, transport, and trading services. And in the later stages of the development trends, the substitution of machines and processes for persons makes the relative fall in occupied persons no exact index of a relative fall in the importance of activities. Measured in the values to which machines as well as men contributed, manufacturers and agriculturists are not being displaced by services as much as appears from the proportion of men occupied in each activity.

Though the exact percentage may exaggerate the change in activities, there is little doubt of the displacement, at the middle and later stages of development, of a way of life based on agriculture. Besides the historical trend, shown vertically downwards in Table II, the proportions based on agriculture of the total occupied population can be compared laterally, region by region, as in the toe of this L-shaped table. The poorer underdeveloped continents are seen to be the continents with a relatively high proportion based on agriculture. While in 1949 (29, p. 39) Australia (Oceania) had 33, Europe 33, and North America 20 per cent of their population engaged in agriculture, Africa had 74, Asia 70, Central America 67, and South America 60 per cent.

3. Science Applied to Industry

For some time now I have presented the application of science as a dominating causal factor in modern industry. A simple chart in my *Investment, Location and Size of Plant* (69, p. 73) developed into an elaborate genealogical tree (72, pp. 72–3) distinguishing economic reasoning and statistical correlation as proving parts of the supposed train of causation. Here I reproduce, as Table III, a still later chart (78, p. 23) which stressed the important self-perpetuating "circular" character of the train of causation, an important element in the take-off. To that chart I add a reference to the material and the product and market conditions necessary for inventive genius or organized research to have affected production, and for scientific inventions to have been applicable as an innovation in industry and transport.

TABLE III

CHART OF CONDITIONS AND RESULTS OF THE
APPLICATION OF SCIENCE

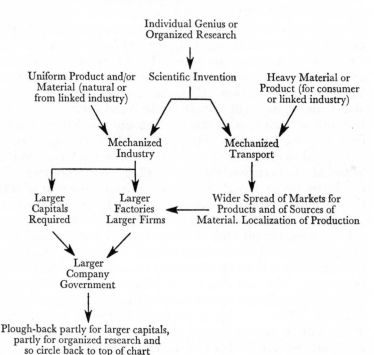

Inventive geniuses certainly existed in all ages and even perhaps among our apelike ancestors, but the application of their inventions to industry is very recent and has not, apparently, happened in history before at anything like the present scale or pace. Many reasons have been put forward why the start of this unique set of events (which is still developing and reaching an extreme form in *automation*) "took off" at the particular time and place that it did, namely, the eighteenth century in England. Scientific knowledge was not enough. As Blackett said in his Presidential Address to the British Association in 1957 (19)—

> During the first two hundred years of modern science, from 1600 to 1800, science learnt much from technology, but taught it relatively little. . . . Despite the interest of the Royal Society in the "useful arts", it was not until the last quarter of the eighteenth century that the impact of science on technology began to be decisively important.

In the countries now developed and, as we shall find, in the underdeveloped countries, it is the *application* of science in society that is the stumbling-block. Particular social conditions are necessary. To quote the chapter headings of Arthur Lewis's *Theory of Economic Growth* (121), they are not only Knowledge and Training but Will to "economize" and certain economic Institutions (such as economic freedom and the right to reward for work), the formation of Capital, and Wise Government.

The will to economize and the reward for work have in the historical past been overlaid by the will to "conspicuous waste", to military power and glory, or to provision for the next world; the institution of true freedom of thought and religious tolerance only just preceded the Industrial Revolution in England.

Even now, not all business leaders or even the majority of them have the will to economize or make the effort to maximize profits; nor does freedom of thought necessarily give them useful thoughts. They are often driven to innovation by sheer need, substituting capital for labour to avoid loss through higher wage demands (138, pp. 64–6), or having to match the innovations of competitors. Certainly those who do not innovate or imitate the innovators are liable to be driven out of business and may fail to survive.

These innovators (Schumpeter (172) confusingly calls them entrepreneurs) might be the owner-managers of a business (entrepreneurs as defined later, p. 138) or just managers, inventors or promoters, or a bit of each. Many empirical studies have recently been published of the way innovation gradually percolates through the firms and plants of an industry. Carter and Williams have shown in successive chapters of their *Investment in Innovation* (33), the variety of business motives (IV) and the grounds for investing (V) or not investing (VI). Much is found to depend on the opportunity offered by available funds obtained, as will be seen (V, §3), by plough-back of sporadically large profits. My genealogical tree (Table III) is, however, meant as a model of the way not only sociological and psychological, but material qualities such as uniformity and transportability (in which industries differ widely) may, by affecting cost, stimulate potential supply and demand, technology and industrial development. The hypothetical arrows of the model are to some extent confirmed by statistical associations indicated in the Appendix (para. (5), p. 267) and Table XIX. Once the development is thus "primed", it may "take off" on its own through plough-back of profits, particularly by large organizations and the research they often undertake.

It is unnecessary further to elaborate the importance of science to industrial development, since this thesis of a dynamic economy has now been generally accepted and built upon as an assumption. But if economic analysis is to be realistic, it must try to measure fairly exactly the speed with which science is being applied in various industries and in various countries, developed and underdeveloped.

To the economist, the main consequence of applying physical science is the growth, compared to the labour employed, of the value of the capital investment and physical capacity, normally appearing as fixed assets in the balance sheet. The growth of capital investment per worker (to avoid confusion with investment in stocks and shares it may be referred to as equipment or mechanization) appears strongly in public utilities, manufactures, transport, and communication, fairly strongly in mining and agriculture, where conditions of work are less uniform, but only weakly in building, trading, and other services. As already suggested, the tapering off in the proportion of workers in manufacturing, compared to services (referred to in the "law of tertiary production") does not necessarily indicate a relative fall in manufacturing production, but rather the growing substitution of machines for men in the manufacturing process.

The amount of the fixed capital investment relative to labour, or more generally, but vaguely, the degree of "capital intensity", is indicated most readily, simply, and without recourse to fluctuating monetary values by the industry's horse-power capacity per worker. As explained elsewhere (69, pp. 90–100) this indicator is unduly influenced as a measure of capital costs by the toughness of the raw material to be processed. A delicate but *expensive* machine used in the second stage of manufacturing would need less power capacity than say a saw used in the first stages of lumbering on logs rough and not uniform (238, Part 4, evidence of Meade). Other indicators are capital expenditure and fixed assets per employee, which Rosenbluth (165, p. 43) finds has only a low correlation with horsepower per worker. I have also used the proportion of net

TABLE IV

HORSE-POWER-A-WORKER IN USE IN MANUFACTURE: PAST AND PRESENT IN DEVELOPED; 1939–54 IN UNDERDEVELOPED COUNTRIES

	U.S.A.	Britain	Underdeveloped countries			
1869	1·1	—				
1889	1·4	—				
1909	2·9	(1907) 1·6*				
1929	4·9	(1930) 2·4				
1939	6·5	—	Brazil	1·4	Mexico	2·1
1951	—	3·1	Brazil (1949)	2·0	Argentine	2·1
1954	9·6	—	Nicaragua	0·9	Taiwan	1·4
			Guatemala	0·6	Greece	1·0
1963	12·7					

* Available: in use approximately 1·3
Sources: U.S. Census of Manufactures, U.K. Census of Production, United Nations (184) Part II.

value of output which is not payroll. This isolates the overhead costs, such as depreciation and obsolescence on capital, but includes profit. The three last mentioned indicators have been combined to form an accounting test of capital intensity in Table XIX, as described in the Appendix.

The wide range of mechanization even within the manufacturing sector is illustrated from the major industry groups of Table XIX. In the group (petroleum) with the highest ratio, the horse-power capacity per production worker was 89·5; in the group (apparel) with the lowest it was 0·22. These differences in the capital intensity of different manufactures illustrate the complex factors explaining the application of science. As lawyers say, it is not only a question of motive, but of the opportunity offered by the material and market situation. If materials are uniform and a uniform product is sold, such as petrol, then mass-producing machines and processing are the easier to apply.

In Table IV, L-shaped like Table II, the upward trend of horse-power-a-worker in manufacture is seen to be continuous for Britain and the United States, though at a lower level in Britain. Other developed countries show the same trend. But the underdeveloped countries, shown at the toe of the L, appear, for the same recent dates, at an altogether lower level. Except in the United States, where 12·7 was reached in 1963, horse-power-a-worker has not recently been recorded.

4. THE INCREASE IN STAFF

The third trend refers not, like the first, to a measurable relation between industries or economic activities generally, but to one within an industry between its occupations. The distinction between industry and occupation is that a man's industry depends on whom he works for, his occupation on what he works at. A bench-hand and a factory manager are in different occupations both in some manufacturing industry; a professor and a college porter are in different occupations both in the educational industry.

The trend now to be noticed is the increase within manufacturing industries of the ratio of administrative, scientific, and technical (including clerical) staff, usually paid a salary, to the production workers, usually paid a wage. If these administrative occupations are considered "services", this trend reinforces the law of tertiary (i.e. service) production mentioned earlier.

This increase in the staff ratio is confirmed by the census taken in various years in all the major countries already industrialized, though it is not easy to obtain data on the ratio in underdeveloped countries. A further difficulty, apart from the poverty of statistics, is that in the early stages of development, with small firms producing the bulk of output, the owner-manager or entrepreneur prevails, and if he is counted as "staff" the staff–operative ratio appears high. In fact, he may, like the "dirt-farmer", be both staff and operative (76) as well as capitalist.

The ratio of staff to operatives in British manufactures has advanced from 11·8 per cent in 1924 to 15·1 in 1935, 20·0 in 1948, 26·1 in 1957 and 30·2 in 1964; in the U.S. from 11·9 in 1909 (about fifteen years in advance of the U.K.) to 20·0 in 1939 (nine years in advance) to 26·5 in 1954, and to 32·7 in 1964 (less in advance). The staff in some industries approaches so close to equality with operatives in number that the ratio is now more conveniently expressed, as in the Appendix, in terms of staff to total employees. To this increase in "white collar" workers in U.S. manufacturing plants should be added the increased employment in administration headquarters of multiplant firms. This trend is sometimes deplored as an unnecessary growth of overhead cost and an example of Parkinson's Law (146). With more forward planning of productive operations, however, the increase of staff per operative may well not be just "empire-building". United States evidence (138, p. 147) is that staff has increased less than the rise in productivity level. In Britain, too, it is probably (72, pp. 139–40) a natural consequence of increased output due to the use of machines which displace the operative, but add to the work of staff, thus increasing the numerator but diminishing the denominator of the staff ratio. In many industries, notably chemicals and electrical engineering, the staff is "scientific" as well as technical and administrative and not wholly concerned, directly, in coping with output. Subtracting scientific staff, the ratio of staff to *output* has in fact probably fallen in England and in the United States.

Though increase in the staff ratio and increase in size of organization are both apparent trends, it does not appear to be true, as often assumed, that staff ratios are greater where the size of plant is greater, measured in total employed. Comparing all the major industry groups given in the Appendix, Table XIX, little rank correlation appears between a group's size structure and staff ratios. It can be said that the staff ratio of an industry is fairly independent of the size of its plants—or firms.

Who, precisely, compose the staff? Both in Britain and in the U.S. the staff (113), or (239) the employees who are not production workers, contain a high proportion of women and consist largely of clerical workers, secretaries, typists and stenographers in the sales, personnel and finance, as well as in the production departments of factories. "White collar" workers is now a phrase officially accepted by the Census to distinguish male and (oddly enough) female staff from the "blue collar" production workers; the term includes managers of all grades, but not foremen. In industries already indicated research workers have recently added to the number of staff.

This trend toward higher staff ratios is likely to continue with continued application of science and greater forward planning, budgeting, and other management procedures; and it has sociological as well as economic implications for the under-developed as well as the developed countries. A cadre of men and also women literates educated at school up to at least sixteen must, for full development, be supplied side by side with the semi-skilled and skilled workers operating, tending, and maintaining the new machines.

5. WIDENING OF MARKETS AND SUPPLY SOURCES

The fourth trend, the widening of markets and sources of supply, and thus the possibility of localizing manufacture, is more difficult to measure and test quantitatively than the trend away from agriculture, the trend to mechanize, or the increasing ratio of staff. Within a single country, measurement of the geographical extent of markets is possible only if that country keeps records of economic activities and structures separately for separate regions. Thanks to the "check-points" that custom-houses present and the detailed publication of imports and exports, quantitative measurement is made easier, however, *between* countries. It is, in fact, possible to measure a common line of development whereby some countries will increasingly import supplies from other countries for their manufacturing industries and will widen their sales of manufactures by export to markets abroad. They thus become differentiated as manufacturing countries—as "workshops of the world".

Though the United States has in fact increased exports of manufactures to markets abroad, and imports of raw material supplies, disproportionately to total exports and imports and also to its increase in total goods produced, yet its inter-regional or inter-state expansion is by far the more significant. The conception of widening markets must not be confined, moreover, to the geographical extension of customers. Markets have an intensive as well as an extensive dimension. As incomes of households increase they will demand more and more goods of particular kinds which they could not originally afford.

Engel's Law, based on the results of statistical inquiries first in Denmark then in almost all countries of the world, is that as the real income of families increases, the proportion they spend on food falls. Thus in the United States in 1950 urban families with incomes between $1,000 and $2,000 spent 36·4 per cent of their income on food and beverages, urban families with $10,000 or over spent only 24·5 per cent in that way (239, 1957, p. 307; 1966, p. 324). To bring the evidence up to date the proportion spent on food, beverages and tobacco by all sampled families fell between 1950 and 1964, when incomes were rising generally, from 30·4 to 25·1 per cent.

This does not mean that the absolute volume of demand was diminishing on food, but that the widening of the market was particularly intense for non-food products. Table XIX (II B) shows that after leather (mostly shoes), lumber and tobacco, food manufacturers grew slowest between 1947 and 1965. And the direction of market intensification is shown by the fast growth (only beaten by chemicals) of the transport equipment group largely devoted to automobiles (the largest single industry distinguished by the Census).

The expansion of exports which has been so frequently described must be seen as only a part of the analysis and measurement of widening markets and sources of supply. Apart from invisible services, about a third the total value of exports, Britain must export manufactures to import food, and also the raw materials for the manufactures; hers may be called a "through-putting" economy in which materials and food from abroad are "put through" her factories, and her factory workers' stomachs, in order that factories and workers may produce for a high standard of living at home *and* for importing the necessary foreign materials and food. It is possible to measure the degree of through-put from official foreign-trade statistics by a summary coefficient which would average the percentages (with a possible range of 0–100) of total rawstuffs and food used that was imported and of all goods manufactured that was exported. A coefficient of 100 would measure complete through-put in which, as in a city state with no rural environs, all food and rawstuffs used were imported and, to pay for them, practically all manufactures had to be exported. The coefficient would be nil in an agricultural and mineral-sufficient country, where no food or materials need be imported and no manufactures exported. Such a coefficient, that I calculated (81) from summary data of the British 1907 *Census of Production,* came to 33. The summary data were not repeated in subsequent *Censuses,* but the British coefficient of visible through-put has certainly gone still higher since, probably to near 50, owing to increased imports of materials, fuel, and food. Saunders (171) considers that nearly all the expansion in industrial output between 1851 and 1950 has been fed from the increase in imports. Since 1907 *fuel* has been imported in the form of oil in place of the home-mined coal; and with the increase of population the need for food imports has not diminished, even though home agriculture has been heavily subsidized. This does not mean that Britain imports a greater proportion compared to her national income. Robinson (160) makes that proportion about the same in 1951–3 as in 1870–80. It means that Britain imports more of the foods and materials that are essential to her life and industry. To that extent, the British economy has become increasingly differentiated and specialized as a manufacturing unit. Belgium, Holland, and Japan, like Britain, increased raw material and food imports and manufactured exports rapidly since 1850 and have a high coefficient of through-put, and such almost completely urbanized areas as Hong Kong, Singapore, or Malta have coefficients still higher, well over Britain's probable 50.

Dependence on foreign trade makes national planning much more difficult, since the demands of foreigners to whom exports are to be sold cannot be planned. Is there a risk in over-development?

This process of differentiation and specialization in manufactures (much of them exported) by countries of relatively small area is associated with high densities of population. Contrary to common opinion, it is not India nor China that has the highest population per square mile, but Great Britain (particularly England), Holland, Belgium, Western Germany, and Japan. All of these countries had by 1957 a density of more than five hundred to the square mile. The increase in density of these smaller countries has outrun their own natural resources for food, raw materials, and fuel production and they must rely increasingly on imports. For the world as a whole, trade between countries has, partly in consequence, been measurably increasing. The *United Nations Yearbooks* (185) give certain index numbers tracing the growth of aggregate international trade since 1938. It appears that in terms of volume total world exports rose between 1938 and 1961 from 53 to 116 per cent of the 1957 volume, though population increased only from 75 to 104 per cent and total production from 67 to 104 per cent.

In Britain and the similar through-putting countries, home markets were also widening. But in countries with a large area and a variety of natural conditions, such as the United States and Russia, these internal markets and also the internal sources of supply are of chief importance. For the United States the coefficient of visible through-put is low. Except for tropical products, such as coffee, sugar, rubber, and for minerals, including oil, not found in large enough amounts within its own boundaries, the United States imports relatively little rawstuff, and exports only a small proportion of its manufactures. It is a self-sustaining, not a through-putting economy.

In countries of wide area certain regions or districts tend to develop as industrial centres differentiated from the mainly undeveloped regions. This differentiation can be quantitatively traced only if regional statistics are published, as they are in the United States. Here, the six New England states employed in manufacture in 1965 between 32·4 and 42·4 per cent of their total non-agricultural employees; the eight mountain states of the West, on the other hand, only between 4·5 and 18·6 per cent. This "localization" and regional development of industries within countries is an important element in development and, in Chapter III, will be analysed further.

Whether a particular industry localizes regionally within a nation or internationally, a developed transport is essential. As early as the Canal Age, Adam Smith pointed out how markets widened largely because of greater transport facilities. A relevant indicator, therefore, which fits into and verifies the argument pictured in Table III, is the increase in the proportion of the occupied population engaged in transport and communication and the growth of mechanical equipment for transport and communication.

With developing manufacture the proportion of the occupied population in transport and communication rose in England (160, p. 459) from 3·0 per cent in 1841 and 6·2 in 1861 to 7·6 in 1881 and 9·7 in 1901. In the United States the number so engaged rose from 4·7 per cent of the total occupied in 1880 to 6·6 in 1900 and to 7·5 in 1950. In Russia the proportion engaged in "transport and posts" has risen from 2·0 per cent in 1938 to 6·0 in 1955 (190). With the increasing proportion of transport going by road not rail, workers constructing and maintaining roads should be included in the transport force, as workers building and maintaining railways are automatically included when employed by the railways. Further evidence of the development of transport is that, recently, the growth of net output of transport and communication equipment has outstripped considerably that of manufacturing generally. In the United States transport and communication equipment formed, in 1937, 8 per cent of the total value added in manufactures, in 1957, 12 per cent. Of the twenty major industry groups listed in Table XIX, transport equipment was shown next to chemicals to be between 1947 and 1965 the fastest growing. These are inclusive figures, from which vehicles used purely for pleasure, if the figures were available, ought to be subtracted and also the *net* export of vehicles to be used for business; but the proportion of total vehicles directed in these different ways did not vary greatly.

A factor that has widened markets almost as much as transport is the art of preservation—overcoming perishability—a physical quality of materials or products equal with portability and gradability (avoiding the need of personal inspection) in basic economic importance. Industries particularly affected are canning and slaughtering, which can now be localized far from their markets.

Before concluding it must be said that this trend toward widening markets internationally has in the last decades been greatly hindered by tariffs, quotas, and other national, not to say nationalistic, restrictions. To quote Myrdal (143, p. 32)—

> International trade was increasing not only absolutely but also in comparison with total production. . . . Beginning with the First

World War, however, . . . and more definitely with the onset of
the Great Depression—all international movements were securely
curtailed by national policies.

The Second World War caused a further set-back, but since
1948 the trend has set in again in general, though not in every
trade—not, for instance, in textiles, where production for the
home market has increased, while exports and imports have
decreased.

6. THE PERSISTENT DIFFERENTIATION OF MANUFACTURING INDUSTRIES

Widening markets and sources of supply bring in their train a
differentiation of industries. So far, the trend in science applied
to industry and increase of staff has been measured only for
manufacturing as a whole. But particular industries have gone
their different ways and the differentiation has been persistent.
In horse-power per production worker, to turn to Table XIII,
apparel was the lowest major group in 1939 and remained
lowest in 1963. The petroleum group was the highest in 1939
and again in 1963. Except for tobacco, no group changed in
fact more than two (out of the twenty ranks) and only two
(textiles and furniture) as much as two ranks, in the twenty-four
years. And the range between the extreme groups actually
widened: from 0·33 to 22·84 in 1939; 0·22 to 89·46 in 1963.
The traits of each of the separate major groups are measured
and ranked in the Appendix, but the process of separation and
the relation of separation to width of market is not easy to
measure by statistical indicators. This relation has been recognized at least since the days of Adam Smith, who devoted a
whole chapter (173, Book I, iii) to the proposition that the
division of labour is limited by the extent of the market. In a
small market there can be little specialization—

> It is impossible there should be such a trade as even that of
> nailer in the remote and inland parts of the highlands of Scotland.
> Such a workman, at the rate of a thousand nails a day, and three
> hundred working days in the year, will make three hundred
> thousand nails in the year. But in such a situation, it would be
> impossible to dispose of one thousand, that is, of one day's work
> in the year.

Without splitting up the work of a smith even as finely as to differentiate nailmaking, the British *Census of Production* was able in 1951 to differentiate forty-one metal industries; and the United States *Census of Manufactures* differentiated in 1954 one hundred and twenty-seven individual metal industries. Though, occasionally, industries coalesce and integrate, increase in manufacture, together with the new applications of science and widening markets, has on balance resulted in increasing differentiation between manufactures.

The first four trends—the flight from agriculture, the application of science, increased staff, and widening of markets—have occurred, whatever the system of *industrial* government, whether communist or capitalist. At this point, however, one of the main characteristics of capitalism must be distinguished—a characteristic not, like control by capital owner, implicit in the word *capitalism*, but conveyed in the phrase free enterprise. Any one capitalist organization in fact controls only a small part of industry; and capitalist industry *as a whole* is not controlled by any single authority but is *controlled*, if that is the right word, by the balance of prices and costs on the market. Under this "market control" if a capitalist firm sees a profit in the difference between revenue from the prices charged and costs in *any* line of product, or process, it is free to take up that line in its plants or, if the firm sees a loss in any line, to drop that line. If enough firms in one established industry take over the products or processes of another, as steel has iron-making, the two industries may coalesce or integrate; if enough drop a product or process, a separate industry may be formed from the activities dropped. As Allyn Young pointed out (206), the progressive division and specialization of industries is an essential part of the process by which increasing returns are realized.

Industries are not in fact preordained. Instead, freedom of enterprise has allowed each firm or plant to develop a set of lines (products or processes) apparently arbitrarily, but usually with technical characteristics which fit together logically and which are adapted to the general work to be performed on the particular materials for the particular market. If the new development does not fit, the firm may fail. One may thus discern an economic logic of events underlying the "mix" within the firms or plants of an industry, and the differentiation between

D

manufactures. The whole process of converting materials into final products is usually split vertically (72, p. 9) by a "Great Divide" into at least two stages: that of refining or producing a uniform substance or stuff out of the raw material; and that of making up or assembling the stuff. Thus, smelting and rolling iron ore, to make the stuff steel, is differentiated from fabricating, working on, or assembling steel and stuffs from other industries. It is this distinction which the U.S. Census uses in its major groups to separate primary metal from fabricated metal and from machinery, textiles from apparel, paper from printing and publishing, lumber from furniture. This separation is logical. Primary metal manufacture is most economically carried on near, or accessibly to, the sources of its heavy and intransportable raw materials, while assembly is most economically carried on near the markets for its products, most of which are of awkward shape and relatively costly to transport and whose producers and customers require frequently to consult together.

This logic of events accounts for the fact that though industries are formed by the policy of single firms, the ultimate scope of the different industries is so similar in different countries that British productivity teams have had little difficulty in finding their opposite numbers in the United States; and that Censuses in the two countries and others use a very similar industrial classification.

It is important for our purposes to define *an industry*; and since an industry is the result of a trend—sometimes a quasi-biological, trial-and-error, fight-for-survival trend—this task may appear difficult. We can accept, however, the official standard census classification of industries as corresponding sufficiently to current usage, yet covering all manufacturing without overlapping. Its basic principle is to assign all establishments (i.e. plants) to one industry or another according to their principal (or "primary") products. Few, if any, industries make only one product, as economists sometimes still assume, but they usually make similar kinds of products. The definition I have adopted (63, p. 5; 72, p. 17) for an industry is *any kind of transactions* (e.g. products or processes) *usually specialized in by a number of plants which do not usually perform much of any other kind of transaction.* This definition can, of course, more appropriately for sociology, be put another way round that "an industry is a group of workers in a number of plants usually specializing in any kind of transactions not usually covered by other plants". To the sociologist, an industry is a *community* of persons, which the persons themselves recognize and to which the employers, at least, may feel a certain loyalty. An industry, however, unless nationalized or a complete private monopoly, is not chiefly, as expounded later, an *association* with an organization and government for general purposes.

Exactly how usual or not usual the specialization may be is a question now answered statistically by the Census (182, pp. 22–5 and 69, pp. 2–5). The U.S. *Census of Manufactures* gives the proportion in which the plants of any one industry (*a*) cover the whole production of their principal or "primary" products, e.g. how far grain is only milled in grain mills, and (*b*) are exclusive and specialize, not making other products, e.g. how far grain mills only mill grain. It is surprising how little most industries' plants engage in products or processes not primary to the industry. Of the 426 four-digit individual industries, only seventeen were recorded in the 1958 *Census* with a specialization ratio under 76 per cent. High coverage is more difficult to attain; but even so only thirty-four of the 426 four-digit industries are recorded as "failing" to cover in their plants two-thirds of all the products primary to the industry, i.e. had a coverage ratio less than 67 per cent. Firms, however, as we shall see (pp. 105–6) integrate production primary to other industries more often and cross the Census boundaries more frequently than plants. They diversify more and become "conglomerate".

My definition of industry is perfectly in keeping with that of Joan Robinson (162), though, to agree with the Census, her *firm* should read *plant*—

> In ordinary language, when we speak of [any industry] we are thinking of a group of firms engaged in a certain type of production, governed by the kinds of object produced and the materials of which they are made.

Later in the article, she adds—

> there are often certain basic processes required for the production of the most diverse commodities (tennis balls, motor tyres and mattresses) and economies in the utilization of by-products under one roof.

It is a great help to definition that industries, even manufacturing industries, differ so widely one from another in their
characteristics. Table XIX illustrates the extent of the range
by citing the measured characteristics of the extreme major
industry groups marked first and twentieth. These characteristics
have, moreover, tended to persist for each industry over several
years. It can be seen from Table XIII that the industry groups
persist almost exactly in their relative rank in horse-power per
production worker. Except for tobacco which ranks second
lowest in 1939, fifth lowest in 1963, and textiles and furniture
ranking fifth and sixth lowest in 1939, seventh and fourth
respectively in 1963, no group changed rank more than one
place. Much the same persistence appears in the *size-of-plant*
differentiation of Table XIII. None of the sixteen major industry
groups that could be defined comparably in 1939 and 1963
changed more than three ranks, except food (changing four),
and ten of the sixteen changed one rank or none at all. The
average change was only 1·4 ranks out of a possible 8·0 in the
twenty years. A similar stability was found by Ramanadham
(152) in India between 1929 and 1949.

There is little, if any, general tendency for industries to draw
closer together in their characteristics. High mechanization or
a larger plant structure does not spread from one to another
industry till all industries are equally mechanized or large-
scaled—in some respects, on the contrary, differentiation is not
only maintained but widened. Among the industry groups in
Table XIII the lowest and highest average of employees per
plant were in 1939 23·1 and 323·0 or just less than fourteen times
as much, in 1963 15·8 and 225·0 or just over fourteen times. The
lowest and highest horse-power per production worker were in
1939 0·33 and 22·84—sixty-nine times as much. In 1963 the
lowest and highest were 0·22 and 89·46—or four hundred and
six times as much!

As well as persistence and stability for different periods in the
same country, these contrasts in the characteristics of the
different industries show a certain ubiquity if tested by similarity
in different countries. Elsewhere, I have demonstrated (72, 79)
the measurable similarity of rank in size of plant, power-a-worker
and degree of localization between British and United States
industries. The United Nations has brought out the similarity

in ranking, even between developed and underdeveloped countries, in net output (i.e. value added) per worker (a rough test of capital intensity), for wide industry groups. Here are the data for the seven manufacturing groups that are recorded for all continental regions—

TABLE V

VALUE ADDED PER WORKER (IN 1,000 1948 U.S. DOLLARS) IN FOUR WORLD REGIONS, 1953

	Asia, E. and S.E.	Latin America	Europe	N. America
Chemicals	1·4	3·0	4·0	9·8
Basic metals	1·1	2·4	2·8	5·9
Paper	1·0	1·3	2·8	7·4
Metal products	0·6	1·1	2·1	6·3
Food	0·5	1·4	2·5	5·8
Textiles and clothing	0·4	1·0	1·8	4·4
Non-metal mineral products	0·4	1·0	1·9	5·9
All manufacturing 1953	0·5	1·3	2·1	5·9

Sources: United Nations, *Patterns of Industrial Growth* (184, pp. 120 *et seq.*)

The seven industry groups are listed in order of their value added per employee in East and South-East Asia; but the ranking is much the same in the other continental regions. None of the first six industry groups ranks more than two places differently in any continent. The ubiquity of their relative differences in net output a worker is evident enough.

7. Four Further Trends and Causal Relation Between Trends

The five trends traced in detail in the last few sections are mainly economic. They describe changes in the kind of work, industry, or occupation which individual persons rather than groups *exchange for pay*, and changes in the technical processes and location of production for exchange. More people were drawn out of agriculture and into manufacturing industries and within those industries into staff occupations, and industries are mechanized and localized nationally, and otherwise differentiated. But the next four trends—urbanization, larger-scale organization, government by manager, and finally, higher living standards—are as much sociological as they are economic and will be taken up in chapters III, IV, V and, finally, VI and VII.

Though partially so, the nine trends are not completely independent of one another. Some of them have been statistically correlated, mechanization and location pattern, for instance, with scale of organization. But before the correlation tests are applied unthinkingly, hit or miss, it is important to put forward, for testing, some theory or hypothesis about the lines of causation, which has some logical probability or plausibility.

The chief train of causation which I put forward as a possible logical sequence of industrial events has already appeared in the genealogical tree model of Table III, and is followed in the sectional arrangement of Table XIX (in the Appendix). The four main "generations" of this tree may, by holding Table III horizontally, bottom next the eyes, be viewed in perspective as, hinterland, background, middle-ground, and foreground. The hinterland (2nd line, Table III, and IA and IB in Table XIX) is the type of work done and its supply and demand setting, the nature, especially uniformity and weight, of the materials used and products made for various markets that are served, and the linkage with the work of other industries, including input and output relations. No word that is ordinarily used covers the study of all these hinterland factors of work done, and I am compelled reluctantly to introduce one of my few technical terms. The Greek for work is *ergon*, so the study of these characteristics will, on the analogy of *erg* and *ergograph*, be called *ergology* and the train of causation I put forward called the *ergological* interpretation of industrial characteristics. Nearer the eyes, the background (3rd line, Table III, IC in Table XIX) is technological; its outstanding feature is the trend toward mechanization of industry, transport, and communication. The middle-ground of the causal train (4th line, Table III, III to V in Table XIX) is largely sociological—one of social or "organic" structure: the trends (soon to be traced) toward the larger-scale organization with, for many industries, localization and urbanization.

In the immediate foreground is the form of industrial government such as the joint stock company or corporation, and their behaviour, for instance the degree of plough-back of profits.

The hypothesis of the importance of the type of work done and its materials-and-markets, supply-and-demand context in determining organization has recently been strengthened by the researches of Professor Joan Woodward into more than two hundred plants in south-east England (242). She found that forms of organization depended largely on whether a mass market was being supplied, or batch, unit or process production undertaken.

This whole perspective in Table III from policy and organization foreground to technology background and demand and supply hinterland or setting is put forward as a "visual aid" in tracing trains of causation. Many such trains have already been explored by economic sociologists, notably Adolf Weber and Karl Marx.

Adolf Weber in his *Standortstheorie* associated location pattern with the physical properties of an industry's materials and products, especially their weight and intransportability. Avoiding the jargon of material or market "orientation" we can say that intransportable *materials* keep an industry like cement-making "rooted" near the source of materials. According to the scatter or concentration of materials, so will the industry be distributed. Heavy and intransportable *products*, on the other hand, keep an industry like brewing "tied" near the consumer. There are two main sorts of consumer. The *final* consumer, such as the beer-drinker, is presumably dispersed among the population; but the *producer*-consumers may be localized. Industries, like machine building, providing the producer with products awkward to transport, will probably conform to the producers' location pattern. Where both materials and products are heavy, the industry may be near the source of materials *or* the market. Where neither materials nor products are heavy the industry may be considered "footloose" and various plans for location are feasible; but as we shall see (Chapter III) loose feet often lead to high localization owing to the economies, external to the plants, of their "flocking together".

Marx's "extension of materialism to the domain of social phenomena", as Lenin put it (119, p. 544), is based less on the hinterland of work than on the technological background. It is summed up in his dictum that the hand mill will give you society with the feudal lord; the steam mill, society with the industrial capitalist. The ergological includes, but is wider than, a technological interpretation. In particular it comprises a consideration of types of market, such as Professor Heflebower (222, p. 304) has proposed. Organization is likely to be different when making speciality goods such as household electrical appliances, or goods where the consumer may go "shopping" to compare qualities and styles, or convenience goods bought frequently—let alone when making producers' rather than consumers' goods.

The association between the external work being performed together with the techniques used, and the internal characteristics of the various industries within the manufacturing sector, is brought out even more clearly when comparing manufacturing with other sectors of economic activity in respect of their location pattern and size of plant. Unlike manufacturing, mining and agriculture have intransportable sources and building has an intransportable product. Services do not work on materials or for a product at all and except for transport and communication are not heavily mechanized. Parker (233, p. 25) states the role of demand squarely—

> The size of units is limited in some industries by the conditions of production and in others by the character of demand. Thus in building repair work and in much road haulage the output is scattered and erratic, while in other industries small-scale operations occur where firms make types of product for which demand is limited.

It would be interesting, but take us beyond *industrial* development, to analyse how these fundamental differences in the work they perform and techniques they use affect not only different sectors' location and size of plant patterns but go beyond that in effecting differences in their organization and government. Mining and building, for instance, have distinctly lower, transport and trade distinctly higher staff ratios than manufacturing. Mining, rail and air transport, communications, and public utilities are nationalized in many countries; at the other end of the scale, building, retailing, and, above all, agriculture retain the small-scale entrepreneur to a far greater extent than manufacturing.

The effect of the hinterland of the work done is also evident in the time incidence of the occurrence of risk. The risks of an industry are high if the products it markets are fashionable luxuries, or durable goods not demanded day by day, and if the material supplied depends on the weather. Seasonal fluctuation can be measured and to some extent the different amplitudes of boom and slump likely to be experienced by plants in the several industries (high, for instance, for *capital* goods) during trade cycles. But uncertainty remains when both nature and human nature are so unpredictable. Where, as in extractive industries, weather or geology affect supplies and where, in industries at large, consumers' and rival traders' behaviour is not planned or predictable beforehand, the cost of wrong prediction will be particularly heavy if much capital has been sunk in special equipment for the enterprise and a slump leads to idle capacity. Social loss will also occur in the form of concentrated unemployment if the industry involved is localized in any one area. To guard against the risk of putting all eggs into one industrial basket, more integration is undertaken by firms than is justified by the economies of *specializing* in large-scale processes or products. Plants and the firm, the unit of government, tend for this reason to be the larger, as we shall see, and large industrial cities are justified by specializing in several industries offering alternative employment.

In the train of events, so far, the capitalist and communist economies show much the same ergological development from the particular work to be done through technology to structure. But in the foreground where I place government (v in Table XIX) the two systems part company. If the firm is small, it is, under the capitalist economy, usually governed by an owner-manager (or entrepreneur) risking his own capital. If the firm is large, its government will probably be of corporate or company form, in which the largest capitalist shareholders may or may not be in control. If the firm is large, not just absolutely but relatively to the size of the whole industry, the result may be a narrow concentration of the control of the industry's production in a few firms, if not a single firm, i.e. an oligopoly, if not monopoly. Even if there are many firms, these may have some agreement and the government of the whole industry may be "confederate" by cartelization.

Thus, a train of causation can be held to extend all the way from the hinterland of the type of materials and markets through applied science, and the technical background, to the social relations of industry, both the structural middle-ground and the government foreground. A *uniform material* like cotton or wool can, for instance, be spun and woven into a uniform cloth for the market. This uniformity accounts partly for the early technical mechanization of the textile industry in England and other countries, developed and underdeveloped. The technology of mechanization led to medium and large plants, and they in turn to joint-stock-company government. On the other hand, clothing, duly differentiated from textile industries, cannot, except for the army, be uniformly produced for its market, and, technically, mechanization is slight. This in turn leads to small plants and the survival of the owner-manager entrepreneur. The ergological train of causation from work to government is seen, again, in metals. Fairly uniform materials such as iron ore and coal are put through high-power blast furnaces and smelted accessibly to the material to form a uniform product such as steel billets. The high mechanization in a "material-oriented" location leads to very large plants and companies, so large as to threaten monopoly of the market and to call for Government control either through some form of regulation or nationalization. Thus the work done largely determines not only industrial structure but the form of government of an industry; and, indeed, in considering which industries are ripe for nationalization and which suited rather for the various forms of capitalism, I have elsewhere (73, pp. 151–9) listed a number of conditions pertaining to the work hinterland.

8. THE SCOPE OF FUTURE CHAPTERS

The chapters that follow bring out the main themes discussed in my Preface: that to forecast the future of the underdeveloped countries, the trends and trains of causation must be studied in countries already developed; that industrial development can and should be analysed empirically and quantitatively to a greater extent than hitherto; that the form of development of particular industries will depend on their type of work and supply-and-demand setting and finally that the findings of such a study can be fully understood and implemented only if sociological is joined to the economic interpretation of industrial organization and behaviour. The first and second themes have already appeared in tracing five of the nine measurable trends and trains of causation experienced in the developed countries. They will appear again when tracing the other trends and trains: urbanization and localization of industries in Chapter III; large-scale industrial organization in Chapter IV; the Managerial Revolution in Chapter V. The bearing of these trends upon standards of living in the underdeveloped countries is taken up in Chapter VI.

The third theme, the importance of joining sociology to economics, will appear immediately in Chapter II with the limits imposed on the full mobilization and mobility of workers and hence on productivity per head of population; it will appear again with the labour problems of the large organization in Chapter IV, with the sociology of companies in Chapter V, and finally, in Chapter VII with the sociological limits to economic progress in underdeveloped countries.

Until recently these themes have been unduly neglected, with unfortunate consequences. In many of their hopes and plans, underdeveloped countries have not studied the past lessons of the developed countries; forecasts have been based on theory rather than observed and measured facts; and economists and sociologists have worked in separate compartments. Marx expressed my first theme in the words (131, p. 13) "the country that is more developed industrially only shows to the less developed the image of its own future". He was a bold forecaster and, in collecting facts from Blue Books, a macro-economic empiricist. As Lenin wrote in 1914 (119, p. 555), "an immense advance in economic science is this that Marx conducts his analysis from the point of view of mass economic phenomena and not the point of view of individual cases". But Marx forecast wrongly when foretelling a fall in profits (119, p. 556) and the increase in the mass of poverty (131, p. 836). More recently, unorthodox theories have indeed proved no more accurate than orthodox. Thorstein Veblen's theory that the control of industry was falling under the control of financiers (192, 193) has, generally speaking, been belied by the Managerial Revolution which has brought the engineers nearer to the control which Veblen imagined as a possibility (193, Chapters IV and V) but did not expect. The theory of Burnham, who first publicized that Revolution, has been belied, in so far as he expected ownership of capital to fall to the State (27, Chapter IX). Of the reasons why facts have belied the Marxian prophecies (particularly that industry would bring mass misery) four, perhaps, can be picked out as the chief: the growth of trade unions, not revolutionary in aim but, to quote Lenin (120, p. 708), with the "bourgeoisification of part of the proletariat", trying for the best bargain out of capitalism; the institution of industrial corporations or joint-stock companies; State policy establishing a national minimum of living and of industrial standards; and, finally, the spread of birth control. All these trends, as we shall see, can be measured empirically and need a sociological as well as an economic approach.

My final chapter will draw together these themes of integrated and empirical measurement with the practical plans for raising standards of living in the future in all countries, particularly in preventing vicious circles from lowering their standards or causing them to stagnate.

ECONOMICS AND SOCIOLOGY OF
MOBILIZATION AND MOBILITY

1. General Economic Mobilization: The Recruitment of Women

Of the nine main trends in industrial development the last, the trend toward higher standards of living, is the "end" trend which leaders of the underdeveloped as well as the developed countries apparently wish to bring about in their country. The aim of development, indeed almost the very meaning now attached to the word development, is progress toward higher standards of living. This aim is primarily economic—to increase the goods and services and consequent real income available to the bulk of the people. Average income-a-head is the crude measure, but the real aim is to ensure that few, if any, fall below a certain standard and a more refined statistical test might be the income of a head nine-tenths down the income scale, i.e. the ninth "decile". The three main factors involved, total national income available, its distribution, and the total population, will be analysed in chapters VI and VII discussing the situation of the underdeveloped countries. It must be realized, however, before proceeding with the less economical and more social trends, that the total available income of a country depends on three sub-elements—differences in which may cut across these trends—

1. The level of productivity-a-worker in its various industries or occupations.
2. The proportion of occupied workers in the population as a whole—its "general economic mobilization".
3. The economic structure or distribution of workers between the different economic occupations or industries, and mobility between these activities, so as to ensure that resources are "deployed" in response to demand.

The level of productivity-a-worker depends largely on the precise economic activity concerned and is discussed in connection with economic structure, in the next section; the present section will deal with general mobilization.

How does the total population to be fed, clothed, and housed compare with the number of workers directly or indirectly feeding, clothing, and housing that population?

The number at work seems an easy matter to find from any occupation census, but there are at least two pitfalls in the way of valid comparisons between times and places.

Occupation to the census-taker means a worker's normal activity and he is "occupied" even though, at the time, unemployed. The effect of unemployment and underemployment will be taken up later.

The second pitfall is deeper. To be occupied economically a worker's activity must be in exchange for pay—must be *gainful*, as the United States Census has it. This qualification is particularly important when comparing underdeveloped countries where subsistence farming by "extended" families is the rule. The economic conception of an occupation as an individual's activity for something paid him in exchange cannot always be strictly applied to the sort of communities (studied by sociology or anthropology) in which work is done in common and as part of general community or of family functions.

Aware of these pitfalls, we must take the proportion of the total population gainfully occupied as the gross, *crude* rate of economic mobilization. In 1950–1 this crude measure of economic mobilization was 47·5 per cent in the United Kingdom, 42·5 in the United States, and the percentage is found to vary fairly widely from country to country. Its variation *is only fairly* wide, because of two usual constants—

(i) Adult men up to the age of about 65 are nearly all occupied, though not necessarily fully employed, in most countries, at most times. In the United States the proportion of men that were occupied in each of the ten-year age-groups between 25 and 54 was about 95 per cent through the period 1931 to 1955 except for the war years.

(ii) The proportion of such men of working age in the general population does not differ very widely from country to country, or time to time.

It is, of course, difficult to lay down the precise ages between which a man can be considered of working age, but 16 to 65 is the range usually adopted. Now the proportion (i) of men in this range of working age who are occupied varies mainly with the proportion of younger men not at work. In the United States a high proportion of young people between 16 and 24 is still at school or university, and though the United States economic mobilization appears lower to this extent, the additional education acquired may well pay off and yield a higher standard of productivity and of living for the country later on. But even among developed countries such long education is still exceptional and in a broad comparison of developed and underdeveloped countries we may neglect the variation due to working-age students.

The proportion (ii) of the male population that is within the working age-range depends fundamentally on migration and on past birth- and death-rates. Since in the United States up to 1940 both birth- and death-rates had been falling, the numbers below 15 had become a lower, and the number above 65 a higher, proportion of the total population. The non-working age-groups at either end of the age-scale acting thus in opposite directions tended to keep the proportion at working ages stable. In fact, up to 1940 the number of children in the United States had fallen faster than that of old people had increased and the proportion of persons of working age increased from 63·7 per cent in 1910 to 68·1 per cent in 1940. Since 1940 the rise in birth-rates has had an opposite effect and the persons of working age were in 1960 down to 59·7 per cent. In most underdeveloped countries, owing to the fall in infant mortality, there is a large increase in the proportion of boys under working age, and here the proportion of males at working age to the total population is falling rather than rising, but again only gradually.

Two ratios that are more variable must be set against these two ratios that are, in practice, fairly constant. We may perhaps neglect (iii) the proportion of men beyond working age who are in fact working, a proportion which though variable involves only a few and hardly affects the aggregate. The other ratio, which does strongly affect the degree of mobilization of different countries is (iv) the proportion of women gainfully occupied.

Long-term and short-term considerations are here again opposed as for secondary school and university students. A high economic mobilization of women might involve children being neglected for the sake of industrial earnings with consequent economic and social loss later on. But not every woman is needed away from industry all her working life. A fair test of the highest proportion of women that could, without long-run loss, be mobilized, occurred in the "combing out" for the British war effort of 1939–45—an effort using combs finer toothed than any other belligerent country. Women in care of children were exempt, and eight million, or about half of the total number of women of working age, were not mobilized in services or industry even by 1944. Since at working ages the population of men and of women is not very different, an addition of about 50 per cent to the (male) man-power may thus form a rough maximum for the economic mobilization of women in the Western economies. In short, nearly 75 per cent of the total population of working age can be mobilized.

The deviations from this standard will be discussed later, particularly as they appear in underdeveloped countries. But it must be observed at the outset how non-economic biological as well as sociological factors affect the degree of mobilization. The age structure of both sexes obviously directly determines the proportion that is able-bodied, but biology affects also the occupation of women, directly and indirectly. Where a community has many children compared to adults, a greater proportion of adult women will presumably be caring for them at home or in crèches and therefore will not be free for economic mobilization.

Biological family checks to women's economic mobilization are reinforced by the sociological checks of tradition and convention. In developed as well as underdeveloped countries unmarried girls, though of working age, are supposed by the traditional social code to live at home even though in their home town or county there is no work available for women. Thus potential women workers are less geographically mobile than men workers and may, in consequence, not be gainfully occupied at all. The majority of women workers live as wives or daughters in a family where they are not the main earners. Owing to the cost of living on their own, they have an economic as well as the sociological motive to seek work where their men-folk work and are less likely to move independently. Thus jobs may in some places remain unfilled and the total mobilized less than it might have been.

An exception to the comparative immobility of women occurs in domestic service. During the English Industrial Revolution country girls appear to have moved into the towns as readily as their brothers who were seeking factory employment in industries where, often enough, women were not employed. The girls found a "home" as domestics in the homes of the industrial employers, the professional classes, or the idle rich. A somewhat similar mobility appears to be occurring in Russian urbanization today, and accounts for an employment of domestics by professional men to an extent impossible to their counterparts in Western countries.

In manufacturing industry, however, it remains possible for women to be unemployed or unoccupied in one region, yet relatively highly paid and possibly in short supply in a neighbouring region, without supply meeting demand. This "anomaly" or "friction" (as an economist sees it) is quite likely to happen wherever mining and heavy industries not employing women are localized, as in South Wales or West Virginia.

Differences in the proportion of women occupied between different regions of the same developed country occur primarily because the economic forces that would level out occupation (unoccupied women moving where their occupation was demanded) are blocked by sociological forces. It is orthodox economic doctrine that women's wages are less than men's for apparently similar types of work, because (though about the same number of women are supplied by nature) much work demanded in industry is unsuitable for them as too heavy. This view ignores the fact that, on sociological grounds, a large "hard core" of adult women, in Western societies at least half of them, is not in the labour market at all. They are not even part of the potential labour supply. No wage that industry could pay would move them from the care of homes and especially of young children. Between married women *actually* occupied and this core (one might almost write the *home-service corps*) of "no-occupation at any price" there are, however, many marginal cases. Recruitment of married women in industry is increasing

E

and is now likely to occur when they have no children, or their children have grown up, or when part-time work is available. In successive decades beginning in 1890 the percentage of occupied to all married women rose in the United States (135, p. 253) from 4·6 to 5·6, 10·7, 9·0, 11·7 and (in 1940) 15·2 per cent. A related series may be continued till more recent times. In 1940 the U.S. Census (239, p. 227) gives the percentage of all women 14 and over that were married and in the labour force as 16·7. In 1950 this percentage was 24·8, in 1960 31·7 and in 1965 35·7. In 1967 over 450,000 women were employed part-time in Great Britain (115), or 16·7 per cent of all women employed.

Definite sociological limits to women's employment will hold, however, where young children and other family dependants are involved. In fact, it is doubtful whether the admittedly smaller industrial demand for women's than for men's labour is not met by a market supply of women still smaller, relatively, to the supply of men. Interpretation of the lower wage-rates of women should in fact be sought elsewhere than in the economics of their total demand and supply. The sociology of family relationships must be called in (62, pp. 19–37) and also the low degree of solidarity and trade-union "organizability" of women with very different family roles—partially dependent, independent, family supporter—involving very different wage demands.

In underdeveloped countries, as Table VI appears to show, the percentage of occupied women varies even more widely than in the countries fully developed. Numerous interpretations have been put forward, but before plunging into interpretation and the tracing of causes, we must recall the deep pitfall in comparing occupation statistics where large proportions are working in agriculture on small farms as part of the extended family groups and where women perform work mostly unpaid. There is evidence, for instance, that the high percentage of Indian women occupied appearing in Table VI is the result of counting in unpaid family workers. Sociological studies, however, show that underdeveloped, apart from the most primitive, countries are less likely than developed countries to mobilize fully their woman-power and to utilize it for the general economy. There are certainly numerous religious taboos. The very low proportion of women shown as occupied in Pakistan may, for instance, be the effect of Mohammedanism.

Hitherto, under the term "crude mobilization", it is the proportion *occupied* that has been considered. *Occupied* indicates persons considering themselves attached or belonging to an industry and so describing their position at the census. It does not necessarily mean that they are fully employed at the time. A further loss in economic mobilization, turning crude into *net* mobilization, will, therefore, appear when we subtract the *unemployed* from the occupied and allow for *underemployment* among the employed.

TABLE VI

	Britain	U.S.A.	PERCENTAGE OF WOMEN TO MEN OCCUPIED: PAST AND PRESENT IN DEVELOPED, PRESENT IN UNDER-DEVELOPED COUNTRIES					
1870		16·6						
1880		17·6						
1900–1	41·0	22·7						
1920	41·9	26·6						
1940	—	32·1						
1950	44·4	36·8						
1950–5		37·2	India	42·3	Pakistan	7·0	Brazil	17·0
			Mexico	15·7	Egypt	11·3		
1960	51·6	50·3	India	46·1	Pakistan	14·3	Brazil	21·8
			Mexico	21·8	Egypt	8.0		

Source: International Labour Office Yearbook, Labour Statistics, 1962, 1966, 1967. For Britain Annual Abstracts; U.S. Statistical Abstracts.

In most developed countries statistics of unemployment rates are published at frequent intervals, and usually these rates measure unemployment at a given moment of time. Part-time workers appear as employed if the count falls at the time they are employed, otherwise not—on balance, part-time employment is thus accurately recorded. Where *few* people are subsistence farmers and almost all work for pay there will be little *under*employment except for this part-time work.

In underdeveloped countries, where much agriculture is carried on by the extended families familiar to the sociologist, the amount of underemployment is harder to assess. Persons occupied may be employed only occasionally (154) or may work ineffectively without sufficient material resources, including land, at their disposal. We shall have to revert to this situation when dealing in Chapters VI and VII with underdeveloped countries. At present it is mentioned only as a caution against taking the crude proportion mobilized as an exact measure of the use of human resources. Part of the occupied population may in reality be unused capacity to be subtracted before computing the net mobilization which will reflect the proportion of the population genuinely at work producing goods and services to raise the community's living standard.

2. Changing Economic Structure and Mobility Between Industries

When the number of workers in each of the economic activities or industries of a country are compared (or any other measure, such as output, of their relative importance), it is common practice to speak of that country's economic or industrial *structure*. To avoid confusion with the *organic structure* of an industry formed by the complex of its firms and plants, I shall, however, speak of the *activity structure*. Usually the total occupied at work is expressed as a hundred, the numbers in each activity as a percentage of the total.

The percentage in agriculture has already been given for various times and places (Table II). Since the value of the productivity-a-worker is usually lower in agriculture than in manufacture, this percentage forms, with a low degree of mobilization, the two elements "double diluting" (as said earlier) the lower productivity in manufacturing activity. The contribution of these two elements in depressing the income of the underdeveloped countries can be roughly measured in comparing continents. Productivity per worker in manufacturing during 1953, as shown in Table V, was about as 5 to 13, to 21, to 59, respectively in East and South-East Asia, Latin America, Europe, and North America; and, unfortunately, these inequalities had been increasing between 1938 and 1953. To make things more unequal still, a much higher proportion of workers were in agriculture compared to manufacture in the Asian and Latin American countries, and as we also know they had fewer workers generally as a proportion of the population.

In agriculture a trend was traced, mining depends on the opening up of a country's natural resources; but in other sectors of the economy, apart from a trend toward the "tertiary" group of services, there is a mobility within limits rather than a trend. Moreover, the structure of activities of different countries will at one time be fairly similar, but that of all countries may change considerably from time to time.

Professor J. S. Bain (209) has compared for a number of countries the proportion employed in the broad sectors of economic activity, and a pattern for the non-extractive activity structure comes out fairly clearly. In each of the five developed Western countries which he cites—the United States, Canada, the United Kingdom, Sweden and France—the manufacturing sector employs most, from 25·8 to 40·1 per cent; services, excluding commerce and transportation, come second, ranging from 16·8 to 22·3 per cent; and third, commerce, ranging from 13·0 to 22·0 per cent. In each country, except France, transportation comes fourth with 6·5 to 8·1 per cent, construction fifth with 6·1 to 7·9 per cent. In France these two sectors, in fact, just transpose rank. (It should be noted that in Bain's original table, the United Kingdom's commerce and transport were transposed in error.)

In contrast to this similarity in the activity structure at a given time of developed countries (the underdeveloped are discussed in Chapter VI), the structure of activities of the same country may differ considerably from time to time. G. C. Allen (3, p. 219) has shown the remarkable changes in the British all-sector structure since 1911; and the manufacturing activity structure of the United States in 1914 seems to differ quite as much from the same country's 1963 structure as the United States structure in 1963 differed from the British structure at that time. This is surprising since, unlike the United States, Britain—a throughput economy—cannot be fed from its own resources and must export particular lines of manufacture or die. The broad outline given in Table VII comprising the two United States and one British structure, show Britain as today exceeding the United States by 1·8 points in the proportion of factory employees in textiles, 3·7 in metals and 2·8 in transport equipment. Much wider differences appear between the United States structure in 1914 and that in 1963. Here the differences run to 6·5 points less in lumber and furniture, 6·6 in other industries and 7·9 in textiles and apparel in 1963, and 5·4 more in transport equipment and 10·5 in metals. Isolated from the need to export, this United States deployment indicates the sheer change in home demand and supplies or in technology, and the continual need for labour mobility.

Aggregating industries into a very few broad groups, to permit comparison between countries, under-represents the very fast change that may occur in the fortunes of specific individual industries. In Table XIX even in the relatively short period of the years between 1947 and 1965 growth in the

TABLE VII

PERCENTAGES EMPLOYED IN BROAD INDUSTRIAL
GROUPS OUT OF TOTAL IN MANUFACTURES

Groups	U.S.A. 1963	U.S.A. 1914	U.S.A. Difference from 1914	U.K. 1962–3	U.K. Difference from U.S.A. 1963
Food, Drink and Tobacco	10·6	7·6	+ 3·0	9·5	−1·1
Textile and Apparel (excluding Footwear)	13·2	21·1	− 7·9	15·0	+1·8
Lumber and Furniture	5·8	12·3	− 6·5	3·6	−2·2
Paper and Printing	9·3	6·5	+ 2·8	7·1	−2·2
Chemicals and Petroleum	5·5	5·0	+ 0·5	5·8	+0·3
Stone, Clay, Glass	3·5	4·8	− 1·3	3·9	+0·4
Metals	31·8	21·1	+10·5	35·3	+3·7
Transport Equipment (including Ships)	9·9	4·5	+ 5·4	12·7	+2·8
Other Industries including Leather, Instruments and Ordnance	10·5	17·1	− 6·6	7.1	−3·4
Totals	100·1	100·0	44·5	100·0	17·9

twenty major groups' value added are shown to have ranged between 120 per cent for leather and 381 for chemicals. Among individual industries even in the shorter period between 1954 and 1963, the range was from a loss of 25 per cent for cordage and twine, 24 per cent for manufactured ice and 10 per cent for millinery to a gain of 186 per cent for toilet preparations, 176 per cent for computing machines and 173 per cent for plastic products. Unemployment can obviously not be avoided or manpower fully used without considerable mobility of labour.

These changes, however, within the manufacturing sector do not constitute a trend since they are erratic and do not follow one line. Textiles moved up last century, the metal industry this, but it may soon be the turn of plastics. The need for mobility is particularly evident when these erratic changes are superimposed on the long-term trend such as mechanization, the trend in displacing occupations (e.g. staff for operative, white for blue collar) *within* the manufacturing sectors and the trend within the non-manufacturing sectors such as that from agriculture to service. Between 1930 and 1964, while the fall in the United States among the agriculturally employed was from 25·0 per cent of the total occupied to 7·6 per cent, in services other than transport the percentage rose from 30·2 to 48·2. In transport, labour has had to adjust to the do-it-your-self movement with the change-over from railroads to owner-driven automobiles, accounting incidentally for the big rise the table shows in the percentage employed making transport equipment.

In a free economy the importance of the various activities depends chiefly on the market demand for their products or services. As demands change with changes in fashion, with consumers' income levels, and also with the type of goods that can be supplied and their cost (and here applications of science are influential) so the relative importance of the activities supplying those demands must change. Textiles and clothing have fallen in numbers occupied, mainly because many people in the developed countries have not increased the amount of clothing they wear (rather the opposite for women) and the increase of clothing per body occurring in the under-developed countries is being met by production at home.

Parallel with changes in *consumer* demand, new scientific techniques and new discoveries have changed the demands *producers* make upon different industries. The use of oil and hydroelectricity instead of coal has stopped the large-scale export of British coal and accounts for much of the drop in the percentage of miners. The use of fertilizers by farmers has increased the importance of the chemical industry. Changes in *public* demand have also affected industrial structure. Armaments, for instance, have played a part in increasing the proportion of workers in the metal industries.

The changes in the demands of the private consumer can be substantiated by comparing family budgets in developed countries at different times and at different income levels. It can be deduced from Engel's Law described in Chapter I, Section 5, that agriculture and food manufactures take up a smaller proportion of income, as the average level of income has risen over time. At any one time different industries will thus have different intensities of demand for their products by consumers at different income levels. As families' income moves up or down so will the structure of their demands. The degree of this "income-elasticity" can thus (as by Prais and Houthakker (150)) be measured for each demand.

Not only do the changes occurring in the structure of demands due to changes in standards of living require long-term deployment and mobility of labour, but forecasting and planning the future of each differentiated industry is fraught with fluctuations, uncertainties, and risks arising from the very trends we traced in the last chapter: the application of science and invention of new goods or cheaper processes, the localization of industry and the need to live by exporting for foreigners in competition with foreigners, and the increases in standards of living.

The risk varies widely between manufacturing industries. Even when we consider only the *major* groups in Table XIX, the amplitude of the fluctuations in production from peak to trough of production, 1947–55, was as low as 1·7 per cent for the food group, but as high as 14·7 per cent for primary metals. Among individual industries the variation was of course wider, from 1·53 per cent for miscellaneous foods to 26·98 per cent for truck trailers (210, pp. 219–22). These fluctuations were not like seasonal variations, certain and foreseeable, any more than the precise direction of growth. It is only in a limited number of manufactures and services that producers can plan consumers' demand as propounded by Galbraith (219) by differentiating products and advertising. Yet, in spite of all this uncertainty, some help in forecasting and planning can be derived from observed connexions between level of income and consumption patterns such as Engel's Law formulates, and also from certain inherent connexions or linkages between industries, particularly those the economist has named joint demand. Forecasting is here akin to the logistics of army supply. Furniture, wall-paper and paints are in joint demand with housing and, with housing booms, were forecast to prosper and (72, p. 115), in fact, did so. Since fashion spreads, it is also possible to argue from fashion-leading countries such as the United States today to fashion-following countries. The relative fall in the textile and clothing industries (excluding shoes) shown in Table VII Column 3, and rise in the metal industries seems, indeed, world-wide. The United Nations gives the world proportion of persons out of all manufacturers employed in textiles and clothing as 29·6 per cent in 1938, 23·9 in 1953; in metals as 26·6 per cent in 1938, 32·1 in 1953 (184, p. 113). From 1953 to 1963 the value of world textile and clothing production rose 54 (under inflation) of metal production 100 per cent.

Thus, in response to the demand at home and overseas, and in reaction to competition with overseas suppliers, a country's working population not only moves out of agriculture but must continually change the structure of its manufacturing and service activities. The example of England, switching from mining, private domestic service, and textiles and clothing manufacture to metal and chemical manufacture is no isolated case. If changing demand-and-supply situations are to be met, no part of the activity structure of any country's economy can be considered immutable.

This changeability applies not only to whole countries, developed or underdeveloped, but also, within countries, to their several regions wherever particular industries are localized. The regions such as Lancashire or New England where the textile industry is, or was, localized, facing loss of employment and falling standards of living, are loud in their calls for political help. Quickest help can be brought by the action of firms themselves developing, with or without State finance, industries other than textile, and diversifying the region. Labour is more capable of mobility from one industry to another when both industries are in the same place and workers need not change their homes. If, owing to the difficulty of changing homes or for other reasons, workers remain immobile when consumers' demands change, they are liable to become unemployed or part-time employed. Many a worker before he became occupied in any new industry may have passed through this stage in his old occupation, and insecurity of employment rather than lower earnings may have been the immediate cause of his change of industry. Correlating increases in employment with increases in earnings for the several orders of industry, A. J. Brown (23, pp. 449–63) shows that in the interwar period there was little correlation in Britain between the earnings and employment changes. The stick of differential unemployment rates rather than the carrot of wage-rates seems to have operated. In the post-war inflationary and full-employment period, however, a differential change in the earnings carrot appeared the chief stimulus to mobility.

Certainly, if an economy is to develop and raise standards of living, mobility must be allowed free play either in response to differences in wages, to unemployment or to other differentials. It is important, therefore, to analyse the factors for and against mobility and the persons who are most likely to respond favourably to differentials.

3. A MODEL FOR FREE MOBILITY ANALYSIS

In time of war, State compulsion was applied to achieve in several countries the industrial mobility required for victory. In peace-time, when free societies do not apply compulsion, thought must be given to the complex of interdependent conditions and inducements that influence a worker to act voluntarily. I first developed an analytical model of such a complex in discussing (57, pp. 96 *et seq.*, and 70, p. 26) possible causes and effects of low productivity and unrest. A similar model could usefully be applied to mobility. The original model traced the effect both upon human capacity and willingness, what a man *can* and *will* do—a simple dichotomy, but supported by high psychological authority (45, p. 22). The effect was measured by specified tests of efficiency (such as output, accidents, and lost time) of a number of particular conditions of employment. The model was used not just as a conceptual exercise, but as a framework for empirical investigations. A summary of some of the evidence collected appears in diagrammatic form in my *Visual Analysis* (215, Figure 20). The multiple conditions can be grouped as "job" or work characteristics, such as type and hours of work on the one hand (to which might be added the environment such as climate where the "job" occurs), and on the other hand as man or worker characteristics—the type of worker on whom work and hours impinge. This confrontation of work and worker is of course basic in the practice of vocational guidance and selection.

Similarly, mobility analysis would trace the effect of job and man characteristics upon human capacity and willingness measured by degree and direction of mobility (industry to industry, occupation to occupation, place to place) or of migration, country to country. The characteristics of the particular type of worker concerned will be taken up shortly (§5) and are particularly interdependent with work traits. Jobs that are attractive or repulsive will not be the same for the intellectual with his characteristic horror of boredom as for most manual workers. It is the intellectual who writes about it, however, and his views about the workers' ranking of jobs must be checked by objective observation.

Just as long hours and intensity of work were shown to cause (a temporary degree of) *incapacity to work* (i.e. fatigue) which was reduced by shorter hours, so *incapacity to move* from industry to industry may be caused by cost of travel, lack of housing near the job, ignorance of opportunities (if the receiving industry is distant), or (wherever the industry) by lack of training or the inborn type of capacity required.

In between the work and worker characteristics this model puts the economic or cash characteristics, including with immediate earnings the cost of learning, if any, and economic prospects and security.

Even if most of the work characteristics cannot, except for hours of labour, easily be changed, many of the man and economic characteristics can. The employer can change rates of wages to attract labour. Many conditions lowering capacity to move, again, can be, and have been (73, pp. 120, 125, 183), overcome by State control over industry and services for industry; by subsidized housing, for instance, or grants for journeys, by information from employment exchanges and (particularly where the workers are young and not committed to any one industry) by technical colleges and vocational training and guidance.

Unwillingness to work is, by definition, overcome through "incentives". *Unwillingness to move* from one industry to another can be overcome by appropriate "attractives". Here economists have, for nearly two centuries, suggested besides the economic attractive of wages, other types of attractives and deterrents, many of them sociological; but unlike the parallel case of

TABLE VIII

MODEL OF TERMS AND CONDITIONS OF EMPLOYMENT INFLUENCING MOBILITY

Characteristics of The Work Itself	Economic Characteristics (Payments in Exchange)	Characteristics of the Worker and his Experience
Hours and Strain of Work	Cost of Learning*	
Type of Work Monotony	Payment Method and amount of Wages or Earnings Perquisites and Tips	Selection of Individuals Intelligence Temperament
Physical Conditions and Hazards	Prospect of Success* Promotion Future Profits	Types of Worker Sex—Married or Single Age
Responsibility and Trust*	Economic Security* Risk of Unemployment Pension Schemes	Education, Training Skill and Experience
Sociability		
Independence		Cost of Moving Home Lack of Housing
Respectability Status, Honour* Prestige, etc.		Ignorance of Opportunities for Work at a Distance

HUMAN FACTOR

(Capacity and Willingness to Move)

Turnover from Plant to Plant in Same Industry	Switch from Occupation to Occupation	Switch from Industry to Industry	Geographical Travel from Home to Home

* Mentioned by Adam Smith, *Wealth of Nations*, Book I, Ch. 10.

incentives to work economists have not been helped much by psychologists. Adam Smith (173, I, 10) mentions agreeableness (including honour), easiness of learning, constancy of employ-ment, probability of success and the trust which must be reposed in those who exercise any employment. Marshall (129, VI, iii,

8) put it that to be attractive a trade's *net advantages* must out-
balance that of alternative trades. "The attractiveness of a
trade depends on other causes besides the difficulty and strain of
the work to be done in it on the one hand, and the money
earnings to be got in it on the other." "One trade is healthier or
cleanlier than another . . . is carried on in a more wholesome or
pleasant locality . . . involves a better social position." Marshall
proceeds to quote Adam Smith's "well-known remark" that the
dishonour in which many people hold the work of a butcher and
to some extent the butcher himself raises earnings in the
butchers' trade above those in other trades of equal difficulty.
Adam Smith, indeed, followed this up with a further illustration of the effect of social disrepute. "The most detestable of all
employments, that of public executioner, is, in proportion to
the quantity of work done, better paid than any common trade
whatever."

Considering the importance always attached by economists
to mobility, it is surprising that so little empirical research has
been done to test the disadvantageous or advantageous effect
upon measures of mobility of these characteristics that form,
according to the economic "classics", the conditions of mobility,
and to verify or falsify classical theories. It is particularly surprising, when most of these characteristics, like hours of work,
as well as their effects, such as labour turnover, are fairly
measurable. Of the disadvantages, cost of learning can be
audited, insecurity tested by rates of unemployment for the
industry, monotony by frequency and regularity of repetition,
physical hazards by accident, occupational disease, sickness and
mortality rates, physical conditions by thermometer and light
meter readings, and so forth. On a modest scale I did once
show, for instance (57, p. 164), that at a large United States
plant, departments with poor air conditions and noise had
turnover and requests for transfer at considerably higher rates
than average; departments with bad lighting and muscularly
strenuous work rates, however, near or below average.

Of the advantages, earnings of occupations are now published, and prospect of success could be indicated by the frequency and extent of promotion. Though less often cited by
economists, sociability is certainly important to some people and
independence to others, for instance, farmers. One could be

measured by the number of contacts with other persons, the other, for a whole industry, by the proportion of persons working on their own account in that industry. Recently, to measure respectability, sociologists have devoted some attention to the way people grade occupations and industrial groupings; and job analysis has tried to measure the strain, and, through the time span during which the use of discretion is authorized (102), even the trust and responsibility of different jobs. Job analysis has assessed the rewards jobs deserve, but presents little synthesis of all these measures and gradings, giving appropriate points or weights to each, either to explain flights from industries known to have taken place or to foster any movements that are required.

A nice question on flights, and one important to the tourist trade, is why domestic services have, between 1931 and 1951, been depopulated of women. In domestic service, though hours of duty were long and often uncertain, there was less hazard, insecurity, monotony, or need of learning than in women's manufacturing jobs. With board and lodging free, the earnings offered today compare not unfavourably with that of factory work. Few industries offer any economic prospects to women, so the answer probably lay in lack of respectability or status, lack of independence of one's mistress, particularly when "living in", and lack of sociability not only by reason of long working hours but by segregation from fellow servants. Hotels employing many domestics could (and still can) obtain and keep staff more easily than the home employing only one cook-general in close contact with the mistress. The personal touch, said to be lacking in large factories, can apparently be overdone. Questioning girls about why they disliked domestic service though no other jobs then offered employment, English interviewers heard the majority explaining without reticence that their mistress "is an old cat" or "an interfering old cat".

More important to industrial development than the deterrents to domestic service are those to business management, and the same question of respectability may again be involved. Among middle-class employments, business enterprise is probably more attractive than the civil services on the score of lower cost of learning, freedom from monotony, chance of financial success and independence; less attractive on the score of insecurity and financial risk and perhaps some physical hazards (particularly gastric ulcers). As to respectability and status, the position varies with the sociological "culture" of a country. In the United States of America business tycoons rank high, but in countries of the Old World, both underdeveloped and developed, trade and particularly manufacture are usually thought rather "low". Their position has risen since the days of Jane Austen or even Ruskin (72, p. 329), but business and works managers are still officially ranked in Britain as of second grade below the first-grade medical officers and country solicitors, and this ranking seems to be supported by popular judgement. Certainly, entries in *Who's Who* of industrialists form a far lower proportion of all entries in Britain than in the United States, though the proportion of men in industry is higher.

Later, in Chapter VI, lack of business and technical enterprise will be stressed as a main obstacle to a country's development. Social gradings, so far as they discourage recruitment into industrial enterprise and management, thus tend to slow down development and the raising of standards of living. This conclusion applies to countries both underdeveloped and developed. One of the main reasons, apart from material resources, for the success of the United States and newer Anglo-Saxon countries in raising the standard of living is probably the greater prestige and respectability of industrial enterprise and management over other forms of middle-class life such as politics. The distribution of ability at birth may be the same in all countries, but in the new countries the most ambitious, best-educated, and able young men become recruits for business instead of for politics, the civil service, or the professions; and business efficiency flourishes. In older countries, like Great Britain, politics, law, and the civil service have superior prestige, and government is "cleaner" and more ably run, perhaps, in consequence. Whatever natural scarcity of talent may exist for industrial management, sociological factors appear likely to maintain that scarcity for some considerable time. Thus do a country's institutions and scale of values, its sociological pushes and pulls, have great influence on its economic life and development. Indeed, a circle is set up, virtuous or vicious according to circumstances, or to taste. An occupation's respectability status pulls in the abler young, and their ability sheds lustre and adds further status to the occupation, thus giving it a push to be yet more respectable and attractive. This circular status pull and push has many other applications —to "crack" schools, for instance, or individual "prestige" firms.

4. THE ECONOMICS AND SOCIOLOGY OF MOBILITY

The economist puts wages, salaries, and earnings in the centre of the model because they form the factor most exactly measurable and also because the possibilities of their adjustment upward will reflect the profitability of any industry and thus ultimately the consumers' demand for its products. But neither Adam Smith nor Marshall were, as we have seen, such all-out believers in economic man as Bastiat, who thought that labour betakes itself automatically to the quarter where it is best remunerated. They both believed in net advantages, of which money payment was only one advantage put in the balance. Money payments, however, are the most easily adjustable of the mobility pulls or pushes, and the wage-structure might be expected to be adjusted according to the changing national needs.

Yet no national policy or plan existed in most Western countries until recently, for changes in wage-structure. The determination of the different wage-rates has been left, as the prices of services and goods are left, to the forces of supply and demand on the market. It is not a policy of *laissez faire* for individual bargaining, however, but for collective bargaining. *Laissez collectives faire* describes the situation in three words. Trade unions are pitted, as controlling supply, against the demand of employers' associations; and each industry has its own organized antagonists. The outcome of the struggle will not necessarily depend on the national demand and the available national labour supply and resources, but rather on the relative bargaining strength of the antagonists in each industry. If the two sides in any industry finally call in mediators and arbitrators, the tradition is for these outsiders not to impose any principles of political economy or national policy. Employers, trade unions, and mediators all have at the back of their minds somewhat similar "human-value" views (such as sociologists delight to study) of relative wages and of what constitutes a "fair" differential. In developed countries their views of a reasonable wage have largely been built up on a long industrial tradition almost dating back to the guilds— views of the just price often more appropriate to medieval than present conditions of supply and demand.

This sociological rigidity has, however, been modified in two directions. Where piece-wages are paid or overtime is extensively worked, earnings—the take-home pay—may vary greatly from the wage-rate for the standard week, and may actually reflect productivity; and in very low-paid occupations or industries, such as were agricultural labour and mining, wages have, by State action, been raised beyond a minimum living wage. These rational departures from the "reasonable", i.e. the traditional wage, have resulted in a narrowing of the earning differentials between the unskilled and the semi-skilled worker (usually on piece-rates) and the skilled craftsman (156, p. 170). Yet this narrowing runs counter to the economic principle of the marginal utility of scarce resources, since the relatively scarce skilled craftsmen, whose cost of learning by apprenticeship has been high, are being paid a reduced differential over the less-scarce unskilled workers.

If we take a wider view and include among occupations within an industry not only unskilled, semi-skilled, and skilled grades but industrial managers, accountants, salesmen, and quasi-professional specialists, then average wage and salary rates of each occupation are found to differ quite radically. Comparing these grades, one might expect a real test of Adam Smith's dictum that economic attractives make up for non-economic terms and conditions, such as dishonour. Some basis for the economists' logic can be found in the cost of professional and management training and in the possible scarcity of supply of the inborn talent demanded, yet on the whole, high rates of pay seem *negatively* correlated with disagreeableness of work —its monotony and hazard—and with inconstancy and lack of prospects and above all lack of honour. As Lady Wootton puts it (204, p. 68)—

> Nearly all the features of the wage and salary structure . . . which are anomalies from the angle of economic theory become

F

intelligible in a broader frame of reference. It is the social factors
which are missed in the economist's interpretation; and what is
anomalous to the economist may make perfectly good sense to the
sociologist. In a hierarchical society such as ours, large issues of
social status are involved in wage and salary scales. Pay and
prestige are closely linked; and (in spite of some exceptions) it is
the rule that the high-prestige person should be also the highly
paid person; and vice versa. Once this rule is admitted as a factor
in its own right, it is remarkable how effectively it explains much
that on a purely economic hypothesis, has to be explained away
... and the same principle explains the importance attached to
the rule that those who give orders should be paid more than those
to whom their orders are given. Where prestige depends on pay,
one cannot be expected to obey, or even, perhaps, to respect,
one's economic inferiors. Again, the positive relationship between
monetary and non-monetary remuneration, which appears so
persistently from top to bottom of our wage and salary structure
and squares so badly with the economist's "balance of net
advantages", is just what one would expect in a society in which
the dirty and disagreeable jobs are left to people whose pay is
appropriate to their humble social position.

Economists have, as Lady Wootton says, "explained away"
this "anomaly" in their theory by the concept of "non-competing groups" between which, "whether from natural causes
or as a result of existing social conditions, the movement of
labourers from grade to grade is not free". Non-competing
groups or grades, though put forward by such classical economists as F. W. Taussig and Henry Sidgwick, are essentially a
sociological concept, and today sociologists are investigating
statistically the precise degree of mobility of persons from grade
to grade. The question usually asked is how many can "climb
the social ladder" beginning, for instance, at the bottom rung
where the father was an unskilled labourer and the potential
climber attended only a primary school. Demographers, in
particular Glass, have shown that in all Western countries, at
least, the chances of getting to the top rung are in favour of the
man who started fairly high, but the exact odds depends on a
particular country's culture, its existing class barriers and
system of education. In England (Scotland has another culture)
mobility between rungs or grades is made harder by the
sociological phenomena of differences in pronunciation and
accent, and the differentiated streams going either through inde-

pendent boarding schools, preparatory and so-called "public", or else through state-aided day schools, where vast differences in family interests and atmosphere will affect the next generation. Thanks to scholarships, many more children of poorer parents now get into universities. And thanks to the falling birth-rates in the last generation of the rich, and to the greater number of upper-grade jobs (the rising staff ratios are one aspect of this) more of these children have a chance of stepping on to the upper rungs of the ladder. It is customary, therefore, to be optimistic about the trend toward greater class mobility and it is possible that Adam Smith's notion of pay balancing the other terms of employment may yet, after two hundred years, be fulfilled. But, as we shall see, the small self-made business man is less frequent today relatively to company managers. Glass points to the possibility (86)—

> that the introduction of joint stock enterprise and the growth in the size of the industrial unit may even have lowered social mobility as compared with the position at the beginning of the nineteenth century. The gradual entry of university graduates into executive and administrative posts in industry may have tended in that direction.

When a change from one industry to another involves geographical movement from place to place, women workers are, for mainly sociological family reasons already discussed, less mobile than men. Young persons of both sexes will, similarly, be restricted in mobility by home ties. On the other hand, the constant biological renewal of the population, youth replacing age, is a factor favouring industrial mobility.

Mobility, after all, is not required of everybody (not *all* textile workers should become metal workers!); and of the number that should move into an industry quite a proportion is represented by young people who have not become (socially or psychologically) committed to any particular industry. Even apart from the number of school-leavers entering industry for the first time, the labour turnover is particularly high among the younger workers. The higher earnings offered by the metal industries, even though only slightly higher, may be enough to attract a youth if he is not tied to some other industry. So, when an ageing textile worker dies or retires, his place may well be taken in the general labour force by a young man attracted to the metal industries. This process may be known as *rejuvenation* rather than mobility, but, by whatever name it is called, it remains an important social process for changing the structure of industrial activity.

Confirmation of the potency of this social process comes from two sources: differences in rates of turnover according to age, and differences in the age composition of workers in the various industries. A number of factories owned by large British firms all showed rates of turnover for men aged not more than 29 to be conspicuously higher than the rates of older men, in fact, on average, two or three times as high. For instance, in a firm owning several factories, turnover in 1950 (123, pp. 64–70) was as high as 68 per cent among men aged 20–24, but only 44, 34, 18, and 13 per cent among men aged respectively 25–29, 30–39, 40–49, and 50–59.

Evidence that the developing industries have on balance been attracting these younger men who "turn over" quickly is given by comparing age-structures. Some industries, by tradition or due to their technical requirements, use *very* young persons, others do not, but the wide age-range 20–39 may safely be taken as the basis of the comparison. In Britain 1962, this age-range formed a higher proportion of the total male working force in the developing chemical (43 per cent) and metal industries (43 per cent in vehicles, 43 per cent in engineering and 41 per cent in metals not elsewhere specified), than it did in the declining textiles and clothing industries with only 35 and 33 per cent between 20 and 39 years of age.

This social process of "mobility by rejuvenation" is more rapid for women than men workers because of the shorter average industrial life of women. The majority, by social custom, not to speak of physiological and housekeeping necessity, leave full-time employment on marriage or at least on the birth of the first child. In consequence, the age-structure of occupied women does not reflect the age-structure of the female (or male) population at large but over-represents the young. Men up to 24 formed 19·7 per cent of the total of men occupied in the United States, for instance, in March 1966; but women of the same age-group 23·3 per cent of the total of women occupied. Moreover, after 24 the number of occupied women fell off considerably faster with age, though recovering later to form a bimodal distribution. Between ages 20 and 24 the average of occupied women in each year was then 692,000, between ages 25 and 45, 506,000; while the number of occupied men remained fairly steady at 1,180,000 and 1,107,000 in the two age-groups. The younger girls who enter industry to take the place of those marrying, are not tied to their particular industry, and if they can reach it from home, may easily choose another industry altogether, thus allowing any required industrial mobility. The particularly rapid rejuvenation of the female working force has been a boon to employers with tender consciences about sacking or, as it is now euphemistically called, declaring a redundancy. It has made it possible to promise no dismissal because of redundancy and yet have mobility and flexibility. As one employer put it to me, the girls, on marriage, sack themselves.

Another form or direction of mobility, like rejuvenation, connected with age and sex, is that of moving right out of a country, in short, migration. Immigrants will tend to move into the industry or occupation paying most. They are usually men of working age and, once employed, will thus increase the degree of general economic mobilization as well as be likely to supply the newer economic demands. Emigrants from the home country who had been at work will, contrariwise, diminish general mobilization, but many will presumably be in fear of unemployment or be underemployed and thus will be leaving an industry less in demand.

We turn now to the observed and measured degrees of mobility. The mere magnitude of the labour turnover generally has not perhaps been sufficiently appreciated in connexion with mobility. A high proportion of the high labour turnover consists in voluntary quitting of jobs by a floating population of workers. Later (IV, §8) it will be shown that most large factories are, for these personnel, far from stable institutions, to which they are committed. Men and women workers are certainly accustomed to leaving their jobs in a factory at rates much higher than is necessary to achieve the degree of mobility required by the economy as a whole. Official records of labour turnover (239, 1965, p. 243) show for the years 1963 to 1965 monthly separation rates averaging yearly between 3·9 per cent and 4·3 per cent, of which 1·4 to 1·9 per cent are voluntary "quits". This would mean a loss annually of almost 25 per cent of factory personnel. But it will be shown later that most of the quitting occurs among "floating" new hands, leaving a fairly permanent core in the plant over the years. A small proportion left because of death, retirement, or, for women, marriage. Of the remaining leavers, the question how many merely transferred to a factory in the same industry, how many changed industries, is more difficult to ascertain.

Another characteristic of the worker besides sex and age which has been found greatly to affect the magnitude of the turnover is his skill grading. Turnover rates are lowest among the skilled, medium among the semi-skilled, highest among the unskilled. Investigating several British factories in 1948, Joyce Long (123, pp. 80–3) found annual rates as different, respectively, as 6, 26, and 65 per cent. Certainly, where redundancy occurs it is the skilled men having to change their place of residence who will be least adjustable and will need high compensation. For unskilled and semi-skilled living in towns which possess a variety of localized industries (a condition shortly to be accounted for) mobility is high. And skilled craftsmen find it easy to transfer, if within the same town, to the same skilled occupation (for instance, toolmaking) even though in a different industry.

To sum up. Except among the skilled workers and where a change of home is involved, an effective degree of mobility is not limited by unwillingness to change employment or industries. In fact, the mass of semi-skilled and unskilled workers are uncommitted to their factories and turn over readily. Often enough they move into an industry toward which mobility is nationally not demanded—may one coin the word malmobility? It is economic *incapacity* to move rather than psychological unwillingness that checks the required deployment. Some incapacity may be inherent, but for most workers incapacity to move as required can be overcome by various forms of state action such as public housing.

5. THE CONFLICTING FORCES IN ADAPTING TO DEVELOPMENT: A SUMMARY

Enough has perhaps been added on mobility to the mainly

economic trends traced in Chapter I to form an adequate background for the realistic analysis shortly to be undertaken of the trends with a greater *sociological* element, such as urbanization, larger organizations and their government by managers. Materials and markets and consequent technological factors have determined economic development and set up a train of events; but so also have sociological factors such as the family, class-distinctions, age-distributions, and the urban growth. The clash of these forces may be represented and summed up with some anticipation of future chapters in the form of thesis, antithesis and synthesis. Theses and antitheses are somewhat monolithic, but syntheses are matters of degree and can best be stated and verified in terms of statistical measures.

The first thesis relates to differentiation of industries traced already as one of the trends of development. This differentiation can be logically planned and administered; but under the free-enterprise aspect of capitalism and the push and pull-back of profit and loss, firms will also tend to reach a logical mix of products, processes and services in their plants. This mix is likely to be similar for some plants which will thus according to thesis form a tidy, neat pattern of industries which the Census can distinguish.

The antithesis to this tidy neatness arises from the mobility between industries involved in development. The frontiers between industries are not only fluid according as the plants that constitute the industry integrate differently; but also according to particular attractives, social as well as economic, offered to workers who may move fairly freely (some types more, some less freely) from one industry to another. New industries evolve, old industries coalesce, grow, or decline in numbers, according as supplies of materials and labour vary and as demands of the consumer change with new standards of living, new wants, and new opportunities offered by new discoveries and inventions.

Between the thesis of tidiness and this antithesis of dynamic chaos, there is nevertheless a *synthesis* differentiating industries —but only to some degree.

Not all the activities of plants assigned to an industry by the Census are in fact engaged exclusively in the principal products of that industry. Firms, as already said, cross the Census industry boundaries more frequently than plants, and not all firms can be assigned to any one particular industry. Nevertheless, when plants, and particularly firms, cross the neat Census boundaries of industries, their activities are usually technologically or, to be more accurate, "ergologically" related. The plants owned by one firm may be in different industries but be performing consecutive processes in a vertical relation like plants in the iron and steel industry and in engineering industries. Or the plants may be laterally "diversified" in different industries, (a) diverging from the same industry supplying the material like plants in the toys or sporting goods, or footwear industries from the rubber industry, or (b) converging on the same market as plants in the batteries and the electric-lighting accessories industries converge upon motor assembly. Or again in diagonal (service) integration some plants may be making the machinery for the plants in other industries owned by the same firm.

The second thesis, evidence for which will accumulate later, is that certain distinctive characteristics have developed for each of the more or less differentiated industries, for instance in the size of their plants or firms, their capital intensity and their plants' location pattern. This differentiation tends to be much the same in different countries, for instance the United States and Britain (69, 72, 79). The range of differentiation is wide even between the major groupings of industry as shown at the foot of Table XIX.

But the antithesis is that there is no uniformity in these characteristics. Certainly sizes of firm or plant and location are, within each industry, of wide variety, and this variety is largely due to sociological factors. Immobility of labour obviously affects industrial location, tradition the use of capital and the application of science, quasi-political empire building the size of the firm.

Nevertheless, in synthesis, there is not a completely random variety, and certain distinctive varieties of size, integration, and location peep through for particular industries. Though some industries, like printing, appear to have no typical size of plant at all, and nearly all industries contain plants of nearly all sizes; yet distinct typical size-*ranges*, where the majority of the workers are employed, appear in most industries. Statistically measured, there are *deviations* from the average size of plant or firm and from a localized centre, but they are usually not too wide or numerous, and we shall be able to speak of typical ranges of behaviour observed by a majority of plants or firms. The synthesis between no uniform organization of an industry and some distinctive varieties is, in short, a set of *variegated patterns* of location, plant and firm sizes, and integration. Statistics may recognize and compare these patterns expressing words like *most, a little, frequently, majority, minority, some* in more exact numerical terms. Statistical inquiries have discovered trends; but even if these trends change the average values, the pattern may stay. Plants in several industries, for instance, are becoming larger on average, and yet they fall into the same pattern of distribution around the average size. A *patterned trend* may best denote the dynamics of the second synthesis.

The third thesis is that these variegated patterns, specific to certain differentiated industries, can usually be logically explained as due ultimately to that industry's technological, material, and market characteristics. A given industry's pattern of organization will take form, persist, and survive when suited to these characteristics. This ergological thesis is particularly evident in the logical train of events set going by mechanization and other technological development based on scientific invention which is applicable (and applied) to yield higher economic efficiency in different industries. This train extends all the way from physical conditions of work and technology, through location and the scale of production and the size of organization, to the form of government and economic policy. It is observable in statistical measures, but it is often obscured by one or other of the multiple factors involved in all human affairs. The need to safeguard against risk is one of these factors, particularly the risk of putting all eggs into one industrial basket. More integration, particularly lateral integration, is thus logically undertaken than the economies of specializing in standard large-scale unit processes or products could justify.

The antithesis to this third thesis is sociological. It is not a new phenomenon, but with the release of powerful technological forces toward change, it becomes more surprising. It points to the slow lag with which human society adapts itself to the train of causation that should follow logically from scientific invention and its transmission. In the underdeveloped countries the sociological traits retarding economic development are most powerful, and a whole chapter (VII) must be devoted to the sociological limits imposed on economic development. Even in developed countries, as we have seen, workers do not move as soon as higher wages are offered anywhere; their mobility is restricted by a whole complex of physical, psychological, and social conditions.

The synthesis between the economic thesis and the sociological antithesis is, as its title implies, a main interest of this book. The pattern into which industry has actually evolved as a result of the conflicting forces has been discovered less from arm-chair deduction on general assumptions than from observation of the real world and the inductive analysis of the data—along the lines of the natural sciences. Considerable progress along these lines can be, and will be, reported in analysing industrial structure and government, both in developed economies, in the next three chapters, and, later, in underdeveloped countries.

CHAPTER III

ECONOMICS OF INDUSTRIAL LOCATION
AND URBAN SOCIOLOGY

1. Relevance and Measurement of
Industrial Location

In tracing the actual development of industrial countries, and
therefore the likely development of countries still underdeveloped, trends were indicated away from agriculture,
toward localization of certain industries and toward urbanization. The three trends are connected but basically independent.
Urbanization refers in particular to the growth of large towns of,
say, over 200,000 inhabitants and is not the inevitable implica-
tion of the trend, already discussed, away from agriculture. The
industries to which agriculturists switch might very well be conducted in small towns or larger villages. Even if the industries
had plants employing, say, up to five thousand, they could still
be accommodated in cities of less than 200,000 inhabitants.
Urbanization is thus a trend independent from agricultural
depopulation, to be separately measured and accounted for. Its
relation to industrial differentiation is more complex and requires research.

Research of realistic type, starting with measured traits and
trends, has, in developed countries, arisen in response to certain
problems that were thought to require solutions. These
problems were high unemployment and poverty in some locali-
ties and areas compared to others; large-scale movement of
people between regions, and loss, in certain age-groups, of
population; congestion of large cities, and sprawl of town into
country, and concentration of population into a metropolitan
megalopolis like that of London or Paris. In 1911 London and
the south and east regions of England, with 17·4 per cent of the
land area of Great Britain, had 32·0 per cent of its population;
by 1961 34·5 per cent. In 1946 the region of Paris covering only
2 per cent of the area of France had 16·5 per cent of France's

65

population, in 1962 18·2 per cent. In the United States similar problems arise in regional development. 1959 income per family in Mississippi was 51 per cent, that in Connecticut 121 of national average. Between 1940 and 1960 West Virginia fell in point of population from the twenty-fifth to the thirtieth largest state; and Kentucky and Mississippi each fell six places. And the same concentration of population can be found. In 1965 the region of the Washington–New York–Boston megalopolis consisting of Massachusetts, Connecticut, Rhode Island, New York, New Jersey, Pennsylvania, Maryland, Delaware and the District of Columbia with 4 per cent of the land area of the U.S. contained 26·0 per cent of the population. But, as we shall see (p. 82), this concentration has in the United States not been increasing.

A landmark in the history of industrial location was the report, issued in 1940, of the British Royal Commission on the Distribution of the Industrial Population, of which Sir Montague Barlow was Chairman. The Commission deals in the second section of its introduction with the "World Phenomenon of Urbanization", and its final conclusion sums up the objectives of national action as the regional dispersal of industries from congested urban areas, the diversification of industry in each region, and the redevelopment and limitation of the congested areas themselves. These objectives have in Britain been partially implemented in New Towns and in development of the old, with Green Belts limiting their sprawl. National policy may thus be summed as the five Ds: dispersal, diversification, decongestion, development, and delimitation.

These economic and social problems and their solution, various as they appear, all involve the location pattern of manufacturing industry. Unemployment is due to lack of industry occurring at a given time; urban congestion and sprawl of people, traffic, and housing are due to too much industry at a given place. The industries whose location is involved in a practical way are not *all* economic activities, but only certain footloose, mainly manufacturing, industries, because few other economic activities have a location pattern that can be altered. Mining and agriculture must take place where the mineral deposits and the soil exist; building, public utilities, and services, with some exceptions, such as the tourist trade, where the population is distributed.

Since it underlies so many practical problems, no apology is required for confining attention to manufacturing location and for beginning with a reference to the exact measurement of the location pattern of different industries. Two measures are required to answer the two separate questions: where, if at all, is an industry concentrated and to what degree, as compared to the general distribution of the population; and what industries, taking countries as a whole, are thus concentrated or not concentrated, and again to what degree. The first question is answered by a series of *location quotients* of any industry in the various areas; the second by one *coefficient of localization* for any industry. The calculation of both these measures has been (69, pp. 34–7; 72, pp. 37–9; 79, p. 9) explained and illustrated very amply in Britain, and the United States (188). Briefly, the location quotient is the degree to which those occupied in any industry in any place are more or are less numerous than would

MEASURING LOCATION AND LOCALIZATION

States in order of location quotient	(A) Total Employees in all Manufactures as percentage of all in U.S.	(B) Employees in Manufactures of Motor Vehicles and Bodies as percentage of all in U.S.	Location Quotients (B) ÷ (A)	Item in Calculation of Coefficient Localization (B) − (A) ÷ 100
Michigan	5·67	37·97	6·69	+0·3230
Indiana	3·60	8·68	2·41	+0·0508
Ohio	7·31	16·19	2·23	+0·0888
Wisconsin	2·73	5·44	2·00	+0·0271
Missouri	2·31	3·38	1·46	+0·0107

Coefficient of localization for the whole country = 0·50.   Total = 0·5004 or 0·50.

be expected if industries were evenly distributed among the occupied population of each area of a whole country. An illustration may be taken from the U.S. *Census of Manufactures* for 1963. Only five states had, for the motor vehicle industry, location quotients above unity calculating on the basis of employees in all manufactures, as in the first column of the above table. If preferred, workers in all occupations may be used as a base.

The single coefficient of localization for any industry in the country as a whole should not be obtained by averaging all the state quotients, since it must give due weight to the extent of the industry in each state. It is obtained simply by dividing by 100, and totalling any excess of any state's percentage of workers in that industry over its percentage of all workers—in the five excess states 31·28, 06·27, 08·88, 03·44, 01·07. If the industry keeps to the same percentage as the total occupied in every region, the differences will be nil; if the industry's percentages deviate as widely as possible, the deviations will approach a sum of 100 and a coefficient of 1. By measuring where an industry localizes, if at all, the quotient throws light on the causes of localization. The coefficient on the other hand throws light, as we shall see, on *what* industries can be planned at all, in one place or another. These summary measurements of the facts will come into use when we trace the effects of particular industries upon urbanization and other developments. Meanwhile, we must confirm the general trend toward large industrial urbanization mentioned at the outset of this book and get some idea of its form and extent.

2. The Trend toward Industrial Urbanization

The earliest known large cities were not particularly industrial. Sociologists (135, p. 314; 98, pp. 164–7) usually attribute their development to the needs for defence, to a surplus of agricultural produce over the demands of the rural population and the funnelling, through the payment of rents and otherwise, of this surplus usually into a capital city of an empire where administrators, priests, courtiers, entertainers, shopkeepers, and merchants congregate, but not necessarily industrial workers. Smaller cities developed at intervals for the marketing of the agricultural produce in exchange for the demands of country folk and also at ports and rivers for the longer distance transport and marketing of produce, and these market and transport towns still persist; but the very large towns that have recently grown did not specialize in these activities. The peculiar development in the last two centuries, first in Britain then in all industrial countries, is that the large cities grew as a result of specializing in some branch or branches of manufacturing industry.

United States experience, statistically recorded, brings out (i) that cities grew faster in proportion than the country as a whole; (ii) that their common characteristic was retailing; but (iii) that most of them had a strong but usually differentiated manufacturing element. (i) In 1860 cities of over 250,000 inhabitants numbered three and contained 5·2 per cent of the country's total population. In 1940 they numbered thirty-seven and contained 22·9 per cent of that population, a 4·4-fold rise. The smaller towns, between 2,500 and 250,000 inhabitants, contained in 1861 14·6 per cent of the population, in 1940 33·6 per cent—only a 2·3-fold rise. Most of the generally fast-growing large cities form part of larger aggregations. The U.S. Census now recognizes standard metropolitan statistical areas (S.M.S.A.) with populations ranging in 1964 from the New York area's 11,260,000 to the 51,000 of Meriden, Conn. These areas are defined as a county or group of continuous counties (towns and cities in New England) which contain at least one central city of 50,000 inhabitants or more, or twin cities with a combined population of at least 50,000. Metropolitan areas, in fact, contain central cities and outside environs of about equal populations on average (239, pp. 19 and 822).

(ii) These standard areas, taken as a whole, differ specifically from the *non*-metropolitan and mainly rural areas in their retailing activities. Their average retail sales per head of population was in 1958 $1,400 compared to an average of $700 in the non-metropolitan areas. But comparing one metropolitan area with another, they do not differ greatly in retailing. In spite of their usually higher income-a-head, the larger areas do not tend to have greater retail sales per head than the smaller. The dozen most populous areas, in fact, had in 1963 average sales of $1,480; the dozen least populous average sales of $1,500 per head.

(iii) The standard areas differ greatly, however, one from another in their types of manufacture. Quoting the largest industries only, the Detroit area specializes in the motor vehicle industry where the industry in 1963 had a location quotient of 7·58; Pittsburgh specializes in blast furnaces and steel mills which had a quotient then of 10·56; the New York area specializes in dresses, measured by a quotient of 4·95. Nearly all standard areas have had a more than national average share of manufacturing generally; though significantly for localization some types of manufacture may be entirely absent from some areas. By 1950 there were sixteen "metropolitan areas" of over a million inhabitants. Exactly half of these had 33 per cent or more of their occupied population employed in manufacture—had location quotients for manufacture, in short, at least 1·27 times the then national average of 25·9 per cent. Only two areas, San Francisco and Washington, had quotients for manufactures below 0·86; their activity structure is that of the pre-industrial courtly and transport pattern.

English cities over 200,000 or 250,000 are sharply distinguished from market towns (and also resort or tourist towns), which have a high proportion of the total occupied in the distributive order of (service) industries. In the smaller market towns, indeed, this proportion is fairly consistently (198, p. 86) around 25 per cent. But in spite of the fact that many of them are ports, none of the eighteen largest English cities, with one exception, had in 1951 more than 17·5 per cent in distribution and nine of them under 15·0 per cent. All of them had, on the other hand, some manufacturing order (usually more than one) twice as great as the national proportion.

After 1931 the populations of the large English industrial cities appear to become stationary or even to fall. But this is an illusion due to the spreading use of the motor-car down the income scale. With the increased transportability of persons the population bursts the bonds of administrative areas to such effect that, whatever extension of administrative boundaries is made, the population is a move ahead. Like a volcano (215, Fig. 34) a city leaves a hollow low density cone at its centre and spreads houses and factories like lava over its boundaries into the countryside. For this reason we shift attention from large cities with legally defined boundaries to conurbations— continuous built-up areas. In the United States the corresponding urban concentrations are the larger "metropolitan areas". The New York–North-East New Jersey area with its population in 1964 of 14,950,000 is one of the most populous conurbations in the world and many consider it only a part of a megalopolis extending from Washington, D.C., to Boston.

The conurbation is certainly now a unit more realistic and significant to economist and sociologist than the single local-authority industrial city, and (in the next section) we will devote attention mainly to conurbations and their industries.

3. SIX PROPOSITIONS IN MODERN URBANIZATION

The original location of any one industrial plant is often the outcome of tradition or of an entrepreneur's or manager's, or even their wives', psychological whim. Nevertheless, associations and correlations have been reliably measured of the surviving plants which can be interpreted fairly logically from economic reasoning.

(a) Certain large manufacturing industries are found localized intensively, as already said, in single metropolitan areas or single states as measured by high location quotients. Many of these localizations occur where the material is extracted particularly if, as usual, it is in its raw state heavy or perishable. The industries are then said to be material-oriented or "rooted". In Table XIX of the Appendix the major groups of industry with the highest input from extractive industry are given as the petroleum and coal products, food, tobacco and primary metals groups; and such input is moderately high in the lumber, paper and textile groups. Compared with the more densely populated European countries of smaller area, the United States has a wide variety of climate and of materials concentrated at distant points. The location of its industries is thus strongly affected "ergologically" by the materials involved in their work.

Many industries are not material-oriented. They may be oriented to the general personal *consumer* market as the apparel, leather (shoes) and tobacco group (Table XIX, Column I a); or oriented to a *producer* market, such as fabricated metals or machinery. Whether they locate near their market depends mainly on the weight and transportability generally of their products.

(b) The growth in population of cities or regions is due mainly to the growth, nationally, of the industries localized there, regardless of whether that region is getting a larger or smaller share of the industry. Thus Pittsburgh grew particularly fast in the 1890–1900 decade when iron and steel production grew fast nationally. Later, with the rise of the automobile

G

industry the population of Detroit rose fast from 1910 to 1940, and that of its metropolitan area between 1940 and 1960—26·9 and 24·7 per cent in the two consecutive decades. Washington grew particularly fast between 1930 and 1950 and the Miami metropolitan area from 1920 onward with the growth, nationally, of public administration and the tourist trade. On the other hand the New Bedford metropolitan area grew only 2·3 per cent from 1940 to 1950 and 0·8 per cent from 1950 to 1960, owing partly to the relative decline or stability nationally of the textile and the shoe industries. In short, the growth of one region relative to another is largely the result of the industrial redeployment nationally, discussed in Chapter II. This proposition is certain enough to enable forecasts to be made of future growth of conurbations based on intelligent extrapolation of the growth of their industries nationally.

(c) Certain service industries and services tend to localize in countries' largest conurbations, such as London, Paris, and New York, and also to a less extent in regional capitals such as, in the United States, Boston, Chicago, and San Francisco.

A table in my contribution to Fisher's *The Metropolis in Modern Life* (54) analysed the employments of all main types including services in which the largest cities or conurbations of Britain, France and the United States seemed to specialize in 1950. This survey included with London and Paris the eight most populous standard metropolitan areas of the United States. In six of them, New York, Chicago, Philadelphia, Los Angeles, San Francisco and Boston, finance showed location quotients of 1·5 or more. These metropolitan areas had at least one and a half times as high a proportion of persons occupied in finance as the country as a whole. But the other two areas, Detroit and Pittsburgh, did not appear to specialize in any particular service employments. Of the six financial centres all but Los Angeles and San Francisco had quotients of 2·5 or over for periodicals, books, etc., and of these four all but Philadelphia and Boston had quotients of 1·5 or over for personal and business service.

New York had the highest quotient in each of these three groups of activity—finance, publishing and personal and business service and it was worth carrying the New York analysis further even into detailed branches of manufacture.

Extremely high location quotients were found in the New York area for fur goods (7·8), artificial flowers (5·3), handbags and purses (5·3), surgical and medical instruments (5·0), women's and misses' outerwear (4·7), books (4·3). Among the detailed occupations high quotients appeared in New York for medicinal chemists (5·3), actors (3·6) and artists and art teachers (3·1).

This list gives an indication of the degree of specialization of a national metropolis in providing six types of activity—

(i) Finance, business services, and commercial communication.

(ii) Publishing and printing of books and periodicals.

(iii) Scientific research and instrument making.

(iv) Arts and their materials and supplies.

(v) Applied art and design, e.g. fashionable clothing, luxury goods.

(vi) Entertainment.

Paris, to illustrate (v), (iii), and (vi), had, besides the *haute couture*, far more than the national share of *garçons de café* and also of the less familiar *garçons de laboratoire*.

Next in rank down this urban hierarchy are cities which appear from their location quotients to specialize, together with the top city, in wholesaling, in specialist professional and public services—such as specialized hospitals—and in daily newspaper publishing, and in department stores. They can also be shown to specialize in industries making containers. Six out of the nine most populous American standard metropolitan areas each had in 1963 a location quotient of 1·6 or over for that industry. This is a service industry the product of which is bulky and costly to transport in relation to its value, but yet an industry which must have plants of a certain size, and therefore not too many, to obtain economies of scale. Almost half the industry's employees are in plants within the narrow size-range of 100 to 249 employees and they make more than half the value added by the industry. At a lower rank are the middling cities or towns that appear to specialize in the more mundane activities, including brewing and bottling and commercial printing. But whatever the rank, the essence of a hierarchy is that the top rank performs, or can perform, all mundane or routine activities down the ranks—as an archbishop can those of a country curate! London and New York retail durables, provide restaurants and general professional services as does any middling town, and for that matter bake and retail food like any village.

The word "hierarchy" has been used loosely by economists to mean just a bundle or variety of things, such as demands, for instance, thus wasting a word that describes a particular relation between structures or bodies and functions or activities which is frequently encountered in the real world. This hierarchy is graphically presented in Table IX by rods, all firmly planted at ground level to represent the mundane activities of *all* the middling and large cities of a model country here taken for illustration to number sixty-five. Only eight of these rods (large cities of second rank) reach the next level of activities specified in the margin and only one, the metropolis, reaches to the top activities.

(*d*) The urban hierarchy is clearly seen *spatially* in countries where industry has not developed and where agriculture is still dominant. A region of fairly homogeneous fertility contains homesteads and villages for the direct producers, market towns for the traders, and a capital or county town for administrators and specialized services. Just such an ideal (almost a sociologist's dream!) was found by the British West Midland Group in the county of Hereford as of 1931 (198, p. 203). Still earlier, I pointed (60, p. 116) to the regularly spaced pattern of market towns along lines west and east, south and north of Cambridge at distances of thirteen to seventeen miles. This type of pre-development pattern has been made the basis of the honeycomb location theories of Chrystaller and Lösch.

The symmetrical pattern of urban spacing is broken, however, by natural features, such as mountains, unfertile areas, or estuaries, and by mining, manufacturing, and also health- or tourist-resort development. Mining develops where the mineral deposits lie, however irregular to the rural pattern; and manufacturing centres which, we have seen, now account for the largest cities and conurbations may not conform to the pattern, either.

Since the sea was for centuries the leading transport "lane" and often still is the cheapest, transport and trading cities develop on navigable estuaries, or harbours. Manufactures are

TABLE IX

MODEL HIERARCHY OF CONURBATIONS AND CITIES

Each line represents one city, its height, the extent of that city's specialization in stated activities

TOP (METROPOLITAN) CONURBATION

(8) LARGE CITIES population 200 to 800 thousand

(56) MIDDLING CITIES population 25 to 200 thousand

ACTIVITIES

Finance and business services
Book and periodical publishing and printing services
Science and applied science
  (medical and scientific instruments)
Arts and their materials
Applied arts: design
  (fashionable clothing): luxury goods
Entertainment

Wholesaling
Specialized professional and
  public services (e.g.
  specialized hospitals),
Newspaper publishing
Department stores

Public utilities
Commercial printing
Brewing and bottling
Construction
General professional services
Restaurants
Retailing durables

less tied to nature than mining or transport, but are likely to settle where cities, with their labour and markets for them, have already naturally developed. Hence, most, if not all, the large industrial cities are found either at estuarine, lake, or up-river sites, or on large coal or other mine fields. In fact, all the eighteen United States metropolitan areas with, in the year 1964, over 1,300,000 inhabitants (the minimum size of five of the six English conurbations), have within their boundaries ports on the sea, navigable rivers, or lakes. Of the six English conurbations, five are either at ports or on large minefields; Tyneside, on both. The one exception is the Birmingham conurbation, and even here, though now worked out, there *once* were large coalfields and iron-ore deposits.

Zipf observed (207, pp. 374–5) that if a country's towns are ranked in order of population a peculiar harmonic degression holds, such as, for instance, that the second town has half the population of the first town, the third, a third of the first's, the fourth, a fourth, and so on. Zipf's "law" indeed fits the facts better in the middle and lower ranks than in the first few, but it has been confirmed even to quite a low limit of city populations by H. W. Singer and G. R. Allen (80, p. 17). The law is compatible with the urban service hierarchy, since the several regions served by regional capitals are of varying size, and the largest *sub*-region may be only just a little smaller than the smallest region. Thus the main cities of regions and sub-regions and sub-sub-regions may well form a fairly continuous series of sizes, with a corresponding series for the sizes of their economic and sociological capitals, just as the archdeacon of the largest archdeaconry within the largest diocese may have work only a little less extensive than the bishop of the smallest diocese.

(e) A small town of, say, 20,000 inhabitants could not contain a factory employing 5,000 persons, together with their families, and the shopkeepers and others to serve them and their families; and it might be expected almost mathematically that the larger the town, the larger, on average, would be the manufacturing plants within it. And there does in fact appear some sort of general law, as will be shown shortly, associating wide dispersion (i.e. a low localization) of industries with industries composed of small rather than large plants. But *big* cities, or the cores of sprawling conurbations, show a reversal of this law, both in the United States and England, and have, on average, the smaller manufacturing plants (99, pp. 49–55). A U.S. Census table showed that, in 1940, cities of 500,000 and over had plants of an average size of only 30·2 employees, and cities between 200,000 and 500,000 plants averaging 38·3. In cities smaller than that, grouped in ten size-ranges, the average size of plant was never less than 54·2 in any group.

More recent data show a similar negative association of size of city and size of plant, though not in the same form. The Statistical Abstract (239, p. 18) ranks all the standard metropolitan areas by their 1960 population; and (p. 776) for seventy-four areas with over 40,000 manufacturing employees gives the total of these employees and the plants. The data permit a classification of areas according to their average size of plants, as follows—

Average Size of Plants (in Employees)	Number of Standard Metropolitan Areas	Average Rank in Population
Over 100	13	57·2nd
80–99	20	57·5th
60–79	20	50·7th
Under 60	21	29·5th

In short the areas with smaller plants employing on average fewer than eighty, and particularly fewer than sixty, rank as the more populous areas. None of the eleven largest areas except two (Pittsburgh and St. Louis) have an average size of plant over seventy-two.

This result is due to two sets of facts. First, within any industry its smaller plants appear to exist in the larger cities. In the second place, the smaller-plant industries are the industries that prefer the city or the core of a very large conurbation. A study of the New York area by Hoover and Vernon (97, p. 50) found that in the central core the proportion employed by industries with, on average, small plants (of sixty or fewer employees) was 61·2 per cent; but in the outer ring only 14·1 per cent. An opposite preference was exhibited by the industries with, on average, large plants of over 240 employees.

Only 7·7 per cent of their total employees were in the core, 38·2 per cent were in the outer ring.

The calculations of Goodrich *et al.* (88, pp. 704–34) make it possible to measure what proportion of workers in various United States industries were employed in 1929 in plants within thirty-three principal cities of the United States. The industries, all with this proportion higher than 65 per cent against 35 per cent for the nation as a whole, i.e. with an "urban quotient" above 1·8, were (highest quotient first): women's clothing, perfumes and cosmetics, men's clothes, gas and electric fixtures, printing and publishing (books and job), and confectionery. Now all these six truly city industries had a much higher proportion of workers in small plants (with one to one hundred workers) than the average of 29 per cent in small plants for manufactures in general, in the order named, 78, 51, 39, 41, 65, and 41 per cent. Some other United States industries combining a high or fairly high localization coefficient with small or smallish plant structure are curtain and draperies, fur and fur goods, cutlery, custom jewellery, clay refractories and fertilizers.

The *locus classicus* of urban manufacture by small workshops is medieval Florence, which still has streets named after the highly localized industries that plied there—the Via Calzaioli or Corso dei Tintori, for instance, once given over to shoemakers and dyers. A special set of cases contrary to a general law is usually referred to as an *effect*. I hope I shall not be considered immodest if this current of localized small plants running counter to the main stream of a positive correlation of size of plant and localization is called, for short, the Florence Effect.

(*f*) The last few propositions have indicated certain specific economic functions of the large urban centre, quite apart from a favourable natural site. To some extent, the city is a local economic unit providing the economic advantages of a single factory. It provides proximity for activities that should for economy be carried on next one another, and accounts for the major part of the economists' *external economies*. It does not, however, provide for the element of *command* exercised over factory operations controlled by one firm.

Elsewhere (54, p. 90) I have listed systematically the economic advantages and disadvantages of large urban concentrations according to specific criteria: current efficiency, future efficiency, income stability, and the offer of a variety of jobs and services. Here, I will only group the main pros and cons in the short and the long run. *Currently* the main economic advantages are the short transport and communication (*a*) with a large consumer market, (*b*) between related or "linked" industries described at length elsewhere (72, p. 87) and the large available pool of labour, management, and finance; the main economic disadvantages are shortage of land at the centre and congestion and hold-ups of goods and of workers, the long and costly commuting to work, and, often, distance from raw materials. For *long-run* efficiency, the city has a main advantage in wider intercommunication of designs and inventions. In income stability the large city has the advantage over the smaller one-industry cities by usually including several localized industries and thus gaining external economies and insuring against mass unemployment at any one time; and it certainly offers a wider variety of jobs and services. On the other hand, local taxes are high, to pay for the wider services. On balance, the *economic* advantages of an industrial city or conurbation probably outweigh the disadvantages up to that size where the congestion at the centre overwhelms other economic considerations. But the *sociological* disadvantages so graphically put (142, p. 122) by Lewis Mumford, including "man-sewers" taking workers from and to their homes, tip the balance against the industrial city at a smaller size.

Both economic and sociological limits must be set higher, however, when it comes to the single metropolis discussed earlier, at the top of the national or regional hierarchy—the city as an intellectual focus. Dr. Samuel Johnson was emphatic (21, 30th Sept. 1769)—

> The happiness of London is not to be conceived but by those who have been in it. I will venture to say, there is more learning and science within the circumference of ten miles from where we now sit, than in all the rest of the Kingdom.
> BOSWELL: The only disadvantage is the great distance at which people live from one another.
> JOHNSON: Yes, Sir; but that is occasioned by the largeness of it, which is the cause of all the other advantages.
> BOSWELL: Sometimes I have been in the humour of wishing to retire to a desert.
> JOHNSON: Sir, you have desert enough in Scotland!

4. CORRELATES OF INDUSTRIAL LOCATION

Before measuring and discussing the various causes and implications of the trend toward larger-scale production, it is essential to grasp the close interrelation of size of plant (if not of firm) with its location. Though simple enough, the inter-relation is often neglected, with consequent confusion when the discussion turns to causes of organization size other than location.

Statistical analysis based on comprehensive census data brings out a main law, to which the Florence Effect forms the exception, that the less localized the location of an industry's plants, the less large the representative plant tends to be. Thus in 1951 (79, p. 7) sixteen out of the twenty-five British industries with low localization (coefficients below 0·30) had representative small or smallish plants (as defined in the next chapter); and sixteen out of the twenty-five industries with higher localization (coefficients between 0·30 and 0·49) had representative large or largish plants. This law was previously suggested by the 1930–5 British data, and confirmed by the United States data in 1929.

The U.S. *Census of Manufactures* of that year when analysed showed thirteen out of the sixteen industries with coefficients of localization under 0·30 to have a structure in the main of small or smallish plants; and twenty-two out of thirty-three industries with coefficients of localization over 0·50 to have a structure in the main of medium or large plants. This positive association of small plants with dispersed location was confirmed also by Bruni (26) in Italy and by later censuses in Britain and the United States (79). The form of the law associating industries having representative small plants with industries of dispersed location was carefully worded because of a possible *second* law (79, pp. 13–14) that industries *with no representative size of plant* tend to be ubiquitous, that is, to be industries with a *particularly* low degree of localization. This *all sites, all sizes* law is logical enough, since industries found in *both* small and large towns might well have plants of all sizes to fit the various sizes of their markets.

The law associating local dispersal with small representative plants extends beyond manufacturing and applies to whole economic sectors. Mining is localized and has large units, building and retailing are dispersed, with, on the whole, small firms and shops; wholesaling is relatively localized, with fairly large warehouses. Banking and insurance are dispersed, with small branches or agents acting as money-collecting services but one or a few centres as we have said (p. 73) in each country.

The professions are dispersed in one-man units or few-men partnerships except education, with its many large-staffed schools.

Of the two characteristics thus found in association the location pattern is more fundamental than the size structure in the sense that it arises more closely out of the unalterable physical qualities of the work involved, especially the weight and transportability generally of the *materials* worked upon and of the product made. These and other "inevitabilities" based on the work in hand were indeed given (I, §7) as illustrations of the ergology of location patterns. Tariffs act like additional transport costs, so that a common market strengthens ergological localization, politically unrestricted. What has not yet been sufficiently thought about is the local incidence of each class of orientation. One would expect market-oriented industries, following the human consumers, to have a low coefficient of localization, but industries oriented to material (usually found concentrated in places not much peopled) to have high coefficients.

Reference to the ranking of major industry groups in Table XIX shows this expectation more true in the United States with its variety and wide scatter of materials than in Britain where much raw material has to be imported. Major industry groups high in ranking of the coefficient of localization are lumber, petroleum, tobacco, and textiles. These coefficients are affected by particularly high location quotients, respectively, in Oregon, in Texas, in South Carolina, and in North Carolina. Other groups ranking high in coefficients of localization are oriented or "linked" to a specialized local market such as machinery or instruments to the industry they supply. Oilfield machinery has (1963) a location quotient of 20·0 in Texas, 24·9 in Oklahoma; textile machinery of 4·7 in North Carolina and 6·8 in Massachusetts (where textiles were once highly localized); woodworking machinery of 10·4 in Oregon. Such links and contacts with other industries are often important and form categories of "communication-oriented" (97, p. 288) and (e.g. around Boston) "science-oriented" locations. Other industry groups have a high location quotient because their plants require to swarm together for external economies. This is probably true of transport equipment and apparel already mentioned, and also of the rubber group. The tyre industry has a location quotient of 5·0 in Ohio and the leather group (mainly shoes) a quotient of 3·9 in Massachusetts and 4·6 in Missouri.

Besides its correlation with the size-of-plant structure, the location of industries affects sociological structure, particularly the geographical distribution of population. During the Industrial Revolution the North of England grew in population compared to the South. In the last forty years, an opposite trend has set in, and now the population of the South and the Midlands is growing compared to that of Scotland, the North of England, and of Wales which have higher rates of unemployment. The consequent congestion of parts of the receiving regions and the age-distribution of the relatively deserted towns are of sociological concern. But the causation is mainly economic—the growth and decline of the industries localized in the different regions. The British regions losing population relatively are regions where the stagnant heavy iron and steel, coal-mining, ship-building and textile industries were localized (largely owing to the presence of the required materials, fuels and estuaries). With the exception of London and the South-East, the distribution of population is now not unlike the position a hundred years ago, before the now stagnant industries led so rapidly to decentralization northward. Today it is *re*centralization and congestion around London that is not only of sociological but also economic concern in Britain, because of the costs of commuting and traffic congestion.

This process of centralization nationally as already indicated (p. 66) has not occurred in the United States. The largest concentration of population, the New York–New Jersey "consolidated area", increased in population between 1950 and 1960 by 14·3 per cent, while the nation as a whole increased 18·5 per cent and the total of all metropolitan areas 26·5 per cent. Put more broadly, much the most densely populated region (the North-Eastern) increased only 13·2 per cent in population, much less than any of the other three regions. Population growth and density were, in fact, inversely correlated, as Table X shows in its first two columns. The third and fourth columns show the connexion of the increase in the proportion of manufacturing activity with this increase in population. One can state that in manufacturing there is still in the United States a moving frontier.

TABLE X

DECENTRALIZATION PROCESS IN U.S. POPULATION
AND MANUFACTURES

Regions of the U.S.	Density of Population per Sq. Mile	Increase in Population 1950–60	Percentage in Manufacturing 1950	1960
North-Eastern	273	13·2	34·3	33·4
North-Central	69	16·1	29·0	30·2
South	63	16·5	18·4	21·4
West	16	38·9	17·5	21·2

Fuchs (216) considers that demand or markets have not been the primary determinant of locational change. Industries most clearly recognized as being market-oriented did not shift as did others. The decentralization of industries did not just follow upon the west and south-west movement of consumers. In the South Atlantic States the abundant supply of unskilled labour appeared to be most important; elsewhere both labour and natural resources played a role; and in the West, natural resources (including climate) were most significant.

5. LOCATION MEASUREMENT AS A TOOL FOR POLICY

Measurements of the pattern of industrial location have often been applied, together with measures of other traits, in the solution of the national problems already indicated. I will pick out three instances, each with a different practical aim: one to repopulate rural areas that were gradually losing population; the converse, to disperse and decongest a conurbation; and another, taken second, where areas have been losing employment in industries in which they specialized to effect a replacement. In all these instances the two main questions, assuming the aims to be accepted, were what industries it was *feasible* and *desirable* to introduce or remove. The desirability or feasibility of any industry depends upon its characteristics; so we fall back upon the measured traits listed and illustrated in the Appendix. But to solve the problem of any given area, the industrial characteristics and the economic activity structure of that area itself must also be measured so that the remedy may fit the disease—and the patient.

The characteristics chiefly differentiating the economic activities of *rural* from other areas, over and above devotion to agriculture, are the low proportion of women and juveniles occupied, the decline of employment generally, and its seasonality.

Among United States farm workers (employers and employed) in 1965, 14 per cent were women; while in non-agricultural occupations 36 per cent were women. Between 1950 and 1965 the total of farm workers fell from 7,408,000 to 4,265,000 (239, p. 229). *Desirable* industries that would fit the situation should, therefore, employ a high proportion of women and juveniles; and would be growth industries flourishing more, or at least no less, in winter than summer. Such a fit was found to be satisfied by a number of industries, but not all such rurally desirable industries would be *feasible* in a rural setting, with its low density of population. To be viable they should, if possible, be linked to agriculture, and not be organized into large plants requiring a high population density within reach of the factory. About thirty industries were found to score sufficient marks as desirable *and* feasible (67) on these various tests.

More pressing than rural depopulation, and a problem, solutions to which have often been found in older established regions, is that of areas suffering particularly from unemployment in their obsolescent industries. A survey of the English county town of Worcester (85, pp. 82–9) had, for instance, to deal with the problem of the loss of employment in the glove industry, which had moved elsewhere. Local resources in agriculture pointed to the feasibility of food-processing and scenery and architecture of a tourist trade. But, then, undesirable industries giving rise to nuisances such as smell, noise, or unsightliness would have to leave, or be put into a special industrial zone. The nuisances analysed were much the same as those listed recently (97, pp. 73–7) as moving industries from the core of the New York region.

A much larger problem in loss of employment was presented by the depressed areas of the British North-east Coast and South Wales. These areas, known officially (and euphemistically) first as the *special*, then as the *development* areas, had been the seat of mining and heavy iron and steel industries. Rich natural resources in coal, iron ore, and harbours had brought great prosperity to these industries localized there, and had made a diversity of industries employing women relatively unnecessary. But these heavy capital-goods industries have the characteristic of strong cyclical fluctuation and the areas lost heavily in employment during the 1932–5 slump. Nor were they growth industries.

Similarly in the United States, of the twenty major industry groups those most subject to the slump of 1947–55 appear in Table XIX (Column IIC) to be primary metal, rubber and plastics, transport equipment, machinery and furniture. Those employing fewest women (Column IIA) primary metal, lumber, petroleum, transport equipment and machinery and those growing least (Column IIA) leather (mostly shoemaking), lumber, tobacco, food and textiles. To prevent poverty where these industries are localized (particularly if, like primary metal, transport equipment, lumber and machinery, they manifest two or all three of these contraindications) it is necessary to diversify by selecting industries that are not subject to slump and which will employ women hitherto unoccupied. British location policy has been in fact fairly successful in bringing the development areas' unemployment rate down near to the national level, though not yet the rate of "unoccupation" of women.

Two birds would be killed with one stone if industries could be moved to the development straight from the congested areas. Unfortunately, many of the areas designated by the Government for industrial development because of high unemployment may also be congested, and planning for the decongestion of a conurbation and decanting industries into New Towns is difficult. It requires a realistic analysis of particular industries' desirability and feasibility for a given area—an analysis which national and local governments are not often ready to undertake thoroughly, or to favour. The chief worry is not to disturb existing linkages and external economies. Industries for removal must not be too closely linked (measured (72, p. 86) where possible by a coefficient of linkage) to the industries staying behind. Nor can plants in the same industries swarming together because of advantages in access to specialized services be feasibly separated. Small plants and firms, in particular, seem to thrive, as we have seen, in large cities.

In spite of these difficulties, about a dozen specific industries were boldly suggested by Midlanders in 1945 (199, p. 136) for removal from the English West Midland conurbation (or their local restriction)—industries where local linkages were not essential. But a brief follow-up (80, pp. 22–3) of the situation disclosed, wherever 1951 Census data were available, that these industries had not on the whole diminished in the conurbation when compared to their national growth.

This technique of selecting industries for addition or sub-traction in a given area, according as its characteristics do or do not specially fit the economic activities already existing in that area, can be carried, over wider horizons, to the industrializa-tion of whole *underdeveloped* countries. The closest analogy is obviously with the planning of industries desirable and feasible for *rural areas*. Industries can be tested for suitability on the score of characteristics, such as are measured and illustrated in the Appendix. And a full-scale survey must extend from the characteristics of the existing economic activity, mainly agri-culture, to the character of the potential material and human resources and markets of the nation as a whole.

The problem of "fit" is not only fitting in with other, possibly linked, economic activities but also with the geology, the geo-graphy, the climate, the social structure and institutions, the psychological attitudes and the size of the market. Most of a chapter (Chapter VI) will be devoted to this problem of "fit" in the industrialization of the underdeveloped countries.

CHAPTER IV

THE SCALE OF ORGANIZATION:
CAPACITIES AND INCENTIVES

1. MEASURES OF THE SIZE OF PLANT, THE UPWARD VARIEGATED TREND

THE seventh of the trends in industrial development noted in Chapter I is the enlargement of the size of industrial organizations. This can be measured in number employed, in horsepower capacity, or in capital assets invested per plant or firm. These measures refer, however, only to one factor of production at a time. A more direct and relevant measure would be the total production of an organization, but the difficulty here is to reduce production to a common unit which, unlike money, is stable in value. The nearest approach perhaps is the U.S. Federal Reserve Bulletin's Index of Industrial Production.

Whatever measure is used, a further difficulty is the very wide variety of plant sizes and (as will appear later) of firm sizes too. In the United States in 1963 for all manufacturing 203,647 persons were employed in 112,036 plants employing one to four persons, giving an average of 1·82 per plant; 2,898,617 in 544 plants employing 2,500 or more, giving an average of 5,329. The difference between the two averages was roughly 3,000 times—as wide as the difference tabulated by Haldane and Huxley in their *Animal Biology* between the size of a carthorse and something half-way in size between a mouse and rat. Very few industries, moreover, show any uniformity of size in their plants.

Of the individual (four digit) industries given in Table XII, two come nearer to having uniform sizes of plant than is usually found. They are the motor vehicle and parts industry with 81·5 per cent of all employed in plants employing 1,000 or more, and the brick and structural tile industry with 65·0 per cent in plants employing between 50 and 249. On the other hand, many industries such as sanitary paper products, given in Table XII, have no visible prevailing type of size at all. For most industries one must be content with a grading shortly to be described, depending (1) on how far the bulk of employees are concentrated in a few consecutive size-ranges and if so (2) which ranges. Many industries do not fulfil the first test, and some of them have concentrations of two sizes. These industries must be declared devoid of any representative plant-size. A bare arithmetic mean size calculated by dividing employees by total number of plants can, of course, always be obtained. But it may be quite unrepresentative, though useful for comparing the trend from year to year. The general trend, in view of these facts, can fairly be described as an upward shift of a variegated pattern. The proportion of persons in each of three wide categories of size of plant for manufacturing as a whole is given in Table XI comparing three years for Great Britain. For the United States four years are given because, as explained below, the statistics for 1909–39 and 1954–63 are not comparable.

Of the minor difficulties the first is the inadequacy of any one easily available indicator of size. Number employed is mainly used here, for reasons argued elsewhere (69, pp. 12–13), but it understates growth, since the increase in power is ignored.

Occasionally, as in the United States, statisticians have worked out with some trouble a value of output per plant at constant prices. One such inquiry (234) shows that in all but one of the forty-six industries able to be exactly computed between 1904 and 1947, the output per plant rose, and that for the total of those manufacturing industries the average rise in output per plant was 15 per cent every five years. In a further list of thirty-five industries measurable over rather shorter time-spans all but three showed a rise, and the (median) average quinquennial rise was, again, 15 per cent. A second minor difficulty also results in understatement of the trend. It is that most countries do not report the number of employees or any other details in plants employing ten or less, and to judge from recent British and also German (100) data, these minute plants have recently lost employees rapidly. Table XI, however, includes all sizes.

From employing in 1935 roughly one-third of all persons in each of the three main sizes of plant, Britain in 1959 employed almost twice as many in the five-hundred-or-more plants than in the less than a hundred strong. The United States distribution goes back farther, and thus starts with more wage-earners in the small plants, but its 1939 distribution shows a swing over to the larger plant.

Unfortunately between the 1939 and the 1947 Census, a change occurred in classifying sizes of plant. The employee, not the wage-earner, became the unit. A plant employing, say, 490 wage-earners is likely to have over 500 employees including the salary-earning staff and thus automatically to come into a higher size category. In short, the 1954 and 1963 distributions cannot be compared with the 1909 or 1939. Accordingly, besides the warning note, a double line is drawn in the table between 1939 and 1954. But comparison is possible between 1909 and 1939 when the proportion of wage-earners was rising in the large plants, and between 1954 and 1963. In this latter period the percentages of employees in the larger plants was falling. This does not mean a smaller total output per organization because, as will appear shortly, the power per worker increased so enormously, bringing correspondingly higher output per worker. In any case firms are still enlarging even in employees by enlarging, as will be seen shortly, the number of plants. Comparing the 1959 British distribution with that of the United States, either of 1954 or 1963, it will be noticed, perhaps with surprise, that a higher proportion of employees are found in large plants in Great Britain than in the United States.

The variety in size of plant is particularly marked when different industries are compared and forms part of the trend toward differentiation already described. Even among the wide major groups of industries surveyed in the Appendix, the range of size extends from an average of employees per plant of 15·8 in the lumber group to 225 employees in the transport equipment group and this differentiation persists. Small-plant industries stay small-plant, large-plant, large-plant. This stability in size is shown clearly in Table XIII for the 16 major groups that can be compared between 1939 and 1963. Possibly due to the relative stability in power per worker (only one industry group changed as much as three ranks in power and only two, two) five industry groups changed rank in size of plant not at all; five, one rank; two, two ranks; three, three; and only one (food), four. On average, the change was thus one and six-sixteenths ranks compared with a possible average of eight.

For purposes of comparing sizes of plant at different dates a simple (arithmetic mean) average is adequate; but such an average is often unrepresentative and we must now introduce the notion of a size of plant grading of industries which allows for some industries having no particular prevalent size. The alternative measure of this structure given in Table XIX in the Appendix (i.e. the percentage of employees in plants employing 500 or over) goes some way toward indicating the results of this "grading", but among the smaller-plant industries more detailed analysis is required.

TABLE XI

SHIFT IN DISTRIBUTION OF EMPLOYEES AMONG MAIN
SIZE-RANGES OF PLANT (PERCENTAGES)

	Great Britain			U.S.A.			
	1935*	1951*	1959†	1909‡	1939‡	1954*	1963**
Plants Employing							
0– 99 Persons	32·5	25·2	24·0	37·8	30·0	25·7	26·2
100–499 Persons	35·3	32·4	30·0	34·2	34·8	29·1	30·9
500 or more Persons	32·2	42·4	46·0	28·0	35·2	45·2	42·9

* 72, revised ed.; pp. 34 and 37.
† *Labour Gazette*, Sept. 1959, allowing for plants employing less than eleven.
‡ Wages-earners only.
** *U.S. Census of Manufacturers.*

Using the test (79, p. 2) of 50 per cent of employees in at least two consecutive size-ranges out of the seven in Table XII (or 60 per cent in the three smaller ranges), industries that have a representative size of plant can be divided into several grades. Large-plant industries are those that have 50 per cent of all their workers in plants employing a thousand or over. Largish-plant industries are industries other than large-plant that have 50 per cent in plants employing 500 or over. Medium-plant industries have 50 per cent in plants of 100–499 workers. Smallish-plant industries have 50 or 60 per cent respectively in plants employing 50–249 or 25–249. Small-plant industries have 50 or 60 per cent respectively in plants employing less than 50 or less than 100.

In other industries the concentration of workers in plants of certain sizes was not so sharp, and supplementary grades can be added for industries showing "bias toward smaller plants" with 60 per cent of workers in plants of under 250, and (a rare case) "bias toward larger plants" with 75 per cent of workers in plants of over 250. All remaining industries were graded as showing no representative size of plant. An example of each of seven more frequent grades is given in Table XII.

TABLE XII

DISTRIBUTION IN CERTAIN U.S. INDUSTRIES OF EMPLOYEES AMONG SIZE-RANGES OF PLANT, ILLUSTRATING THE SYSTEM OF GRADING. 1963 CENSUS OF MANUFACTURES

Industry and Code Number	Percentage of Employees in Plants Employing Stated Number							
	Total of employees in each industry = 100 Percentages in contiguous columns qualifying for grading are underlined							
	1–19	20–49	50–99	100–249	250–499	500–999	1,000 plus	Grade*of Size of Plant Assigned
Sawmills and Planing Mills (2421)	24·7	19·3	17·6	16·6	9·6	7·0	5·0	Small
Brick and Structural Tile (3251)	3·0	21·7	39·0	26·0		10·2		Smallish
Wool Weaving and Finishing (2231)	1·7	4·0	7·1	26·6	33·0	27·5		Medium
Mechanical Measuring Devices (3821)	3·7	5·1	6·0	14·2	13·4	12·7	45·0	Largish
Motor Vehicles and Parts (3717)	1·0	1·4	1·9	3·2	4·5	6·5	81·5	Large
Brooms and Brushes (3981)	14·1	17·0	19·4	20·8		28·7		Bias to Smaller
Sanitary Paper Products (2647)	1·8	2·8	4·6	18·1	24·6	28·9	19·2	

*"Bias to Larger" grade has been omitted as very rare.

Table XIII compares average of all employees per plant and power per production worker in 1939 and 1963 for all the major groups of industry where the two Census classifications allow comparison between the two years. The rank of the sixteen groups is also given for each of the resulting four columns. It will be seen that the size of plant has for *manufacturing as a whole* increased slightly, increasing in some, decreasing in other groups, but that for each production worker the horse-power capacity has almost doubled. It should be borne in mind that with rising staff ratios the power capacity per *employee* has not risen quite so fast. The ranking of the groups, however, remained, as just noted remarkably stable over the twenty-four years, particularly in horse-power capacity per worker.

At least four salient features, displayed by the facts, thus require to be explained. Two are seen clearly in Table XIII: the trends in all groups of industry (except apparel) for a rise in the horse-power per production worker; but for all manufacture little if any increase in employees per plant. Thus the output per plant though rising, rises only slowly.

Two other sets of facts are brought out by Table XII, the

TABLE XIII

CHANGE IN AVERAGE (ARITHMETIC MEAN) EMPLOYEES PER PLANT* AND HORSE-POWER PER PRODUCTION WORKER, U.S.A. 1939–63

	1939				1963			
Major Industry Group	Rank	** Average Employees	Rank	H-P. per production worker	Rank	Average Employees	Rank	H-P. per production worker
Food	1st	23·1	10th	6·85	5th	43·9	10th	10·70
Printing	2nd	25·8	4th	2·38	2nd	23·8	3rd	3·07
Lumber	3rd	35·2	11th	7·71	1st	15·8	12th	15·84
Furniture	4th	41·3	6th	3·55	3rd	36·0	4th	4·08
Apparel	5th	44·0	1st	0·33	6th	45·2	1st	0·22
Chemicals	6th	45·0	14th	13·19	7th	61·4	15th	43·54
Stone, Clay and Glass Products	7th	48·6	12th	10·56	4th	36·5	11th	14·13
Machinery	8th	72·5	8th	4·99	8th	65·0	8th	8·90
Paper	9th	96·7	15th	15·60	11th	100·4	14th	26·73
Metals (not Machinery)	10th	98·0	13th	12·10	9th	65·5	13th	23·50
Leather	11th	102·0	3rd	1·40	10th	81·2	2nd	2·17
Tobacco	12th	129·0	2nd	1·15	15th	196·0	5th	4·39
Petroleum	13th	143·0	16th	22·84	13th	128·0	16th	89·46
Electrical Machinery	14th	169·0	7th	3·97	14th	153·0	6th	4·77
Textiles	15th	182·0	5th	3·39	12th	126·0	7th	6·52
Transport Equipment	16th	323·0	9th	5·31	16th	225·0	9th	9·60
All Manufacture		54·7		6·42		55·6		12·69

* Plants employing at least one wage-earner (according to the 1963 definition).
** In order of average persons per plant, 1939. Certain major groups appearing in 1963 are not directly comparable with the 1939 grouping. Rubber, which included plastic products in 1963, excluded them in 1939. The instruments group had not been formed in 1939. Miscellaneous included in 1939 many of the instrument industries. These groups have accordingly been omitted from the table. The transport equipment and the automobile group distinguished in 1939 but not in 1963 are merged. The 1939 iron and steel and non-ferrous groups and the 1963 primary and fabricated metal groups are merged to form a comparable "metals" group.

variety of plant sizes *within* each industry; but the distinctly different levels round which variety of size occurs as *between* industries, allowing most of them to be graded according to a characteristic size of plant.

2. MEASUREMENT OF THE SIZE OF FIRMS, THE CONCENTRATION OF CONTROL

So far, it is the size of the plant (the unit of continuous physical building) that has been traced. What, however, is the trend in the size of the firm or unit of business government? Information on this trend is less abundant and more confused, but certain conclusions can be drawn from Census data and official reports. Information is confused because some data refer to simple concerns or companies, possibly subsidiary, others to composite units of control. Owing to holding companies and other devices, these types of governing body are by no means the same, and caution must be exercised in comparing different series of data, particularly between countries. The simplest and most distinctive word to cover the unit of accounting and of government in industry is *firm*, and *within* each country six conclusions can be stated about the size of firm—

(i) Most of the larger firms own more than one plant, but the smaller firms have only one plant. The average firm is, therefore, larger than the average plant and the dispersion of sizes still wider.

(ii) The plants owned by these multi-plant firms are on average considerably larger than those owned singly by a firm identical with the firm. In 1958 the plants of multi-plant firms employed on average 241, single units only twenty-one. Compared to plants firms are therefore *very* much larger on average and their range of variation in size very much wider. In manufacture *generally* the smallest firms will be no larger than the single plant they own and some will employ only one man. But in 1963 in point of employment, the largest United States industrial firm, General Motors, employed 640,000. The next two largest industrial firms were Ford Motors and General Electric employing 317,000 and 263,000. The largest purely British industrial firm was the (nationalized) Coal Board employing 550,000, and Imperial Chemical Industries employing 143,000. If plants range in their size as mice to cart-horses, firms range as mice to elephants!

(iii) Comparing single industries, the average size of firm varies more widely than the average size of plants. Evely and

Little (50, Appendix H) list 219 British manufacturing trades
for 1951. Their arithmetic mean size of plant varies as 1 to 67
from 30 employees (in fish-curing) to 2,010 (in rayon, etc.,
yarn and staple fibres); the arithmetic mean size of business
units or firms was, in these two industries, as 1 to 101—40
employees to 4,030.

At U.S. Senate subcommittee hearings, Blair (238, Part 4)
submitted detailed information on the divergence between
plant and company concentration in 1958 in 166 industries.
The eight largest *plants* in metal cans accounted for 19 per
cent of output, but the eight largest *companies* for as much as
89 per cent—a divergence of 70 points. The eight largest
beet sugar *plants* accounted for 20 per cent of the output, the
eight largest *companies* for 94 per cent—a divergence of 74
points. These are two of the extreme cases, but 63 industries
out of a total of 166 had a divergence of over 20 percentage
points. In a further measure of divergence, the percentage of
all employees that are in multi-plant companies, for all the
twenty major groups of industry are ranked in Table XIX.

(iv) This multi-plant statistic of the U.S. Census of Manufactures (236) gives perhaps the most detailed and significant
information on differences in size between firm and plant.
The data confirm the eighth trend listed in the first chapter
(toward enlargement in the size of industrial organization)
as measurable not only by output or mechanical power in
use, but by persons employed. We may trace the trend from
1929 to 1939 and again from 1957 to 1963. Between these
two periods measurement changed from wage-earner to

All Manufactures		In Single-unit Firms	In Plural-unit Firms	Percentage out of Total in Plural- or Multi-unit Firms
Wage Earners	{ 1929	4,524,000	3,845,000	48·4
	1939	3,472,000	4,414,000	56·0
		In Single-unit Firms	In Multi-unit Firms	
All Employees	{ 1954	6,165,000	9,456,000	60·6
	1958	5,317,000	10,077,000	65·5
	1963	5,219,791	1,014,715	67·8

employee and the organization measured from plural unit under a central administrative office to "multi-unit". The increase in the proportion of workers in multi-plant firms was fairly general, and the ranking of industry groups, in Table XIX, for 1963 was not very different from that for 1929, when allowance is made for the different grouping of industries.

The largest change was in the printing major group which showed the lowest proportion of workers in firms with several plants in 1929, but rose to fifth rank in 1963.

(v) Though data are scarcer, the four conclusions reached concerning plants seemingly apply to firms and often more strongly so. There is (*a*) a rise in their size but (*b*) a slow one and (*c*) a wide variety of size *within* each industry, but yet (*d*) characteristically different levels (round which the variety occurs) as between industries.

(vi) Any absolute increase in size of firm as well as plant, however, does not necessarily involve an increase of size of the largest few firms *relative to that of the whole industry*—does not, in short, involve a concentration of control over whole industries.

The *absolute* size of both plants and firms is important, as we shall see, in questions of costs and efficiency and also of management and labour relations. For *firms* at least, *relative* size is also important in questions of monopoly or oligopoly control. Where one or a few firms sell practically all the output, and monopoly or oligopoly reigns, these firms' policy on prices and production may become the policy of the whole industry and their government its government. The concentration of output in a few firms is certainly very high when compared with other well-known concentrations, such as income among individuals. Particular industries differ very widely, however, in this concentration both in the United States and Britain. In the United States many industries had in 1958 high concentration of the market accounted for by four firms (the proportion for less than four may not be disclosed): $92\frac{1}{2}$ per cent in electric lamps, 84 per cent in primary batteries, 79 per cent in cigarettes to name only familiar products. On the whole the smaller industries are more liable to high concentration. As to the trend, the evidence is that concentration of firms in manufacture *generally* has been tightening though not within individual industries

(187, pp. 22–49). We may quote Blair's evidence on the percentage of the *total value added* by all manufacture accounted for by a few large firms in 1947 and 1962 (238, Part 1, p. 81)—

> Over the entire period [the share] for the 200 largest [firms] increased from 30 to 40 per cent . . . for the 50 largest the increase was from 17 to 24 per cent. . . . In 1958 according to the Census Bureau a total of 269,834 companies were classified in manufacturing. Thus less than one-tenth of 1 per cent of the total number of companies accounted in that year for two-fifths of the total value added.

Not every manufacturer competes with every other, so the issue significant for monopoly or oligopoly is concentration among firms in *individual industries*, making more or less for one and the same market. In a table covering the period 1947 to 1958 the following changes are reported (238, Part 2, p. 80) in concentration ratios among the 360 industries—

Increase 5 per cent or more	96
Increase less than 5 per cent	71
No change	21
Decrease less than 5 per cent	73
Decrease 5 per cent or more	99

This combination of greater concentration of firms in manufacture generally, but no greater concentration industry by industry, points to firms each spreading their activities into more industries and widening their scope, i.e. "integrating", "diversifying", or in the latest phrase, becoming more "conglomerate". This behaviour is in keeping with the growth motivation to be stressed later (IV, §7; V, §2). If a firm cannot grow because of limited demand in its own industry, the solution is to spread into other industries.

In Britain concentration is also high in many industries, and often the same industries as in the United States. Taking industries employing at least ten thousand, explosives and fireworks, cement, dyes, ordnance, electrical equipment for vehicles and cotton thread all contained *three* firms (British disclosure rules are more liberal than United States) which made, in 1951, more than 85 per cent of the added value of the industry. From 1935 up to that year Armstrong and Silberstone (*Statistical Journal*, Part 3, 1965) found concentration on balance to have been tightening. Out of all the industries that were comparable between the two years, 27 had increased in concentration, 14 had diminished. Between 1951 and 1958 Shepherd (235) finds a further increase of concentration in more British industries than decreases. Out of industries comparable between the two years 1935 and 1951, 27 had increased in concentration, 14 had diminished.

3. CORRELATES OF SIZE OF PLANT AND FIRM

Before advancing theories to interpret the four salient features which appeared when measuring the size of plants and which are equally, if not more, applicable to firms, let us examine other measurable facts and trends that might hypothetically be expected to be correlated with these sizes.

Two characteristics of industries that, unexpectedly, are little correlated with their plant-size are their total size and their staff ratio.

It is far from true that the larger industries have the larger plants. The bread, newspaper and women's dresses industries are among the eight largest industries, but they have small or smallish plants prevailing. Their average number of employees per plant was in 1963, 42, 38 and 39, compared with a U.S. average for all manufactures of 55. Evidence and reasons have already been given for dissociating higher staff ratios from larger sizes of plant when discussing, in Chapter I, the two simultaneous trends. Here we may take an overall view and compare the twenty major groups covering all manufacturing industries. The rank correlation between average size of plant and staff ratio (obtainable from Table XIX, columns VIIA and B) is as low as -0.08. Closer correlates of plant-size that research has, however, disclosed are localization, already discussed (III, §4), degree of mechanization (one measure of technical progress), and the earnings of workers and of capital, which may be taken as measures of efficient performance.

Mechanization and size of plant appear positively related. Comparing industries, I have claimed (69, 79) a fair correlation of plant-size and mechanization in British industry in 1930–5, and again in 1951, and in United States industry in 1929 and again in 1947. Dr. L. Bruni (26) has found a similar fair degree of correlation in Italian industry. Mechanization was measured by horse-power-a-worker, allowing for the fact that in assembly industries less power is normally required for a given degree of mechanization than in other (particularly process) industries. Considering assembly and non-assembly industries separately, it was found, in these countries and years, that industries, typically with large-size plants, tended to be industries with high horse-power-a-worker. Evidence for this correlation is also given in the Appendix, Table XIX. Though a factory with few workers might, as already stated, have machinery idle much of the time and thus show a high horse-power-a-worker, yet industries typically with small plants were found to be low-powered. Steindl (175, p. 22) sums up (and supplies some supporting data) that "there is a good deal of evidence to show that the amount of fixed capital employed, both in relation to output and to number of employees, increases with size of plant (*and* with the size of the firm)".

The correlation of higher earnings of labour with larger plants has been observable for some time (72, p. 67) though perhaps less observed than it deserves in either Britain or the United States. In 1954, annual wages and salaries per worker in British manufacturing plants (182, 1954) rose fairly continuously from £400 in plants employing 11–24 to 415, 435, 486 and 529 in plants employing 100–199, 500 to 1,000, 1,500 to 2,500 and over 5,000. In the United States, dividing payroll by number of employees, size-grades showed in 1958 the same consistent pattern of higher pay per employee with larger sizes of plant. The pay per employee in the plants employing 1,000 to 2,499 and 5,000 upwards was 136·6 per cent and 142·3 per cent of that in the plants with 1–49 employees; and in the intermediate grades of sizes of plant, earnings per employee rose consistently between the two extremes. In that year *firms* showed the same progressive trend size by size (236, Part 1, p. 34). The average pay per employee in manufacturing companies employing 10,000 or more was $5,825; in companies employing fewer than 20, $3,834—a difference of 152 to 100. The increase was continuous throughout the nine size-ranges of company.

The rise of pay with increased size of plant is, in both countries, associated with a rise in "value added" or "net output" and, where data are available (as in the United States), with capital expenditure per worker. All manufacturing plants employing over 500 accounted in America, 1958 (239, p. 767), for 42·8 per cent of the employees, 48·7 per cent of the payroll, 51·6 per cent of the year's capital expenditure and, in output, 48·5 per cent of value added. In Britain, however, unlike the United States, the value added (or net output) per worker appeared to increase progressively only up to the larger plants employing fewer than 2,000.

Correlation of size with the earnings of capital in the shape of profits can only refer to firms, not plants. Moreover, correlation is not scientifically possible except *within* an industry, since industries differ so widely in their capital intensity and profits cover risks and other factors, not proportionate to the amount of capital. What clear-cut evidence exists points on the whole to higher profit of the larger firms (72, p. 62). In the course of trade fluctuations, however, the profits of smaller firms vary more widely and in the boom phase are often higher than the profits on average of the larger firms. This correlation, apart from slumps and booms, appears as far as the evidence goes also in the newly developing countries. In India, for instance, where the average size of cotton firms was fast increasing between 1905 and 1944, Mehta (137) found the larger size on average the more profitable.

4. INTERPRETATION OF THE FACTS, THE LAW OF INCREASING RETURN

When all the relevant details of the trend itself and of its correlates are measured and assembled, how can this general trend toward large-output manufacturing plants and firms be interpreted?

The explanation that held the field in the hey-day of classical economics was the Law of Increasing Return. Marshall (129, IV, xiii, 2) worded it "an increase of capital and labour leads generally to an improved organization which increases the efficiency of the work of capital and labour". The correlation we have found of plant size with intensity of capital provides reasons for holding this law to be probable. With increase of capital and labour the possibilities open out of full use of more specialized power-driven machines and greater division of labour. In manufacture (as against agriculture) land, limited as it is by nature, is not important and *all* factors of production can in the long run be increased. Three principles apply (63, pp. 16 *et seq.*), those of bulk transactions, massed reserves, and multiples. The cost of large containers is per contents less than that of small containers, and the cost of dealing in *bulk* quantities less in proportion to units; when items are *massed*, deviations are more likely to cancel out and reduce the risk that the final result will widely diverge from expectation; and when the capacities, e.g. of specialized *indivisible* machines, are different, balancing production, so that no capacity is idle, requires an output that is a multiple of the several capacities. These principles have been found to apply not only in the technology of the plant but (especially with the disproportionate growth of reputation with size) in marketing, advertising, and finance by a firm. Indeed, more agreement is found about the economy of these activities in a large firm than that about the economies of the large plant (159, Chapters IV and V) and, as the facts indicate, firms extend to a larger size than plants. This extension through finance or advertising by some firms may, however, proceed so far as to involve a high concentration of power within an industry. The possibility of monopoly or oligopoly amounting to a monarchy or oligarchy will be taken further in the next chapter, devoted to industrial government. Recently, research has been added as an activity with large-scale economies accruing to the large firm. Villard (195, p. 360) shows a much higher percentage of larger than smaller American firms undertaking research.

A further point that has been neglected is that large firms— thanks to their marketing and financial strength—can afford (and take the risk of) setting up large plants often in a location new to the industry concerned. Thus the correlation of large plants with large firms may well be interpreted as a two-way causal train. Large plants are partly the cause of large firms. But, also, large firms may sometimes be the cause of large plants.

5. FACTORS LIMITING INCREASING RETURNS IN PARTICULAR INDUSTRIES

The law of increasing return can be squared with one of the four salient features brought out by the facts, the growth in average power per plant in all but one major group—apparel; and with the correlation of size and greater earnings by labour and capital. But can the law be squared with the other correlations and the remaining salient features?

Economists have naturally asked themselves why, if the law of increasing return is true, do the sizes of manufacturing organizations, as the statistically measured facts show, change in the different industries at such diverse rates? Why, in fact, does not the largest firm in each industry with its supposedly superior efficiency not overwhelm its rivals completely, incidentally gaining what additional advantages there may be to itself in a monopoly? As Robertson puts it (158, p. 847)—

> The root difficulty about increasing returns has always been to understand how, while they prevail, equilibrium can exist without the whole supply of the commodity in question becoming concentrated in the hands of one producer.

To resolve that awkward question, we will first inquire into the causes underlying the salient feature of the differences in size of plants and rates of increase in size, *between the different industries*. Here several of the correlations traced earlier will help the inquiry, though correlation by itself cannot determine which correlate is cause, which effect. Why do so many industries still employ so many workers in the smaller plants; and why have so many industries not greatly increased the typical size of their plants?

Discussing the trend toward the differentiation of industries in the first chapter, weight was attached to certain physical qualities (on the supply side) of their materials and to their techniques; and (on the demand side) to their types of market —in short to the supply and demand setting of the work confronting the producer. These ergological factors were correlated with differences in the location pattern. Heavy materials root an industry near their sources, heavy products tie the industry near the market. In its turn the location pattern, as duly demonstrated, affects the size-pattern. The more dispersed that plants have to be, in relation to the population, the smaller their accessible market in areas not urbanized and the smaller their size. Where material and product are transportable, the larger their accessible market and sources of supply, the larger plants can (but not necessarily will) be.

More directly affecting size of plant than this transportability (which in the first place affects location pattern) is the uniformity of the materials and conditions of supply and the uniformity of the product and conditions of demand. Demand may be large extensively because many possible customers live within the area where the product can be transported, and intensively because many customers demand a lot of the product. Thus plants are small when the whole demand for their product is neither extensive nor intensive and (e.g. in the U.S. (1958) lapidary work with 1,904 employees, or the U.K. (1951) incandescent mantles with 769) the whole industry is small. The lack of correlation of size of plant and size of industry when we considered all industries indicates, however, that this cause, on the demand side, of small plants applies only for very small industries. On the supply side the rule probably goes farther that the less uniform the conditions, the smaller is the plant or firm. The outstanding example is outside the manufacturing sector, namely agriculture, where seasons vary and the behaviour of weather and livestock is not uniform or easily foreseen, and where also, sure enough, the scale of organization is smaller than in manufacture. Uniformity allows *full use* of specialized machines and other technological economies. Agriculture employs high-powered machinery, but most of it has to be idle much of the year.

Summing up a comparison of the characteristics of corresponding United States and British industries, I found (79, p. 23) a "stronger international agreement in industries' power-a-worker than in degree of localization". This I attributed "mainly to the wider differences between the geography of the United States and Britain than between the techniques employed in corresponding industries in the two countries. The United States is large, has more varied climates from place to place and weather from season to season, and has a greater variety of minerals". Technology, on the other hand, is transferable from one country to another provided that uniform materials and products are similarly supplied and demanded.

Uniform materials allow for mechanization, uniform standard products for large-scale increasing-return operation, and both mechanization and standardization give some industries big plants. In a free economy the sovereign consumer who wants to be different and special puts a severe limit on the extent of any uniform market. Producers may either pander to the consumer with special goods made on a small scale; or may try by extensive advertising (63, p. 85; 72, p. 121) to stimulate the consumer to demand the article which by large-scale methods is the most efficiently produced. Either policy is costly and not apparently encouraged in Communist economies, where what people are (or are not) to consume, as well as to produce, is planned on a large scale. My discussion of the limits imposed by the consumer's whims was cut out, as only "of bourgeois relevance", in the Russian translation of my *Logic of British and American Industry*!

It is true that the manufacturer does not deal normally with final consumers, but either (when making capital goods) with another producer or with a wholesaler or retailer. The vagaries of the consumer will still be felt, however, by the retailer and, in his turn, by the wholesaler.

Table XIX, Columns ia, i and ii, citing the input–output tables compiled in 1958, shows that of manufactures as a whole only 19·3 per cent went directly, but 68·0 per cent indirectly, into personal consumption expenditure. As in so many of their characteristics, however, industry groups vary widely from one another. In direct personal consumption they range from 0 in the primary metal group to 74·2 per cent in the apparel groups.

Fashion goods will tend to present small and short-lived markets, and industries producing them, like the clothing trades, to be on a smaller scale. Nevertheless, increasing return may make itself felt in large-scale communities or organizations *somewhere* in the whole process of converting materials into goods in use. Large cities have already been noticed in the Florence Effect as allowing small localized plants to flourish. Similarly, if both factories and retailers are small-scale, large wholesalers will usually (72, p. 102) be interposed between them. Further research should test the hypothesis that if an industry has small plants, a large-scale stage is usually present somewhere in the whole productive-distributive process.

6. FACTORS LIMITING INCREASING RETURNS IN GENERAL

So much for the differences and different rates of increase, in size of plant between different industries. The salient statistics bear out the law of increasing return in featuring the growth in size of plant generally. But how can we explain the third salient statistical feature, namely that this general increase is so slow?

The law, it must be observed, is a long way from saying that large plants or firms are more efficient than small ones. It applies, in the first place, not so much to the size of organization through "internal economies" as to the size of a whole industry through the "external economies", largely of localization, as already described. Such external economies can be obtained even though plants remain small.

In the second place the law applies to the scale on which a single commodity is produced, to its mass-production. Large plants, and still more so, large firms, in fact provide a wide variety of different products, processes, and services, many of them on a small scale. Of the thousand largest United States manufacturing companies in 1950, only 118 were confined to one (four-digit) census industry, 480 were in two to five industries, 332 in six to fifteen, and 70 straddled over fifteen industries. Two-thirds of these thousand companies even straddled over several of the twenty major groups into which all the 450 U.S. census industries are classed, 227 of them over four or more groups of industries. Analysing 111 of the largest U.S. manufacturing corporations in 1959, Gort (220, pp. 13–19 and 23–5) bases several measures of integration, including diversification, on this very straddling. To define an industry in the first chapter we accepted the census assignment of all plants to one industry or another, according to their "principal products". One of Gort's indicators of integration is the proportion of workers in the firms of an industry who are straddling into other than the principal primary products of that industry— who are, we might say, "poaching". Comparing thirteen major industry groups, he found (p. 33) that the tobacco group of plants integrated or diversified least, with only 16·8 per cent of its employees at work assigned to other industries; the petroleum group integrated most with 69·4 per cent of its firms' employees in other industries (mostly, in this case, extractive). If, however, vertical integration is excluded and lateral integration, "diversification" or "conglomeration" thus isolated, the ranking is different and appears in Table XIX, Column IVE. Tobacco remains least diversified with only 0·1 per cent of its firms' employees in other industries; electrical machinery now appears most diversified with 33·3 per cent of its firms' employees in other industrial groups.

For manufactures as a whole, diversification has certainly been increasing as already surmised. Between 1950 and 1962, more of the largest 1,000 corporations had diversified into more products (238, Part I, evidence of Houghton). The number making only 1 (five-digit) product fell from 78 to 49, and the number making 2 to 5 from 354 to 223. But the number of corporations making 6 to 15, 16 to 50 and (the few) making 51 products upwards, rose 11, 84 and 88 per cent.

A similar though less detailed tale of integration is shown for Britain in Roskill's *Who Owns Whom* (166).

Integration, like specialization, is a relation between an organization or structure and an activity or activities or, as Talcott Parsons would say, between actors and acts. In measuring its extent we must be careful to specify the structure —exactly who the actors are—and also the category of activities we are talking about. In the preceding paragraph the reference was to firms not plants. The plants, as already said, stick to one industry and certainly one *group* of industries more closely than do firms owning several plants. It would otherwise not be possible, as the Census does, to assign plants definitely to one industry or another. Nevertheless, there is some degree of deviation from this assignment duly measured in the proportion already mentioned (p. 25) to which plants specialize in or cover exclusively the industries' principal products. It must be remembered, however, that this particular indicator measures the relatively modest integration by the plants of an industry not by its firms, as measured by Gort.

Using his statistical measure of integration or diversification, Gort found (220, pp. 65–74) only a moderate correlation with the size of the firm. Thus the integrated firms not being significantly larger but straddling several industries may have pursued each industrial activity on a smaller scale. Size of firm and increasing returns are here not necessarily connected. At present we can only surmise that the connexion often depends on the reasons for integrating. If a firm or plant integrates because it fears to put all its eggs into one basket, then it checks the increasing return of enlarging a single line of activity. In fact, a smaller plant or firm taking the risk of specializing in one line and putting its eggs all in one basket, may provide that line on a larger scale and with increased returns compared with the lines which a large but integrating firm or plant may provide. Some large firms have in fact "disintegrated" (72, p. 74) in order to increase their returns.

On the other hand, (i) a small plant or firm is obviously precluded from providing any one line beyond a scale employing all its resources, and (ii) if integration uses up spare capacity, acting on the principle of multiples, increase in size should go hand-in-hand with increasing return. The fact that some resources useful in producing one product are also useful in producing another extends to resources besides the purely material. These resources, to quote Gort (220, p. 58), "include research and development staff, the availability of experienced salesmen and the requirement of common managerial skills for two or more products". Finally, (iii) aggregation within the same plant of related operations may yield increasing return, for instance cutting out transport and reheating between the vertically related processes of iron and steel making, or working up heavy chemical by-products on the spot.

Pending further statistical correlation, one may conclude that though the law of increasing returns does not necessarily involve the large integrated plants or firms, the law may well have been a factor in the increase, but only slow increase, of the size of plants and firms. Integration will presumably, at the time it is introduced, increase the number employed in any particular plant or firm, but it may not lead to the same increased return that extending one particular line of activity would, and thus to the overwhelming of competitors in that line.

The fourth salient feature of the statistical data still remains to be explained. Why is there such variety of plant-sizes *within* almost every industry?

Two of the factors already used in explanation exercise some influence here. Even within the same industry, as officially distinguished, different plants may integrate different activities to a various extent. And ergological factors of materials, markets, and technology will again affect variety of sizes of plant within a particular industry. Many of the industries listed will include plants with local markets of different size, extensively and intensively, and somewhat different materials and technology.

Even where an industry is fairly homogeneous in technology, materials, and markets, however, the sizes of plants and firms differ. While differences in scale between industries are largely the result of external ergological causes, such differences within a homogeneous industry are largely humanly caused, and the human decisions involved are in turn largely independent of the particular industry, and internal to the particular plant or firm. They may be conveniently distinguished by the standard four economic categories—

> Land
> Capital
> Labour
> Management

(i) Some plants within any industry are often unable to grow for the simple reason that their site is cramped and the management decides no further suitable land can be found.

(ii) If the firm is a one-man business, a partnership, or a private company, no one may be willing to make more capital available, and the smaller public companies also often find difficulty in finance. This is an orthodox explanation (159, pp. 54–63), but, as we shall see, is not always so important to the management as assumed.

(iii) Possible labour supplies may be physically too scattered to be available without costly and time-consuming transport. Thus, plants in rural areas with a low density of population are limited in size. It is often stated that labour morale is lower, the larger the plant, and morale is then confused with efficiency and high return; but the evidence is conflicting and will be taken up later.

(iv) The theory still orthodox (at least in elementary textbooks) is that management is the great stumbling-block to larger size. I consider this theory not proven. My reasons, being heretical to textbook dogma, must be elaborated in the following section.

7. MANAGEMENT AS A LIMITING FACTOR

The diagrams of economic textbooks show not a continuously

falling curve of costs per unit of output in consonance with the law of increasing return, but, after a point usually placed near the middle of the range of output, a rising cost resulting in a U-shaped curve. This rising cost with size is often offered as an explanation of the persistence of small plants and firms. Troughton (181), inquiring among managers of a number of firms, could, however, find no evidence or grounds for the rising-cost phase of this U-curve, which textbook theory connects with management both in the short and in the long run.

In the short run, after exceeding a normal output (as usual drawn in the *middle* of the output scale) the well-known textbook he quotes assumes that—

> Management problems will increase and managerial efficiency will decline. The entrepreneur will be unable to deal with the very large output and management problems will get out of hand. There will be too many workers per machine for really efficient production.

But the managers' answers pointed to the contrary of these assumptions. Costs fell as fixed capital and overhead staff became utilized nearer to capacity. Each machine took so many men and no more and there could be no question of overcrowding. In the past the ten-hour working day, often followed by overtime, undoubtedly caused sufficient fatigue to affect costs (57, pp. 231–3). But today, with high machine costs, overtime pay is probably cancelled out by the lowered overhead machine costs *per unit* of this greater output. At worst the cost curve is L-shaped—flattening out at the very high outputs.

In the long run, according to the textbooks, the same U-shaped cost curve with increasing size again appears and again is attributed to increasing difficulties of management—the ultimate incapacity of one man to co-ordinate the multifarious activities of very large firms. It is probably true that the variegated pattern of plant sizes *within* almost all industries, though largely due to varying size of markets and sources when goods are costly to transport, is partly due to the variegated capacities of managers, some of whom, previously perhaps skilled workers or foremen, may not be able to cope with the accounting, finance, buying or selling involved. Many an owner-manager entrepreneur starting a business may never get beyond employing more than ten or, say, fifty workers.

Most of them eventually go out of business; but meanwhile they appear in the "snapshot" of the Census if the business still survives at the date the Census is taken.

At larger sizes of plant it is incapacity *to delegate* or to adopt new techniques, not all-round incapacity, that might make management limit size. But theory should not deny, or even ignore as it often does, the possibility of delegating co-ordination, capably and successfully. Recognizing that management is divisible, it does not follow that the total cost of all administrators (delegator and legates) would increase more than proportionately with size. And as Andrews points out (5), management is not static, but with increasing output will in the long run change its techniques just as in the long run the type of technical equipment is changed. The U-shaped average cost curves are presented in textbooks as though they were the findings of empirical research, but actually little attempt was ever made by economic theorists to verify what is a mere assumption. The more sophisticated economists now admit that the U-curve was a mere deduction from the unrealistic concept of perfect competition. Empirical research like that of Joel Dean (46, pp. 292 *et seq.*) has not in fact found any such curve. According to J. S. Bain (7, p. 155) "over the observed range of firm sizes, the largest firms appear not yet to have become big enough to suffer perceptible diseconomies of very large scale". Melman (138) has summed up official U.S. data for 1937 to show *administration* expenses per dollar of sales actually *falling* as the asset size of firms rises. The analysis was repeated for more firms in 1941. Table XIV compares for both years the proportion of administration expenses to total sales for different sizes of firms.

The *capacity* of management, though its variety results in a variety of sizes of plant and firm within an industry, does not then appear to limit the increase in the general level of size. But there is the other side of management, as of all human activity—a side unduly neglected in economic theory—the manager's *willingness* to expand business. Management may well result in both variety of size and in *slowing down of increases in size*, not from incapacity so much as from unwillingness. Here motivation enters in, and we must be definite about the person whose motives are involved.

In the first chapter a trend in development was discerned (to be detailed in the next chapter) toward the divorce of management from ownership. This trend, popularly known as the Managerial Revolution, is more accurately an evolution and is only slowly being accomplished. Industry in most developed Western countries is still left at present with two main categories of manager: the owner-manager or true entrepreneur risking his own family or friends' capital, and the manager owning little capital and paid mainly by salary. The two categories of

TABLE XIV

PERCENTAGE OF ADMINISTRATION EXPENSES TO SALES
ACCORDING TO SIZE OF FIRM

Assets $	1,034 Firms 1937	4,107 Firms 1941
Under 1 m.	17·8	14·1
1–5	15·8*	12·3
5–10	13·8	10·9
10–100	13·5*	} 10·0
100+	10·5*	
Weighted average	14·7	13·0

Source: S. MELMAN, Applied Statistics, Vol. III, 1954, pp. 1–11.
* Weighted average of several asset ranges.

manager will have a different motivation, and in considering past willingness to expand we must, to be realistic, make a distinction between the two. Several subdivisions of these two categories can and have been (72, pp. 298–315) distinguished. The entrepreneur can be the self-made founder of the business or the head of a family business which he inherited, or simply an influential large shareholder in a company; the salaried executive a promoted employee or a technocrat brought in from outside or a trained administrator. Each type has a different outlook, but for the sake of a simple tabulation only the two main categories will be assigned a separate column in Table XV. Attention will be drawn to the subdivisions (in brackets) when especially relevant.

As great a weight of motive against expansion appears in the table under the modern entrepreneur as under the salaried manager. This corresponds to the facts and business men's attitudes observed by Mackintosh (125) and Barna (10). The entrepreneur managing his own capital has been particularly unwilling to expand if it involves calling in outside capital and possibly sacrificing his own control.

Orthodox theory is probably wrong in the weight it attaches to management incapacity rather than unwillingness to expand;

TABLE XV

MOTIVES FOR EXPANDING THE SIZE OF FIRMS

Motives	Entrepreneur		Salaried Manager	
	For Expansion	Against Expansion	For Expansion	Against Expansion
Economic A Cash nexus	Maximum profits from increasing return (especially self-made entrepreneur and financier)	Marginal revenue becomes less than marginal cost	Chance of greater salary with expanded business	Not *his* profit maximized
Economic B Real-cost nexus		Desire for ease. Owner has no fixed hours. Long week-ends in country possible (especially family head) Tax burden		Desire for ease, but must show results. If expansion unsuccessful *risk* of sack. But no profit if successful
Psychological Boss nexus Hobby nexus Freeman nexus	Power-seeking Empire building Love of work	Independence from others' financial control Preoccupation with *public* work	Power-seeking Love of work	Fear of others' power. Fighting an expansion by takeover
Sociological Name nexus Gang nexus Sport nexus	Prestige Status-seeking in industry	"The gentleman-ideal" "Fair" competition Sportsmanship	Identification with firm (especially old employee) Prestige of expanding firm	Professional loyalty Matey with competitors
Alogical "Drifting"		"His own money to play with"		No initiative or ideas from outside

and when it does look at willingness it is wrong, again, in confining attention to just one incentive. Maximization of profit still stands in too many economic textbooks virtually as the only motive for industrial operation. In reality, particularly where the top management is paid not by profit but salary, quite a complex of motives has influenced business decisions.

In this complex we may distinguish at least five sets of motive: two types of "profit" or economic motive, psychological motives, sociological motives, and no apparent motive at all!

(i) *Economic Motive A*

Profit maximization with shorter or longer horizons (e.g. to keep goodwill) but regardless of Marshall's "real costs" (129, V, iii, §2) may have been the motive that ruled the founder entrepreneur of Industrial Revolution days who apparently allowed himself (and his workers) no rest and ploughed back nearly all the profit on his capital. But, with the spread of the salaried manager and the inherited business, it is probably rare in Britain today. In the United States it reputedly still occurs even under management control. Many a manager though not paid by profit apparently identifies himself heart, soul (and duodenum?) with the organization and its profit.

(ii) *Economic Motive B*

Here, profit is considered in some relation to the real costs involved. "A firm may fail to develop" to quote Mackintosh (125, p. 50) because "the rewards for development are thought to be insufficient". This limit he continues "may be found particularly where the rewards to the firm are identified with rewards to the persons in control, which are subject to income tax, and surtax, and eventually to estate duty". The entrepreneur owner-manager may, in general, balance his profits from expansion against enjoyment of his leisure. He will try to maximize his total happiness, in which monetary profit will no doubt still loom large in his calculations. He will weigh the trouble involved in expansion against the risk and uncertainties of profit and, often, the balancing will point against expansion. The *non-owning* manager has no profit to weigh against trouble and risk and may well prefer ease of mind, and showing results to the shareholders in the shape of balance-sheet strength, security, and liquidity together with a reasonably increased but not necessarily maximum profit. In taking risks he will realize that if unsuccessful he may lose his job, but unlike the entrepreneur, if he achieves success, get no profit from it. Many mergers or agreements between firms may probably be accounted for not by the desire for a monopoly profit but by the desire to shelter from the worries of competition. The owner-manager *entrepreneur* can go further in taking his ease than the salaried manager, since he is playing with his own money. Examples of a leisured gentlemanly, "satisficing", attitude which I have given elsewhere (72, pp. 302–4) referred largely to heads of family-owned firms.

(iii) *Psychological Non-economic Motives*

Many a motive beside the cash nexus (and the cash-minus-real-cost nexus) affects the managers' will to expand. Some will affect the entrepreneur, some the salaried manager, and some both of them; but as the entrepreneur is his own master, his *un*willingness to work hard can be carried to greater lengths. The hobby nexus—the love of work in itself—stimulates both types to expand, and so does the love of power. But the negative form of this power nexus, the will to be independent and *not* to be in the power of others (the freeman nexus) exerts a particular force on the entrepreneur. Considerable empirical evidence has been collected by Mackintosh (125, pp. 71–5) of the *unwillingness* or lack of ambition of small firms to expand business by bringing in outside capital. Both entrepreneurs and salaried managers will usually fight against a merger if they are to be the submerged party, even though receiving compensation and the "golden handshake". But in a merger by take-over the salaried manager (as pointed out in the next chapter) is likely to be overridden by the holders of the majority of the voting shares, and loyalty to their management is not usually up to the strength of shareholders' economic motives.

The existence of small firms has been interpreted psychologically, also, in terms of a gambling attitude combined with the freeman nexus. To quote Steindl (175, pp. 60–1) "small entrepreneurs . . . accept unusually high risks at very low remunerations. . . . The social position of the entrepreneur ('to be his own master') is valued as such and any small entrepreneur will struggle to the last to retain it!"

(iv) *Sociological Motives*

Empirical research has been disclosing more and more how powerful are these motives, particularly in the large organizations. The motives involved in social relations are not only the gang nexus (so potent, as we shall see, in labour relations) but the fame and the sporting nexus. Which way the nexus pulls the entrepreneur depends on whether his bond is with industry or with outside public and social life. If he wants to win a name as a public figure, it is unlikely that the industrial effect will be toward expansion. But for the non-owning manager the important question is how far he identifies himself with the interests of the firm he serves. If he regards the firm's success (though not necessarily its profit) as *his* success, then expansion may well result. This tendency to expand will be supported by any desire he may have for fame and status, and also for winning in a sporting capacity.

I have often (e.g. 72, p. 309) stressed this identification of salaried executives, though shareless, with their firm and their consequent striving for its increased volume of business. Marris (230) has assumed volume to be the main objective and (163, p. 143) Joan Robinson has put the point forcibly—

> The main cause that has falsified Adam Smith's prediction that joint-stock enterprise would be impossible, and Marshall's dictum that limited liability companies stagnate, is this capacity for managers and boards of directors to project their egos into the organization that they happen to belong to and care for it just as much as if it were a family business.

Katona certainly found (103, p. 233) that top executives of large corporations remembered their own and their competitors' volume of business and share of the markets, rather than the profits. On the other hand, the gang nexus, connecting the salaried manager by ties of loyalty to his fellow professional managers, may well restrain all-out competition, especially price-cutting, to secure business. And the sport nexus itself may restrain the salaried manager, since sport must abide by certain rules of the game. Indeed, regard for his good name as a sportsman among the gang—his fellow entrepreneurs in the trade—may limit the extension of business even by the entrepreneur owner-manager. He wants to be thought (if English) a gentleman, (if American) a "regular guy" not, respectively, a bounder or a chiseller. A sociological impulse will creep in to share business with potential competitors rather than expand.

(v) *No Apparent Motive: "Alogical" Behaviour*

It must be recognized that many managers, whether owning capital or not, just follow past tradition. Their outlook, as Carter and Williams (33, pp. 38–53) put it, is parochial and their behaviour does not express any particular desires except to carry on. The entrepreneur feels it's his own money and the salaried manager may have no initiative. Many of the firms thus inefficiently managed will eventually go out of business; but there is a lag, often due to the goodwill of an equally alogical customer, and as already said these businesses while they survive appear in the "snapshot" of the Census. Lack of motive is likely to hold out longer in owner-manager business, since there is no one in authority to dismiss the manager lacking in motive-power and, anyway, it is the entrepreneur's own money to play with.

Thus, on top of some plants' physical limits of land (particularly within conurbations), on top of costly transport of materials and supplies and of product to market, and on top of costly communication with linked industries, slow expansion is explained by many factors (as Table XV shows graphically) that are not of this ergological type. These factors affect management motives. Some are economic and some psychological and sociological, particularly the ethical principles and general sentiment against too cut-throat a competition by such "low" practices as cutting prices. It is true that a few firms not subject to these psychological and sociological restraints might grow fast; but to raise the general level of size they would have to grow *very* fast, and here, in *rate of growth* rather than a given large size, as Robinson (159, pp. 120–33) and Edith Penrose (148, *passim*) have stressed, there certainly are considerable management limits.

8. LIMITS TO LABOUR COHESION

The supply of labour was considered, in Chapter II, as its adaptability and mobility affects different industries in different countries. Attractives and repulsives, psychological and sociological as well as economic, were considered which would move workers and potential workers into, or out of, jobs, newly demanded, or no longer demanded. The present chapter deals specifically with the larger-scale trend and concentrates on attractives for labour to "cohere" and stay, and on incentives for labour to work efficiently, in the larger manufacturing plants and firms. For the size of his firm, plant, or department of plant probably has more effect on labour than the ultimate control analysed in the next chapter. Certainly the attitude of labour seems not very different in large co-operative, large nationalized, or large capitalist plants or firms.

As organizations become larger it might be expected that cohesion between their members would become more tenuous. Contrasting larger and larger plants, I have pictured (72, pp. 272–6) the gradual loss of "matiness" between employer and employed, of first names and of the team spirit (few teams known to sport have more than fifteen members); and the emergence, often by necessity, of check-numbers, of output records, clocking in, office segregation, and a bureaucratic hierarchy—in short, of "depersonalization", paper-work, and institutionalism. The larger plants and firms of modern industry with their mechanization and minute division of labour have presented the worker with four Rs likely to repel rather than attract him—repetition, routine, red-tape, and risk. The risk of unemployment has to some extent receded, though redundancy in certain factories still rears its head, particularly in declining industries and in prosperous industries that are introducing automation. But the place of unemployment risk is being taken by another R—remote control due to the operation by larger firms of several plants from headquarters office.

Thus the trend to larger-scale industry might be expected to raise (and to be limited by) certain labour losses. In my model of the train of causation of industrial fatigue and unrest mentioned earlier (II, §3) six types of labour losses were distinguished. Two refer to the very constitution of the organization: the turnover of labour, in which labour is lost (either by a worker quitting on his own initiative or the less frequent discharge) and *has to be replaced*; and absence (including strikes). Four, quantity, quality and economy of output, and accidents, refer to the behaviour of members of the organization, once they are mustered.

Losses are constitutional or "organic" in the sense that, if every member of a factory left or was absent, that body would (temporarily at least) not, in fact, exist. Some minimum absence is unavoidable, due to ill-health, and some minimum turnover, due to death and retirement. Indeed, a certain turnover beyond the minimum is necessary for the economic adjustment and mobility discussed earlier.

In practice, labour turnover has been found to vary widely from factory to factory, and occasionally the rate rises to fantastic heights. Comparing seventy-one factories owned by a British chemical firm (and whose records were kept on a comparable basis) Joyce Long found a range from 7 to 700 per cent. Seven hundred per cent turnover means that in the course of the year seven times as many workers left and had to be replaced as were employed on the average at any time during the year. This particular factory was not large; and in general the expected lower morale in the larger factories was not very evident, at least in the men's labour turnover. Long's inquiry into the factories of the chemical *and* other large firms, and a contemporary inquiry by the British Institute of Management did not, in fact, reveal (123, p. 79) any marked or consistent relationship between size and turnover.

An important revelation, however, from these studies of labour turnover in large plants is the high rate among short-service green hands compared to long-service employees, constituting a vicious circle. Turnover is high among newcomers, requiring the hiring of more newcomers, thus leading back to high turnover. "Most industrial organizations seem to consist of a nucleus of tried hands who have served their employer like old family retainers, surrounded by a floating and fleeting population of newcomers. A large factory, indeed, is rather like a boarding-house that takes 'transients'." This conclusion, derived from an inquiry I undertook at a large United States "ten-hour" plant in 1917–18 (57, pp. 166–9), was based on the number of persons leaving after a shorter or a longer service, namely, less than three months or more than a year. This turnover was then compared with the number of persons of similar length of service at work at any given moment during the same period. Thus 53 per cent of those employed had a length of service of over a year, 28 per cent of three months or less. But among the persons leaving the plant only 12·6 per cent had over a year's service; 68 per cent had three months or less. In short, the risk of leaving was far higher among the newcomers than among the older hands, in this case a relatively higher risk of 68/28 to 12·6/53, or about 10 to 1. This experience of a "floater-cum-nucleus" structure intensively investigated in a single large United States plant was confirmed at much the same time (57, pp. 169–74) by extensive data from other United States factories and in two English factories.

Some thirty years later, in 1948, an inquiry I initiated in Birmingham showed the floater-cum-nucleus structure still being reproduced and thus deserving the name of a pattern. In a count at a large factory (123) 663 men were found to have been employed over a year, but only 98 of them left during the year; 131 men were found to have been employed under three months, but during the year 265 in this short-service class had left. The count also found that 557 women had been employed over a year and 130 of them left during the year; 148 women had been employed under three months, but during the year 267 in this short-service class had left. The greater risk of leaving among the short- as against the long-service class was thus, for the men, 265/131 to 98/663, roughly 13 to 1; for the women, 267/148 to 130/557, roughly 8 to 1.

This floaters-cum-nucleus composition of large plants is a sociological fact of considerable importance to economic efficiency. To avoid the high cost in loss of output and in training of the many replacements due to this high "infant mortality" among newcomers, special care is required immediately after a worker's enrolment in order to turn them from floaters into nucleus permanencies. So important is permanence and stability that many employers work out a "stability rate", dividing the number (possibly forming a nucleus) who have survived a year by the total originally employed. This stability rate was suggested by the British Industrial Fatigue Board (57, p. 156), who found during the First World War that in six factories, excluding night-shifts, the survivors of a year's employment ranged among single women from 72·2 to as low as 27·6 per cent and among married women from 58·8, even lower, to 16·7 per cent.

Once persons have joined an organization, the next question is how far they will always appear at the time and place appointed—in short, their rate of absence. A minimum absence is unavoidable owing to temporary sickness (say up to six months), accident, and reasonable leave. Sickness varies with age, but in manufacturing normally averages five working days a year for men, equivalent to 1·7 per cent of working time, six for single and perhaps twelve for married women, equivalent to 2 and 4 per cent of working time (70, p. 39). Absence from accidents varies widely from industry to industry. For all U.S. manufactures the severity rate per million employee-hours in 1963 was 689, or 0·689 per cent, of working time. In the lumber group it was 2·94 per cent of working time, in stone, clay and glass 1·52 and in primary metals 0·88. But in the food industries it was as low as 0·146, and in apparel 0·169 per cent (239, 1966, p. 244).

In large plants, absence follows the turnover pattern. Its actual level usually far exceeds the unavoidable minimum; and some individuals, or classes of individual, are more prone to be absent (whether from sickness or otherwise) than others, in particular, the unskilled and semi-skilled rather than the management or staff. Among the 33 plants of a British firm (13, p. 37) absence with no excuse, damned as "absenteeism", but carefully analysed, averaged over ten times higher in some than in other plants.

The costs of absence, though they do not include training new workers, are like those of turnover considerable, particularly if the lost time is not known, and, therefore, not organized for, beforehand. With the mechanization and high staff ratios involved in development, overhead costs of idle equipment and of unused services of overhead staff are particularly heavy. There is also disruption of teamwork, which may in assembly industries reduces the output by far more than the absentee's normal contribution (70, p. 38).

It has been maintained (1) that absence rates show a significant correlation with size, being higher in the larger plants, presumed to be due to lower morale. This thesis is plausible in view of the "depersonalization" of the large plants. To test it, we may again appeal to the many factories owned by the British chemical firm whose records were kept in standard form. Absence records were kept of the men employed in thirty-four factories where their total absence rates ranged (13) from 2·5 to 7·1 per cent in 1947, 2·5 to 5·8 per cent in 1948.

K

Women's absence rates were recorded in twenty-five factories and ranged from 3·1 to 11·0 per cent in 1947 and 2·5 to 9·3 per cent in 1948. Eight of the factories were outstandingly large, each employing a total of men and women over 1,300. But instead of their showing the highest absence rates, many of them had rates among the *lowest* two-thirds: for men, four of the eight in 1948, six in 1947: for women, seven in 1947, six in 1948. One can hardly say that these eight largest plants tended to have the highest absence rates, and the hypothesis certainly requires further evidence in proof.

Whether absence rates are higher in larger than in smaller plants, a more significant fact about absence from large factories is the "Blue Monday Effect". If fatigue was the most prevalent factor in absence one would expect the last day of the working week to show most absence. This seems in fact true of school-teachers. But among English unskilled and semi-skilled factory workers on no more than a forty-eight hour week, the reverse was found true. The highest rates of lost time occurred not at the end of the working week but at the start, on Mondays. Baldamus (8), who drew attention to this unexpected phenomenon, suggested it may be due to the reluctance of a worker to return to a dull remote-control job after his week-end off. *Skilled* workers, presumably with more interesting jobs, did not show the higher absence rate on Mondays. Possibly the ratio of Monday to Friday absences may be the most handy indicator of morale in large plants, and considerably more reliable than the total absence rate.

The extreme degree of absence, often, indeed, bringing the whole plant to a stop, is the strike. A strike is an organized absence, either "wild cat" organized unofficially or else organized officially by a trade union, which will then supply strike-pay. The working time lost by strikes in manufactures has been on the whole very much less than that lost by individual absence and has shown little sign of increasing. From official United States and British statistics, I calculated (57, p. 191) that from 1881 to 1905 only 0·38 per cent of working time was lost in the United States and from 1899 to 1913 only 0·23 per cent in Britain. In both countries the percentages rose sharply in the hectic years 1916 to 1921, but since then have returned to one-third per cent or below. In 1949–55, in the seven

Western industrial countries reviewed (101) the days lost annually per employee varied in manufacturing between 0·5 and 0·9, or 0·17 and 0·3 per cent of total working time. The heavy cost of strikes to industry arises indeed not directly but indirectly from disorganization of linked occupations and trades.

There is little evidence to show whether industries with the larger plants or firms are more or are less strike-prone than average. Kerr and Siegel (106), examining the actual strike records of eleven countries, conclude that it is location pattern rather than scale of organization that is significant. Industries or sectors highly localized, like textiles, lumbering, mining, and docks, appear more strike-prone than industries, like clothing or food, scattered among the general community.

The phenomenon of strikes or organized absence draws attention to the trade unions who organize official strikes and sustain them by strike-pay. Trade unions, themselves, have been subject to the larger-scale trend. The average (arithmetic mean) membership of a British trade union was in 1939 6,181, and in 1960 15,077 when seven unions out of a total of 650 held almost exactly half (49·5 per cent) of the membership (116). The number of unions with headquarters in the United States and affiliated to the American Federation of Labor and the Conference of Industrial Organization fell, between 1940 and 1964, from 147 to 129. But the membership, including Canadians, rose from 7,872,000 to 15,150,000. The average per union thus increased from 53,600 to 117,400 members (239, p. 246).

Western society is pluralist—and large-scale pluralist. Each large-scale sub-society has different aims: management to obtain growth, perhaps, or more income for a given cost; trade unions to obtain greater equality in incomes. But the two aims do not necessarily clash and, as I shall maintain in a later chapter, development toward a higher standard of living implies both aims. In this chapter I am concerned with employees *within the large plant* blocking its cohesion so far as to agree on restriction of output.

Early in my inquiries into industrial fatigue I noted the restriction of output by whole groups of workers within both large English and large United States factories. The output of individuals doing the same work without imposed restriction should, in view of the distribution of human capacity, naturally fall into a normal distribution curve in which the average output was more frequent than either a low or a high output. I certainly (57, p. 221) found examples of such distribution. But among other groups I found a lop-sided curve when no output appeared above a certain figure and that figure was by far the most frequent. Apparently output was restricted at a stereotyped amount which practically all workers could fairly easily make, an output recognized by the group, and given a name, such as *doggie* in North England, or *stint* in Connecticut. Recently Kilbridge (110) has used this shape of output frequency curves in testing for the continuing effectiveness of wage incentives. The classic study of informal groups, however, was made by Elton Mayo and his associates in the Western Electric's large plant at Hawthorne, near Chicago (164). Here the group of men bank-wirers were found to have their own code—by no means following the employers' "party line" of maximum possible individual efficiency. The four rules of correct behaviour in this American factory group are a reaction to large factory conditions detailed in the model on page 50, particularly to the uninterrupted hours on monotonous types of work. Though differently named the same reaction was found in British factories (not to mention Public Schools). Here are the American and English names, respectively, given to four types of violator—

1. Rate-buster, swot
2. Chiseller, slacker
3. Squealer, sneak
4. Act officious, swank

This etiquette is almost as inviolate as primitive rituals. To break it was taboo, simply not done; or, if done, the violation would lead to social ostracism. The school slang for ostracize "to send to Coventry" is, indeed, now common usage in English factories—even in Coventry itself!

Large-scale employers try to strengthen plant or firm cohesion by personnel or labour departments and industrial relations officers, often using techniques suggested by the Mayo experiments. Where they are successful in holding an ever-growing staff together, *Organization Man* (201) is often the consequence; and they have widened the staff conception by giving "staff status" not only to foremen but to long-service operators—the type forming the nucleus in contrast to the high turnover floaters already described.

The informal group attitude among workers in large factories, neutralist to increased productivity, has been contemplated with equanimity by sociologists and they are, of course, playing their legitimate role as scientists in neither praising nor condemning what they observe. But it is difficult to escape the feeling that sociologists realize they are professionally "on to a good thing". Groups are their speciality, and the presence of groups in the midst of industry has certainly been neglected by economists. Elton Mayo, himself, called the economists to task for holding "a rabble hypothesis" of workers in factories as completely atomized individuals. The theory of sociological man in industry appears, in short, to be replacing that of economic man; and the theory, curiously enough, seems, as Peter Drücker notes, to be oblivious of industry (25, p. xv)—

> It has been fashionable of late particularly in the human relations school to assume that the actual job, its technology and its mechanical and physical requirements are relatively unimportant compared to the social and psychological situation of men at work.

But as Professor Eric Trist adds in quoting from Drücker—

> good human relations as a management philosophy is giving place to what may be called the task approach. In this both instruments and people are considered, but in relation to the work that has to be done.

This "task" approach, which has always been my own, will be followed up in the next section, dealing with incentives to productivity. But, meanwhile, it must not be thought that sociologists and psychologists wrapped up in group study, and economists observing the loss of individual output occasioned by group behaviour, are utterly segregated or that their several approaches cannot be integrated. Indeed in case-studies, recently, of operations in two contrasted English factories, Lupton (227) has cogently assessed the balance of economic and sociological forces. He appreciates the "logic" of social group "norms"; but also the "logic" of the nature of the work including market conditions (along the lines I have ventured to call ergological interpretation). Many psychologists, including Freud, are quite as critical of groups (83, p. 11) as any economist—and particularly of their intellectual capacity—

> When individuals come together in a group all their individual inhibitions fall away and all the cruel, brutal and destructive instincts, which lie dormant in individuals as relics of a primitive epoch, are stirred up to find free gratification. But under the influence of suggestion, groups are also capable of high achievements in the shape of abnegation, unselfishness, and devotion to an ideal. While with isolated individuals personal interest is almost the only motive force, with groups it is very rarely prominent. . . . Whereas the intellectual capacity of a group is always far below that of an individual, its ethical conduct may rise as high above his, as it may sink below it.

Economists, keeping in view the total national income, which so many psychologists ignore, realize the incompatibility of high personal incomes with output-restriction and consider the behaviour of many factory groups unintelligent and unrealistic, indifferent to the interests of fellow workers, and destructive of the national economy. All three of these economic comments on groups agree with the modern psycho-analytical approach as propounded by Alix Strachey (176, pp. 194–5)—

> The *dis*value of regressive group-mentality is considerable. In the first place, it induces an unrealistic state of mind in the subject on all matters connected with it, so that the ends he aims at in regard to it are often bad, from being mistaken, and the means he adopts to attain them are inexpedient. In the second place, it makes him indifferent to persons outside his group, since his libidinal impulses are mostly directed to persons within it, and most of his identifications are made with them. Nor has he any sense of duty or compunction about outsiders, since his group super-ego is not concerned with them. Indeed, if he happens to dislike them there is nothing to prevent his wanting to injure them and trying to do so, if he thinks it possible and safe.
>
> This brings us to the third and perhaps the most serious objection to group-mentality. Much of the large amount of libido which a group-member expends . . . is got by withdrawing it from non-members, and that makes him not only indifferent to their welfare and happiness but actually desirous of their destruction and unhappiness.

9. INCENTIVES FOR PRODUCTIVITY

The study of cohesion and its opposite in large factories has led on to that of restriction of output, particularly by informal groups of individuals. The failure to achieve possible outputs must now be considered on its own. Any individual worker's quantity and quality of output, and his accident records too, depend broadly on three circumstances: his selection for the job, his training and capacity for the job, and his willingness to work at the job once selected and trained. All three have been separately analysed, but are interdependent. A capable and willing worker *mal-selected* for a repetitive job may suffer acute boredom, have more accidents, and attain a lower output in that job than one less capable and willing than he, but impervious to monotony.

Vocational selection and training is investigated by individual psychology; sociology and economics are involved more in the task of getting workers, once hired, willing to produce reasonably up to their long-run capacities. So, always bearing in mind the possibility of more effective selection and training, we will focus attention on capacity and willingness at work.

Relative physical incapacity may be permanent or, as when fatigue occurs, temporary. Industrial fatigue was important while hours of work were long, and output was found to fall in quantity and quality and accidents to rise as hours got longer. Reliable evidence on this was collected in Britain between 1913, when the British Association for the Advancement of Science set up a Committee on Fatigue from the Economic Standpoint, and 1924, when the Industrial Fatigue Research Board (the successor of the Health of Munition Workers Committee) substituted in its name "Health" for "Fatigue". Evidence was also collected in America, beginning with Josephine Goldmark's *Fatigue and Efficiency* published in 1907, and continuing till 1920 with the U.S. *Public Health Bulletin* No. 106 (189), in which Miss Goldmark with Miss Mary Hopkins presented my own investigations contrasting plants with a ten-hour and an eight-hour working day.

During this period hours of work were never less than forty-eight a week and during the 1914–18 war sometimes rose to seventy-two a week, even for women. But since 1919 shorter working weeks have become established and physical fatigue less evident. There was no reason, in fact, for Elton Mayo and his associates to have been so surprised when a resumption of a mere forty-eight-hour week, after experiments in shorter hours, did not lower output. There is no contradiction between his results obtained in 1928–32 and the earlier long-hours-falling-output findings of 1907–24.

The size of plants does not in itself affect capacity, but has been held, as we know, to affect *morale* and the will to work. Special stimulants to the will have been introduced by employers—stimulants usually known as incentives. A vast literature has grown up to help boost productivity or to explain or justify labour's often "negative" reactions ranging like a spectrum (57, p. 384) from the yellow of ill-will through the green of envy and unrest to the blue of frustration and the violet and red of fatigue and positive ill-health.

One of the chief questions involved is the relative strength of economic and of psychological or sociological incentives. In the past, no doubt, employers have believed too exclusively in the strength of the incentive provided by the amount of wages and the method of wage payment. Recently, however, the general sophisticated view, influenced largely by Elton Mayo's work, has swung over to the socio-psychological side; and in the literature, as against the practice of incentives, this side now holds the field. This swing away from economic man was justified up to a point and is still needed in explaining management behaviour. But on labour incentives, as on labour groups already considered, that point has been passed and the balance has tipped too far against economic interpretations. The practice of British business men has indeed been somewhat ignorantly criticized by sophisticated *literati*. The following passage appearing in an American University quarterly and written by an "English Research Fellow" is not an unfair example—

> British business men have been far slower to adopt (certain) techniques than their American counterparts. . . . A recent study has shown that British managers are still firmly wedded to incentive payment schemes for workers, although they can give no objective evidence for their commitment and it is now over twenty years since a series of classic studies carried out at the General [*sic*] Electric Company's Hawthorne Works, in Chicago, first gave evidence of the greater effect of work-group norms on output.

It is true that till the publication of *Productivity and Economic Incentives* (45) there was little scientific evidence (to be summed up shortly) on the effect of incentive payments upon output. Psychological investigators, no doubt, found the subject dull, and economists just assumed the economic motive without empirical evidence. But though the group norms of Mayo's relay assembly girls rose temporarily under the stimulus of social limelight, his output-restricting bank-wirers hardly support the case for norms as incentives.

The controversy has been bedevilled, as so many controversies have, by sociologist and economist being interested in different aspects—norms, for example, as against efficiency—and trying to answer quite different questions. Thus J. A. C. Brown (24, pp. 188–90) maintains that work is attractive in itself—a retired worker will haunt the gates of the factory where he used to work. Undoubtedly, most people find life boring without *some* productivity. This, however, is not the question economists want answered, but rather how to get people to work *more* productively. Every individual has his own pace of working, for which no special incentive is required: or there may be some conventional group tempo. But the problem in the large factory is to get individuals to work beyond this often jogtrot pace, without cumulative fatigue, and to work in co-ordination. In spite of sociologists' discoveries, it is probably still true that paying so much a piece of work is the most direct way of getting *more* pieces made, and that the more individual the appeal as against *large*-group incentives or profit-sharing, the greater the incentive effect upon output. Amidst the welter of controversy it will be useful steadfastly to narrow the issue to the effect of larger-scale organization, and to keep close to some generally established correlates of size and incentives—

(i) The earnings of workers, as already shown (p. 98) are higher in the larger than the smaller factories. This may be the result of greater efficiency of the large plants, but it might also be a means of compensating workers for otherwise less attractive conditions in large plants, such as monotony cited in Table VIII.

(ii) Payment by the piece is more frequent in the large factories. Thus in five successively larger sizes of plant employing from one to twenty-four right up to one thousand or more, the percentage of workers on systems of payment by result was, in Britain in 1961, 13, 24, 39, 49, and 56 per cent (114). This fact is connected, of course, with the earnings difference, since workers usually take home more when on piece-rates than on time-rates.

(iii) In large factories very great increases in output have been obtained by changing from a time- to a piece-rate system (45, p. 267) when other conditions, such as method of work, remained the same, and always provided workers' representatives had previously been consulted. Among eighty-eight workers with records of many operations before and after the change in several British factories, fifty increased their output 67 per cent and over, and another twenty-nine over 34 per cent. While no worker's output fell, increased earnings are, as to be expected, correlated with increased output, but their pay did not increase exactly proportionately. Thus the cost of labour in general fell. All the workers were interviewed. Few complained of this lack of proportion or of fatigue and the majority were satisfied, by various tests, economic, psychological, and sociological. No negative association was found between increased output and greater satisfaction, in short, there was little evidence of the more the increase, the less the satisfaction; and those increasing output *and* earnings were positively associated with most satisfaction.

(iv) The piece-rate system is not spreading in industry generally. In April 1961 the percentage of all workers that was paid by result was 33 and showed little change from 1951, 1953, and 1955, when the percentage remained at 32. For manufacturing only, however, the 1961 percentage was 42.

In contradiction to the sophisticated English view that piece-rates are being abolished in the United States, the percentage of manufacturing workers on incentive plans in the United States, though at a lower level than the British, also tends to be stable. To quote the U.S. Department of Labor's *Monthly Review* (May 1960, p. 463)—

The various forces at play appear to have produced a comparatively stable situation with respect to the proportion of factory workers under incentive wage plans.

A later article in the *Review* finds a negative relationship of piece-rates with degree of technology which may explain the lower level of incentive payments in the United States—

> The more technologically developed an industry the lower the percentage of production workers paid on an incentive basis.

The main question raised by these four sets of fact, established statistically, is why, if more output is obtained by the economic incentives of piece-rates and if the higher earnings (in the larger plants) are associated with more workers on piece-rate, the piece-rate system has not been extended further and, particularly, into the smaller plants.

Two logical reasons apply, one at one end of the trend of development, the other at the other end. In the smaller plants, not mass or even "batch" producing, it is often economically not worth while to make the complicated calculations to find the correct piece-rates when so few pieces are to be made on any particular job. At the other end, with mass production and technological development, mainly in large plants, piece-rates may be unnecessary. Speed is automatically set as by a conveyor belt, or by automation, or accurate records are kept and workers dismissed if their record is poor. In short, piece-rates appear to be an intermediate occurrence between the small-scale, low-mechanized and the large-scale, highly mechanized plant on the way to automation.

The expansion of piece-rates is also limited by the difficulty of measuring the exact difference in effort, skill, responsibility, and working conditions (including safety), required to make a piece in the course of one job as against a piece in the course of another. Unless the time-study and the job analysis are very carefully conducted, some jobs will be found to be "gravy" or loose, others "tight" for earning a given sum of money. On some jobs the day's wage (or earnings) will be thought unfair for the "fair day's" work done. In consequence, workers assigned the "tight" jobs will be envious and liable to accuse the foremen of favouritism to the others. Instead of brimming with high morale, the whole department will be rent with ill feeling. This besetting difficulty drew my attention early in my inquiries (57, p. 89) to the correlation of little confidence in time-study and the type of piece-rate system.

Analysis of the motives actually observed in the real world of large-scale industry (45, table, p. 32) has led me to divide the varying reactions of labour into three general attitudes, A, B, and C, of which C was the unambitious attitude of not wishing to increase the amount earned whatever the wage-rate. This is parallel to the Sargant Effect (170, p. 77) of wanting to secure only a certain fixed future income from interest. In either case, the higher the rate of interest or wages that is fixed, the less is the principal, the time worked, or the output required to produce it; and therefore a higher rate of interest or wages tends to lessen the amount supplied, saved or worked. The supply curve is backward sloping. The A attitude, on the other hand, is largely "transpecuniary", since the workers look beyond their pay-packet to what they can buy with it, either for their direct satisfaction or to "keep up with the Joneses". Occasionally workers may think of saving or (especially managers) of the prestige of a high gross salary regardless of the high surtax standing as a status symbol. In any case, the A attitude leads to more work for more pay. In the B attitude the pecuniary or transpecuniary A motives exist, but have no absolute priority. The worker might fear a cut in piece-rates or might be a complete "Organization Man" keeping "in" with his foreman; or group solidarity with his mates and fear of taking work away from them might come first. To this scheme I have since added (81) a D attitude, which is not infrequent in large factories, namely, complete failure of motive owing to not understanding the system of payment. Plenty of evidence exists of this situation (57, p. 256) when complicated premium bonus systems are used, though more effective communication and consultation could easily alter it. Here I may quote a summary (45, pp. 273–4) of the approach that was almost standard practice in several large-scale factories—

> The first step was to persuade workers who were to be directly affected by proposed changes to consider the proposal. In every case the first step had the backing of the official trade union representative, and in some cases the official had been consulted before the workers were approached. If opposition was raised, the next step was more intensive persuasion and exhortation by both

management and trade union officials. At some stage there was a voting procedure to discover whether there was a majority in favour of acceptance. If this failed, a number of solutions were possible. But whatever the method of persuasion, if the workers concerned are not convinced that they are getting a "fair" deal, then there will be trouble at some stage. . . . Engineers, business managers and practical economists can certainly hope greatly to increase the national product by economic incentives but only if they take account of the social climate, particularly its liability to storms.

After their intense concentration upon groups and human relations, including communication and consultation, industrial sociologists are now realizing, we saw, the importance of the specific industrial task or job. We must, therefore, refer back to the considerable research done in the occupation field before the somewhat exclusive cult of "sociological man" set in. Two features of special significance to present and future development may be picked out—the monotony of large-plant jobs and the need for human adjustment to machine costs.

Development has included not only large-scale organization but mechanization, and this has, of course, altered and will continue to alter the types of work mainly found in factories. In 1917 I analysed the distribution of all the workers in a large and (then) up-to-date U.S. brassware factory, according (57, p. 64; 70, p. 66) to their relation to their work, and its "physiological and psychological requirements"; 4·1 per cent of the workers were related to the machine "as toolsetters" and about 2 per cent more for machine maintenance, and 35·8 per cent were actually on machine work—but their relation to the machine differed significantly.

The largest group (13·8 per cent of all workers) were operating semi-automatic machines mainly pulling levers to bring the tools into contact with the material and to engage and release the material. The feeling of monotony and boredom in this highly repetitive semi-skilled work, indicated by its falling hourly output curves, can usually be relieved by various policies singly or combined. Practicable policies are to select men and women less monotony-prone, to introduce rest pauses or tea-breaks, to allow a variety of jobs during the day and to teach easier-work methods that will allow rhythm and other forms of what Baldamus calls "traction" (45, p. 13), giving a feeling of being pulled or drawn along by the inertia or momentum "inherent in a particular activity, and the opposite of distraction". In "object" traction "the worker . . . feels impelled to reproduce or complete (an object) without interrupting the complete job cycle; in *batch* traction . . . to complete a given batch of work; and in machine and line traction . . . to 'keep going' smoothly with a machine and conveyor belt or just a chain of consecutive operations".

The next largest groups were merely "tending" either a chemical treatment (9·0 per cent of all workers) or an automatic machine (6·9 per cent) (usually after filling a hopper with a store of material). This type of work is probably becoming more frequent together with that of maintenance. When automation is introduced into a factory it should certainly increase the fairly skilled and responsible jobs of maintaining and tending machines and reduce the mere operating jobs, and will certainly increase the staff ratio. This conclusion is important, since the monotonous job has so far been the most frequent type in a large plant, and monotonous work is hardly a basis for intelligent enjoyment of life.

As well as changing the structure of factory jobs, mechanization, and automation still more so, introduces an economic need for working shifts, as in some chemical, the petroleum and the primary metal industries. This is a further example of an ergological train of causation. Machines are now so expensive an overhead, and they are so likely to become obsolete before they wear out, that they must be used to their fullest capacity sixteen hours in the day if not twenty-four. This can be achieved without fatigue or other physiological harm to workers by two or three eight-hour shifts or even six four-hour shifts. The main limit to shift work as to so many ergological requirements is social and psychological: the natural unwillingness of workers to be at work when their friends are at leisure, thus breaking up their social life. This unwillingness has to be overcome by an economic motive, the chance of earning more per hour at overtime rates on the unpopular unsocial shift.

To sum up, developing industry seems to require economic incentives not only for productivity on a given job which is often monotonous, but for adjustments to new circumstances, particularly to costly mechanization. Economic incentives are not always feasible, but, where feasible, they result in higher production and are worth the "labour trouble" admittedly involved. Only when work is sufficiently automatic that the machine sets the pace can large plants, with their depersonalization, usually afford to abandon some economic individual or group incentive.

CHAPTER V

ECONOMICS AND SOCIOLOGY OF INDUSTRIAL GOVERNMENT

1. THE FIRM, ITS POLICY AND RISKS IN THE MARKET

THE last two chapters have dealt with industrial structure in the strict sense of the site, size, and scope of activities of the plants and firms of an industry. The facts and the trend were observed essentially by snapshots of the situation taken at particular moments, as by a census. The sociology and particularly the economics of industry require, however, for a realistic analysis, continuous "movies" as well as "stills". Men in industry are continuously at work exchanging goods, services, and titles to goods and services in the outside market; and inside certain organizations that engage in this exchange, men are continuously at work giving (and obeying) commands. Economics is primarily interested in demand and supply leading to exchange; industrial sociology in power relations—the command and reply—within a unit of organization. For a grasp of its movement and working as well as structure, the classic capitalist free-enterprise system may be pictured as a number of unit firms, great and small, being steered "in a sea of troubles".

Outside these firms there is assumed the anarchy of the market. Though firms and industries are linked and interdependent —the input of one, the output of another—yet no authority is assumed set over them. Instead, there is competition (however imperfect), trade fluctuations, uncertain supplies, and uncertain demands for which firms must produce in advance, investing in specialized capital equipment still more in advance.

For the smaller firms the risk of loss and eventual extinction is high. Beesley found death-rates of metal establishments in two zones studied in the West Midland conurbation (12) during 1923–39 43·8 and 53·4 per thousand annually—about three times the contemporary human death-rate. In larger industrial firms taking the company form, extinction was no

134

more rare. McGregor (134, p. 168) gives annual rates of liquidation between 1885 and 1912 varying from 5·5 to 3·0 per cent of all companies. In large companies today total loss is uncommon. In 1959–60 Marcus (229) found losses among older and larger United States corporations considerably less than among the younger and smaller. Yet the gain or losses to shareholders of large going concerns by dividend plus changes in the market value of their shares show a wide dispersion. Between 1936 and 1951, for instance (78, pp. 161–87), a sample of 304 large English manufacturing companies ranged from a total gain of 1,535 per cent to a loss of 82 per cent on the original investment. In 16 per cent of the companies shareholders gained in total less than they would have gained had they invested in the safe British Post Office Savings bank, i.e. 37½ for the fifteen years at simple interest.

Apart from some peripheral control by the State (73, *passim*) and some auxiliary institutions and services, to be detailed later, the main co-ordinating factor in this anarchy is through the price-mechanism. When firms are all small in relation to the size of their industry, price is determined by the whole industry's supply and demand on the competitive market and this situation was, in the nineteenth century, the fact on which classical economic theory was built. Analysing industrial structure and concentrations today has, however, turned economists' attention to the possible power of a few leading firms selling as oligopolists or buying as oligopsonists a high proportion of any product. Prices may not be settled by demand and supply, but as Gardiner Means has it (136, pp. 10–13), may be "administered" by these firms. It becomes important to inquire further with the help of sociology into the internal organization of large firms and the motives of those found to be their prime managers, as we shall call the top executives. They have in fact a board of independent directors more like the British than the United States Cabinet. This internal analysis is taken up in the sections (2 and 3) that follow; but first we must look into the external economics of the market, and particularly costs, in relation to risk. The necessary empirical investigations are slow to appear. Only a few economists, such as, in England, Hall and Hitch (92), Hague (91), Andrews (5) or Barback and, in the United States, Bain (7), Kaplan, Dirlam and Lanzillotti (224) and

Baumol (210), have taken the trouble to inquire from business men what is their price policy in relation to their costs, and what costs they take into account. Among other discoveries, Hall and Hitch found that the rate of interest, and Andrews that marginal costs, do not loom as large as theory would have it. Where oligopoly prevails, no firm is likely to reduce prices for fear the others will retaliate similarly, leaving shares of the market where they were, but reducing all oligopolists' revenue. As Bain (7) maintains, the prevailing object may well be the highest price consistent with not encouraging, by the resultant high profits, the entry of new firms into the industry or the poaching by old firms from other industries. Thus Means (136, pp. 236–48) speaks of a "target price" adopted by the large United States steel companies.

The main policy question for most firms is whether, through price policy or otherwise, to expand or not and if so, by how much. This question was taken up in Chapter IV when interpreting the actual facts and trends in the sizes of firms, and stress was then laid on the motives of the different types of prime managers (including entrepreneurs) deciding on policy.

Where the firm wants to expand, by no means always the case (125, p. 7), the central problem when fixed capital is so important in industry is the supply of capital resources, including credit from banks or from linked industries and wholesalers, i.e. bank or trade credit. But the main sources of fixed manufacturing capital in developed economies today are the plough-back of a firm's own profit or new issues on the capital market. *Market* is here again used of the relatively unorganized relations outside the firm where the goods, services, and titles are bought and sold or, in the *labour market*, hired and "declared redundant". The original owner-manager entrepreneur (117, pp. 275–80) raised most of his capital by ploughing back profits, and this seems to be recurring; for some years after 1947 English industrial companies' boards of directors succeeded in ploughing back 60 per cent of the shareholders' profits (78, p. 144). In the United States, Berle states (14, pp. 25–6) that only 6 per cent of capital expenditures (including provision for depreciation) by firms between 1946 and 1953 came from issue of shares and 64 per cent from the firms' own savings out of profits. The remainder came (18 per cent) from current borrowing and (12 per cent) from bonds or debentures.

In the middle, nineteenth-century, period of capitalism, however, the capital market was, in the view of economists, the normal and assumable main source of capital supply, and the savings of the public still have their effect on industrial capital. Individuals save extensively through voluntary insurance, and the insurance companies buy shares on a large scale (78, pp. 117–18) in industrial companies. Sociological inquiries into the identity and habits of individual savers are thus relevant. Madge (126, p. 100), for instance, found in 1943 the highest savers in Glasgow to be country-born, Presbyterian, right wing politically, and of smart and mentally bright appearance. But buying shares in industrial companies does not extend, in Britain as it does in the United States, very far down the income scale. The movement for wider shareholding is sociologically up against the poorer man's desire for security and his suspicion of the Stock Exchange.

The investment of capital involves risk, as we have illustrated, either to the entrepreneur or to the shareholder. This measurable risk is due mainly to the capital investment being specific to certain products and to a certain scale. The expectations of the manufacturer as to the market demand for that product on that scale are most uncertain of fulfilment. Controversy, in which psychologists have joined with economists such as G. L. S. Shackle, has ranged round the questions how the risk-takers or risk-bearers form their expectations of the probabilities of any eventuality and whether there is any basis in past experience for valid expectations. Though, popularly, risk conveys both senses, economists distinguish between risk as a probability that can actuarially be estimated and the kind of "uncertainty" with which business is also faced—probabilities which cannot reliably be estimated. Table XIX ranks industries by liability to seasonal fluctuations which are the more predictable, and cyclical slumps the less predictable risks. There are in fact three dimensions in the term *probability* and as I have put it elsewhere (60, p. 91), it is possible to make such a statement as that "this probability is probably improbable", i.e. this particular eventuality is fairly reliably calculable as relatively infrequent! In this three-dimensional complex of probabilities the risk-taking and -bearing entrepreneur may psychologically form some image to simplify his expectation; but the gambling temperament or merely, as Keynes puts it, "animal spirits", makes for confidence and favours optimism over pessimism. Adam Smith (173, I, x) also thought that "the chance of loss is . . . by scarce any man who is in tolerable health and spirits, valued more than it is worth". But the shareholder and his advisers certainly have statistical data of past experience, some of which are probably relevant. His investment is not unique, nor all-out, nor once for all.

Even apart from the gambling nexus, the cash nexus or financial incentive to risk is difficult to calculate for the entrepreneur, but it is not so hard to calculate for company shareholders. The entrepreneur's income includes pay for management as well as risk-bearing, but for shareholders who do no managing the risk factor is more isolated. The average compensation in capital gain and dividend received by groups of shareholders in different industries or different sizes of firm do in fact (78, pp. 172–6) seem to vary, as economic theory has assumed, with the risk in those industries and with the various sizes of firms.

Economics now includes a "theory of the firm", but the assumptions of economic models do not sufficiently recognize that a large modern firm is complex in structure and government, and contains many conflicting interests, particularly between ownership and management. The term that is normally used by economists for all prime decision-makers is entrepreneur. The explicit definition of this term (Sir Hubert Henderson's (94, p. 116)) is a man who manages, owns the capital, and takes risks, but in most large firms, particularly if of company form, no such person is identifiable. To be realistic we must look into the various forms of the firm and their relative prevalence, and the way those various forms may alter economic theory.

2. The Form of Government of the Firm

Differences in the behaviour and decisions of firms are not unconnected with differences in their form of government. And firms are found to differ significantly in form according

to the type of their industry and their size (78, pp. 87–92).
Of the main legal forms, sole trader and partnerships govern
most smaller firms and are found to prevail in building,
retailing, agriculture, and the professions sectors; corporations
prevail in banking, insurance and manufacture. A further step
in industrial government, largely determined "ergologically"
by the nature of the material and markets, is the participation
of the State in the control of so-called "natural" monopolies.
In Britain mining, transport, public utilities, including communication by telephone and radio, are nationalized, in the
United States regulated. The precise policies will be detailed
shortly in Section 4. Here we must analyse the situation of
companies within the manufacturing sector more closely.

The degree of prevalence of companies (or corporations)
varies considerably with the particular manufacture concerned. In Britain I found a variation from 65 per cent of the
industry's taxable income going to companies in clothing to
100 per cent in heavy industries (78, pp. 1–2).

In the United States even among the "major groups"
combining many manufacturing industries, there is a distinct
differentiation. The lumber group, ranked in the Appendix,
Table XIX, as that with the least percentage employed by
corporations, had in 1958 65·9 per cent so employed; the
apparel group next least, 80·5 per cent, and the food group,
third least, 86·8. At the other end of the scale primary metals
had 98·5 and transport equipment 98·7 per cent. The ranking
and its discussion in the Appendix point to a close correlation
between percentage employed by corporations (Table XIX,
Column v a) and percentage employed in plants employing
500 or more (Column iv b). The Spearman coefficient of
rank-correlation for 1963 is as high as +0·87, where +1 is
positive, −1 negative perfect correlation.

This correlation tends to confirm one of the links in the
chain of causation set forth hypothetically in Table III. We
have argued, and presented evidence, that certain physical
qualities in material or product, such as uniformity, favour
mechanization and that mechanization is linked with larger
factories. We are now putting forward evidence that manufacturing groups with a large factory structure tend to be industry groups subject to the company form of organization,

If we define an industrial segment to refer to the prevailing form of government of a firm, we can sum up that certain segments are associated with certain sectors—for instance, the company segment with the manufacturing sector, particularly that part using capital intensively. Much of this association can be interpreted logically enough, since the main purpose of the joint-stock company (as British corporations are named) is to join stock, that is to aggregate large capitals; and nationalized industry, with the taxpayer available, can raise large capitals still more easily than the company.

As firms become larger they must consider enlarging the sources of their capital; also of their recruitment of labour and appointment of staff by the various methods open to them, separately or combined, old or new: patronage, nepotism, examination, interview, co-option, even election (as for the full-time paid co-operative wholesale society directorships). They must also consider their internal organization, once the staff is found. Analysis of large-scale industrial organization will require much the same political science categories and conceptions as are needed for studying State administration and constitutions (139): decentralization and delegation, the span of control, the chain and unity of command, sanctions, budgeting, arbitration, co-ordination, and the various references of control—to verify, to compare with a standard, to restrain, to regulate, and often to govern generally. Company or corporation law and the articles of association of particular companies form the basis of company constitutions, but the board of directors that is set up will create, or "structure", at least the top positions of the executive hierarchy (and their rate of pay) to which staff are to be appointed.

The simplest but most inclusive term to cover these problems in internal organization is rule-sharing and, in the large-scale industry to which development has led, the problems focus upon the delegation of power. The size of plants and firms, which was noted in the last chapter, has been supposed to be limited by the capacities of the prime manager. If he does not delegate, nervous breakdown or ulcers are supposed to threaten him. In some sense he can now delegate to the newer statistical or econometric techniques, and more reliably and copiously than to the traditional rule of thumb. Linear programming, for instance, can help him allocate given resources to the best advantage, or the theory of stochastic processes allow for chance events in estimating risks.

But responsibilities which a computer, mechanical or human, cannot take must also be delegated. Here, span of control and chain of command both play their interdependent parts. If an administrator can control only four subordinate administrators, and empirical evidence suggests this figure, then mathematically a total administrative staff of eighty-five requires a chain of command of four links (i.e. $1+4+16+64$) involving that much additional communication in the course of the rule-sharing.

Rule-sharing I originally put forward (60, pp. 412–28) as a useful neutral term not referring to any particular doctrine of the separation or the division of power. The more familiar and seemingly synonymous term "the separation of powers" refers to the particular doctrine enunciated by Montesquieu and wrongly attributed to the British, but carried out in the United States constitution, that the processes of legislating, executing, and adjudicating be allocated to different and independent bodies. In the company-form firm these processes, or at least two of them, are discernible. As Haney put it (93, p. 263), the body of shareholders are "roughly comparable to the voters in a democracy, the directors to a parliament, the executive head to a prime minister and the other executive officials to his cabinet". The constitution is usually pictured in the familiar hour-glass diagram (215, Fig. 56), the large number of shareholders represented by the wide top, the few directors and the fewer chief executive officers at the narrow waist. The policy or laws decided upon at this concentration of power are executed by a hierarchy of managers spreading out down the lower half of the hour-glass into the foremen and the total operating force.

In a book describing his organization one industrialist, at least, frankly uses as chapter headings the executive system, the representative system, the legislative system, and the appeals procedure. Mr. Wilfred (now Lord) Brown claims in fact that his company has a written constitution (25, p. 225) in which shareholders and customers as well as labour are given a part.

Usually, however, firms show little separation of the vertical stages in the process of government and their assignment to independent bodies. The executive is also the legislative organ.

Company constitutions follow the British rather than the U.S. political pattern here as well as in restricting to some extent the powers of the chief executive in appointing the Board of Directors. It is for this reason appropriate to speak of the leading individual person, as far as there is one, as the prime manager, suggesting a relation to his board akin to that of the prime minister in the British Cabinet.

A second doctrine in rule-sharing, often called the division of powers, does, however, apply very completely to industry. This separation refers to some balance in the horizontal division of labour between central and local governments; or, in a confederate or federal constitution, between the confederation or federation and the states or provinces. Large industrial firms have to find solutions of a similar problem. Many holding companies own all or a majority of voting shares of subsidiary companies. The existence of holding companies is largely a matter of history, and the way in which the company was originally enlarged. The modern development is the deliberate use of the holding-company device, usually combined with interlocking directors, to create a federal constitution by which responsibility is delegated to subsidiaries for the different regions where the firm operates or different divisions for its different groups of products. The holding company has in many books (including my own) been accounted a device for pyramiding control by the ownership of a bare majority of voting shares. But holding companies today seem anxious to hold 100 per cent, not just 51 per cent of the votes of their subsidiaries and to avoid the complication of independent minority shareholders. In short, freedom in organization now seems valued above capital leverage—a logical consequence, perhaps, of the Managerial Revolution.

In this free organization the question of the reserve powers of the central control in the parent holding company looms as large as in political federations and the answers vary as widely. Some industrial firms, like political confederations, reduce these powers to a minimum, which usually includes decisions on capital expenditure above a certain amount, and making the higher appointments.

Andrews (208, pp. 88–9) points out that economists still assume firms to be monolithic and "this monolithic analysis abstracts from what happens in business and how that is directed as a going concern". In reality a large firm usually contains not only a segregation of owner and managers as already said (p. 109) but different "divisions" making different products, and a functional diversity of outlook and interest among managers as between buying, production and selling.

Once the details of internal organization are known, the industrial sociologist might be able to get away from the legal form and classify the government of firms into the Aristotelian types. Monarchies, oligarchies, and aristocracies will certainly be found in the family business. Democracies will be rare, except perhaps in co-operative societies. But new post-Aristotelian types could be added such as plutocracies, where large shareholders have control; or bureaucracies, where the management reigns, and technocracies, where the reigning managers are, in fact, engineers or chemists.

In attempting this realistic search into the seat of power, we must proceed from the known to the unknown—from the measurable to the hitherto non-measurable. The important measurable elements are—

(i) The degree of divorce of managership from ownership.

(ii) The type of attractives offered managers to come and to stay, and incentives to work effectively.

(iii) The antecedents of prime managers.

(i) Ownership and management are, by definition, married in the owner-manager entrepreneur. He is usually still in charge of the smaller firms, and many companies, even large companies, are still found where the directors hold between them the majority of shares and often bear the same family name. Even among the 98 very large English industrial companies in 1951, five appeared from the names of the directors and the holders of large shares (78, pp. 136 and 223–65) to be family firms. Among medium and smaller large industrial companies with over £200,000 nominal capital that I analysed (but owing to the cost could not publish) many more family firms appeared. But, on the whole, statistical analysis confirms the development trend, numbered eight at the outset of this book, of the emergence of a governing hierarchy of top managers who, even in a capitalist economy, do not necessarily own the capital.

(ii) When management is divorced from ownership its financial incentive is in the form of a secure salary together with the
hope of promotion to a higher level particularly if growth is
achieved. The United States practice of offering managers
bonus options to buy shares whose value will vary with profits
or dividends is not generally adopted in Britain, so that profits
are not in fact a direct payment for management.

In this question of incentives for industrial management
sociology and economics are particularly closely integrated.
In my *Logic of Industrial Organization*, published in 1933, I
devoted a number of pages to the English Public School Man
as Manager, and subsequent work by sociologists on "motivation" and "attitudes" gives no cause to withdraw this integration of motives and economics behaviour with the study of
institutions. Industrial Sociology is being systematized. March
and Simon in their analysis of organization (128, p. 84), adopt
an equilibrium theory of inducements balanced against contributions presumably affecting measures of attraction or deter-
rence such as labour turnover, and thus somewhat similar to
my mobility framework or model (II, §3). They, too, hope that
hypotheses may be empirically tested.

(iii) The types of top prime-manager I originally distinguished and have subsequently retained (72, pp. 298–315),
based on measurable antecedents, were the self-made entrepreneur, the family head, the financier, the large shareholder,
the part-time director, and finally, the full-time executive
directors, probably owning little of the capital, who might be
ex-employees of the same firm, ex-other business, ex-technicians,
or trained administrators.

Many investigators have since tried to find the frequency of
these types, though they usually confined inquiries to company
directors or managers, thus omitting the self-made entrepreneur
and some family heads. In Britain Copeman (43, pp. 57, 148
et seq.) found that, with increasing profit plough-back, the
financier was becoming less important and the executive
director, often an engineer or accountant, more so. Most
directors were sons of business men (5 per cent were Etonians)
and had begun work in a large firm; and a bare majority had
been employees of the same firm throughout. Training for
executive posts was closely associated with a father who was a

director of the same firm. Thus, the ex-employee (originally either a clerk, or accountant, or an engineer) and the family head appear to be prevailing types.

The Acton Trust (2) found that in large organizations employing over 10,000 men, nearly half of the near-top managers aged 45 or more had started from the bottom either as operatives or clerks, although only a third among similar ranking younger men. Of such of these managers who held degrees over half took their first degree in science and technology and were presumably ex-technicians. Summarizing these English, and comparing them with foreign inquiries, Granick (221) devotes five chapters to the Technocrat and the Heir, the first of which contrasts Manager and Entrepreneur. He makes several references to the "parachutist", who, in contrast to the ex-employee or "Organization Man", drops into the top of an organization from elsewhere. These sociologically different types of leader or prime-managers are mainly of interest to an economist as causing differences in policy. Any ex-employee from the same or another business, as Andrews and Brunner (6) point out, would, on his way up the hierarchy, have learned in a hard school to cut costs and thus indirectly to maximize profit. But this conditioning process may not take place with other types, such as the hereditary family head or the ex-technician. Elsewhere, I have assigned marks to each type (72, p. 302) in respect of five sorts of policy and some research has been undertaken that might test my no more than plausible hypotheses. Carter and Williams (34) examined firms they rated as technically progressive or unprogressive to find how far they compared in twenty-nine specific characteristics. Many of these characteristics are akin to the five policies I selected: large-scale innovation, co-operation with other firms, reinvestment of profit in fixed plant, large-scale co-ordination, and top appointments. The technically progressive firms rated far higher than the unprogressive in taking trouble to base investment decisions upon quantified data; and rated relatively high "for forward-looking tendency", "anticipating development during a considerable period"; but their position was relatively low in recruitment policy and readiness to co-operate. If the technically progressive firms were led by ex-technicians (and on average they rated high in "status of science" and "top manager a scientist") their result would agree with the high points I gave this type of leader for innovation and reinvestment and with the low points for co-ordination, and *no* points for top appointments. On co-ordination this ex-technician, though not rated very efficient by Carter and Williams, proved more so than my hypothetical mark allowed.

3. ECONOMICS AND SOCIOLOGY OF COMPANY GOVERNMENT

The corporation is undoubtedly the most important institution in the United States economy, and it has its counterpart in the British Joint Stock Company, the French *Société Anonyme*, the German *Aktiengesellschaft*, and, in fact, in all developed capitalist economies. Until recently, however, its study has fallen between the stools of economics and sociology. The economist was concerned with decisions and risk-taking in the market by firms regardless of their form, and the sociologist seemed to scorn the materialist interests involved in firms, whatever their form. Yet there is a somewhat intriguing sociology of the corporation or company. In political-science terms the company has a constitution, and Lord Salisbury, subsequently Prime Minister, thought (203, p. 211) its particular constitution ideal for the government of the State. As gradually worked out, this constitution has some peculiar features. Ultimate power is supposed to reside in the shareholders, but they vote not by heads but by the amount of shares—normally the "common stock"—they hold. The directors for whom they are supposed to vote are in fact appointed by co-option; new directors are nominated by the board itself, and thus the board is normally self-perpetuating. There are no invariable rules, however, and realistic sociologists are needed who will proceed by observation of cases and statistical enumeration and summary. Within the company they must look into the number, the appointment, the organization, the status, roles and powers of bond holders and shareholders of different categories, of directors and of managers with different functions and at different levels. These inquiries should tell us which of these persons forms part of top government.

Outside the company sociologists are needed, too, to examine

the workings of the institutional entourage—the financial intermediaries—auxiliary to the company. Economists have since
Lavington (117) studied the structure and behaviour of the
Capital Market realistically and statistically, notably A. T. K.
Grant, R. F. Henderson, or in a more general view of city
institutions, Lord Balogh. Prominent at the launching of the
company are the promoter and merchant bankers issuing shares
on the market and at its breaking up the Liquidator and
Receiver. Throughout the life of the company it is helped by
further institutions, particularly the Stock Exchange with its
brokers and jobbers or specialists, bulls, bears, and stags. Here
stockholders can at any moment sell their shares at some price,
and get rid of the risks shares carry, thus making their purchase
more attractive. Next (and here sociologists might have a field
day) to advise the shareholder on his possible risks and chances
of gain come the financial journals, and a host of investment
services. These institutions have built up a certain folk-lore, the
validity of which does not always stand up (53, 77) to statistical
testing. The Stock Exchange is often pictured as a haunt of
iniquity, but the fact that, whether folk-lore or "scientific", no
system of price-prediction seems very sure, suggests that Stock
Exchange values take account of a multiple complex of causes
which develop in the long-run and are not accounted for in any
simple "system".

To return to the companies at the centre of Wall Street or the
"city" entourage, they have at long last been examined socio-
economically in the United States, Australia, and England.
Berle and Means's *The Modern Corporation and Private Property*
published in 1934 (15) was the American, path-breaking,
investigation. Since then Gordon's *Business Leadership in the
Large Corporation* (89) has provided a realistic and largely
statistical analysis, and in 1959 economists, lawyers, political
scientists, and sociologists combined in contributions to *The
Corporation in Modern Society* (132). From Australia came
Wheelwright's *Ownership and Control of Australian Companies*
published in 1957 (200) with a wealth of information. In
Britain the National Institute of Economic and Social Research
sponsored Tew and Henderson's *Studies in Company Finance* (180)
and, in 1960, Evely and Little's (50) *Concentration in British
Industry*. My own *Ownership, Control, and Success of Large Com-*

panies published in 1961 (78) was preceded by a pilot study (68)
in 1947. It refers to the structure and experience, 1936–51, of
industrial, commercial, and brewery companies registered in
London (and thus omitting Scottish companies), i.e., to 109
"very large" companies of over £3m. nominal capital in 1951,
indirectly by sample to about 258 "medium" down to £1m.
and about 1,350 "smaller" large companies down to £200,000
capital.

The conclusions which follow both on organization (i–viii)
and on the implications (*a–e*) are equally applicable in the
United States where R. A. Gordon is the main authority (89)
and in England where I inquired into the ownership and control
as well as investors' success in the largest industrial and commercial companies in 1951 (78). Both sources go some way in
establishing the eighth trend noted in the first chapter; the
surprising fact of the emergence of a governing hierarchy of top
managers in industry who, even in a capitalist economy, do not
necessarily own the capital and are not always responsive to
the shareholders—legally the owners. Does this lead to an
"irresponsible" industrial society?

(i) Shareholders as a whole cannot be expected to govern
their company. As an extension of the sleeping partnership
device they may be called sleeping shareholders and are
the prime example of Veblen's "absentee ownership".
Apart from their qualitative unfitness as too scattered, busy,
or unbusinesslike, shareholders own shares in several companies, and run into thousands for the large companies, too
many to take decisions. Their only effective power comes
when a take-over bid is made and every shareholder has the
choice of selling shares and votes to parties in opposition to
the existing directors.

(ii) Shares are held very unequally. A test of inequality
significant for government is the proportion of voting stock
held by a sufficiently small number of stockholders to form a
coherent governing group or junta. Quite independently the
U.S. Temporary National Economic Committee (241) and I
chose the largest twenty stockholders as a reasonable number.
Summarizing this committee's results for 1937–9, Gordon
(89, p. 32) found that in ninety-eight of the largest manu-

facturing corporations the twenty largest stockholders out of
an average per corporation of about 35,000 held a (median)
average of 18·52 per cent of the votes, but some corporations
were more unequal than others. In twenty-seven of the
ninety-eight corporations the largest twenty stockholders
held less than 10 per cent, in thirteen more than 50 per cent.
It is significant that in England I found much the same
situation. On average, the twenty largest vote-holders in the
very large companies (about 0·02 per cent of all voteholders)
held about 30 per cent of the votes, but in a substantial
proportion they held 50 per cent or more (78, pp. 184–5).
These percentages are more reliable and comprehensive than
in the United States because in the United Kingdom all
shareholding in public companies must be legally registered
and open to public view.

Thus in both countries corporations present as Gordon
says "a dual picture" (89, p. 157) regarding the distribution of
ownership. On the one hand there is the great mass of small
stockholders each owning but a minute fraction of any one
company's stock. At the other extreme we find a substantial
fraction of corporate ownership concentrated in the hands
of relatively small groups of large stockholders. The many
small holders are fairly helpless, but the critical question is
not only the precise dimensions of this "substantial fraction"
but, as quite a conflict of interests may arise, the connexion
between large ownership of stock and directorships.

(iii) The evidence I found in the largest English industrial
and commercial companies in 1951 was that the average
percentage of voting shares owned by the total of directors
was only 2·3 per cent and only three directors for every two
companies appeared among the largest twenty shareholders.
Statistical tests of the distribution of voting shares as well as
the share-owning of directors indicated that these large
companies fell into two groups. In two-thirds of them control
was divorced from ownership in a managerial revolution, in
one-third control may still have rested with the large shareholders—a possibly coherent twenty holders possessing at
least 30 per cent of the voting shares.

In America the T.N.E.C. analysis of the largest corporations, summarized by Gordon (89, p. 32) found that in

sixty-seven out of the ninety-eight manufacturing corporation issues, the twenty largest shareholders held 30 per cent of the voting stock or less, and that a governing group of owners was less likely. All the officers together held only 0·81 per cent of stock and all non-officer directors 2·33 per cent of the stock of 115 large industrial corporations. Within most large modern companies quite a conflict of interests may thus arise.

(iv) In this conflict the board of directors is probably gaining in strength. Marshall, in his *Industry and Trade* (130, pp. 316–18), discusses realistically the important question of company policies likely in view of the balance of internal forces at the time he wrote. This type of discussion was not followed up by subsequent economists, an omission particularly unfortunate since the actual balance of forces has been changing radically since Marshall's day. He realized that "the distinctive conditions of joint-stock administration come into view only when the ownership of capital is effectively divorced from its control"; but his conclusion except for the first sentence now reads somewhat doubtfully—

> Those who are in control have not nearly the same pecuniary interest in its economic and efficient working as they would have, if they owned the business themselves. Its higher officials may watch its lower officials, and its directors may watch its higher officials. But its directors can generally keep their positions by faithful, steady work, without showing special initiative; and they often content themselves with that.

Today few directors are content with mere watching; directors are mostly full-time managers and often the initiators of policy.

The growing independent strength of the board of directors is attested by the small size and full-time employment of the board (78, pp. 82–92). In contrast to the British boards of banks and insurance companies with possibly several guinea-pig directors, the boards of industrial companies are small. The average board membership even of the very large industrial companies was, in 1951, nine; and the great majority of the members appear to be full-time working executives. The size of boards did not grow out of proportion to the growth in size of companies and here there has been little sign of Parkinson's Law (146) at work.

In the United States Boards of Directors are larger, in keeping with the companies' larger assets and in the eighty-four large industrial corporations cited by Gordon (89, pp. 117–19) averaged in 1935 nearly fourteen members. Of these only 43 per cent were executive officers, but Gordon considers the power of the officers to be increasing.

(v) The recent trend has been toward further divorce of control and ownership. Among the very large English companies, compared in 1936 and 1951, inequality in ownership was diminishing and fewer had a small group of owners with a high proportion of the votes and thus likely to be in control. In fact, the virtually shareless directors increased—

> In 1936 the average proportion of the total votes held by the largest twenty shareholders was 30 per cent; by 1951 19 per cent. Forty-nine of these very large companies showed a fall in this measure of concentration; only sixteen showed a rise. . . . The proportion of shares held by directors, . . . fell between 1936 and 1951 and also the number of directors among the largest twenty shareholders. There were more directors holding no more than their minimum share qualification (78, p. 186).

In the United States, Larner (226) has brought out the trend toward management control very clearly by looking back at Gardiner Means's analysis of the 200 largest non-financial corporations in 1929 and contrasting a similar analysis of the 200 largest in 1963. The critical question is the proportion of corporations that were known or could reasonably be thought of as immediately management controlled. In 1929 the percentage was $32\frac{1}{2}$; in 1963 Larner makes it 80. Of the remaining corporations 14 per cent were probably immediately controlled by a minority of shareholding, 4 per cent by an actual majority and 2 per cent by two or more minority interests. When the two hundred largest non-financial corporations are subdivided into five groups of forty each according to size-rank, both in 1929 and 1963, it appears that rule by manager has spread consistently from larger to smaller. In 1929, the number out of forty so ruled were, largest first, 27, 21, $15\frac{1}{2}$, $15\frac{1}{2}$, $9\frac{1}{2}$; in 1963 in all sub-divisions as high as between 33 and 37.

The 200 largest non-financial corporations of 1963 were not, of course, the same as the 200 largest in 1929, though it is

M

remarkable how many (in fact, eighty-one) of the largest 100 had been in the original list thirty-four years earlier. Of the nineteen newcomers thirteen had existed in 1929 but were not then among the 200 largest, six had not existed at all in 1929. Even among the eighty-one fairly stable companies listed, thirty-six changed from stockholder control to management, and only three reversed the trend. Recent controversy questions whether twenty shareholders owning voting stock of at least 30 per cent is really necessary for controlling the whole company, particularly if the owners are interested parties such as the trustees for the company's own pension funds. Larner (226) in both the years he compares, accepts a percentage as low as ten per cent if held by an individual family corporation or group of business associates.

(vi) The sharing out of the net profit between dividends and plough-back obeyed no single expected principle, such as a fixed proportion between them, as some authorities (90, pp. 274–5) suppose, a fixed rate of dividend or a fixed rate of reinvestment on assets. In 1948–51, when the share-outs were analysed intensively in England, the fixed dividend rate was, however, the nearest principle approached.

> Analysis . . . showed that not the assets but the shareholders had priority and that the assets were the residuary legatee. . . . The principle actually adopted by 1948–51 appeared to be for a company to distribute to shareholders just over 1 per cent of assets whatever its profits, and for companies making higher profits to allow their shareholders in addition only about a fifth share of the profits. This policy resulted in a certain stability of dividend but violently fluctuating plough-backs. The amount of the plough-back to reserves and consequent investment thus seems to depend almost wholly on the opportunity offered by the amount of the profit of the preceding period . . . (78, p. 187).

This conclusion, based on the statistical analysis of a large number of English companies, is paralleled by Mackintosh in his recent intensive study of small English firms (125, p. 108)—

> In the policies of all these firms there is present to some degree an idea for the minimum dividend. . . . In the simplest example it can be assumed that there is a minimum satisfactory dividend; if the firm's earnings exceed the amount required to pay this

minimum dividend and to meet its requirements of finance for internal use, it will add to the dividend some fraction of the surplus earnings.

(vii) The size of the company affected, in the years studied, policy and working constitution. The larger the company, the greater the proportion of plough-back and lower the dividend and the wider the divorce of management from control. The average percentage of ordinary shares owned by the board was 2·9 for the smaller, 2·1 for the medium, and 1·5 for the very large English companies. The proportion of directors among the twenty largest shareholders was 30 per cent for the smaller, 21 for the medium, and 16 for the very large companies. Analysis of seventeen giant companies with over £8m. nominal capital in 1951 made it appear that control by personal or family ownership compared with institutional ownership, e.g. by insurance companies, was not possible beyond a certain size.

(viii) The effect of the work being done, the "ergological" effect, can be observed even though the question of the top management of a firm might be supposed far removed from materials and markets. For instance (78, p. 189), large English metal companies, compared with very large breweries, had distinctly larger boards, more interlocking directors, more divorce between ownership and control, and higher plough-back of profit. These contrasts may be connected with the types of markets (e.g. linked industries as against consumers), with the growth of the industry and new capital requirements, and with the need for technologically trained leadership. We have seen (pp. 28–9) how recent research by Joan Woodward (242) stresses the dependence of forms of organization upon types of market served, involving mass, batch, unit or process production.

The realities of the company organization, particularly control by a few inside capital-owners or co-opted shareless directors, thus appear very different from its legalities. Somewhat similarly the implications of the real organization of a company upon its policy are very different from those drawn from some of the assumptions of orthodox economic theory.

(*a*) The divorce of ownership of capital and its risks from control and management—risk-bearing from risk-taking—

contradicts what Robertson (157, p. 89) considers a proposition so important that it might almost be described as Capitalism's Golden Rule, "where risk lies there lies the control also". Marshall, indeed, laid it down in his own italics (130, p. 645) that *"decisions as to the taking of risks generally and of new departures in particular should remain, for the present at least, in the hands of those who will bear the burden of the risks".*

(*b*) If the managers and owners of the risk-capital are different people and the prime managers, unlike the entrepreneur as usually defined, have no capital, then they cannot maximize "their" profits. They might wish to maximize other people's profits, but this wish would depend on motives different from that assumed in Economic Man—motives such as loyalty to and identification with the company apart from its shareholders, and most fittingly studied perhaps by sociologists and psychologists. This is in fact what I suggested in the last chapter and Table XV when considering the motives for expanding the size of firms.

(*c*) Contemporaneously with the increase in management control, the proportion of profits ploughed back (which is the direct responsibility of the directors) has increased considerably. This may be coincidence, but could be interpreted rationally as cause and effect. If managers identify their interests with the company and its growth, not with the shareholders' interests, the way to grow is to restrict dividends and plough back capital, though not necessarily into the same industry. The actual increase in integration in large companies' activities may thus supply a link in interpreting the chain of events. The reserves ploughed back from an industry not expected to grow will be invested elsewhere.

The trend toward plough-back, though noticeable, is not in fact growing very fast or consistently. This is probably due to the risk prime managers run of so depressing the Stock Exchange prices of shares by paying out low dividends that their shareholders might easily accept any take-over bids from would-be prime managers. G. R. Fisher (53) certainly found that prices depend largely on the last year's dividend.

(*d*) The division of work in the large company should simplify rather than complicate economists' theories of distribution. The question is still asked in some textbooks what are company profits paid for, and the answer is usually somewhat dusty. But in the large company no person is currently paid any profit, and the baffling question of profit as an incentive for what function does not arise. Debenture or bond holders are paid interest, shareholders dividends, managers salaries, and the work that is being paid for is in each case fairly clear: capital, risk-capital, and management respectively. Profits or losses will, of course, accrue to the company as a whole and to any bodies or persons buying and selling at different prices. But a realistic analysis should settle the structural question of payment to precisely *whom*, before speculating on the function of a vaguely conceived profit.

(*e*) Economics has in the past been concerned with price and rates of exchange generally, more perhaps than with any other single aspect of the economy. Under the competition that was assumed, the prices of goods were held to be determined by the total of the demand and supply conditions in the market, and the policy and behaviour of *individual* firms was not taken into consideration.

The assumption that the form of industrial organization is relatively unimportant from the economic point of view (e.g. 195, p. 94) and that structure has little effect on functioning and behaviour must be reconsidered in the light of industrial concentration. Further research is called for, not just describing industrial institutions, but integrating their forms with their policies and behaviour.

With the growth of large organizations, threatening monopoly, a *micro*-economic theory of the firm is now drawing attention to decision-making by the government of individual firms which might be determinative for the whole industry. Instead of a simple solution actual inquiries from those directing large corporations as to how they devise prices reveal a wide variety of policy. Policies vary, especially in capital-intensive industries, according to the degree to which the capital plant is utilized (211) and greater or less production is aimed at. But the target may lie beyond that of utilization of capital.

Besides the target mentioned earlier in the chapter (that of charging the highest price consistent with discouraging more firms entering the industry) economic targets are found to be aimed at achieving a certain return on investment, or stabilizing prices or margins, or maintaining or improving market shares. Prices may be set simply to meet or follow competition, or price policy may be considered secondary to the differentiation, branding and advertising of product. Professor Galbraith (219) goes as far as to say that prices reflect production decisions taken as part of a large corporation's planning, other parts being the large reinvestment of profits and the integration, away from the market, of the services, supplies and materials the corporation requires.

In any realistic analysis of price determination, two of the main themes of this book come into play; the need for other social sciences besides economics, and the ergological interpretation according to the nature of the work being done.

Purely *economic* targets are often not a full explanation of price policies. Particularly where a few large organizations are in control of an industry, cautious diplomacy and consideration of moves and the reactions they will provoke, as in a game of chess, are the order of the day. As Professor Mason (231) puts it "economics will be found to have little to contribute . . . the psychologists, the sociologists and possibly the political scientists will be the main contributors". In any case, price decisions are in fact considerably limited by the nature of the product to be priced. Kaplan, Dirlam and Lanzillotti (224, p. 254) found that "the character of the product—the type of demand to which it caters as well as its physical attributes, production requirements, amenability to differentiation and stage of maturity—sets boundaries to the pricing discretion of the company big or little". They cite perishability, durability, transportability, diffusion of raw material supplies, the extent of the market, and vulnerability to substitution.

How far even the very large manufacturing firms can really determine prices and thus profits depends largely on their share of the output of each of the products they make, in short on the products' concentration ratio; and the control of prices and profits by any one multi-product firm may be different for ergological reasons, according to the nature of each particular product it is making.

Evidence analysed by Bain and summed up by Cave (212, p. 108) suggests that profit rates on capital are measurably higher in industries with similar barriers to entry but with higher concentration ratios. Among the medium barrier industries, profits in 1936–40 averaged 10·2 per cent in industries where the largest eight sellers controlled 70 per cent or more of the sales, 7·0 per cent where concentration was lower. With low barriers to entry the profit rates averaged in the concentrated industries 10·5 per cent, in the less concentrated, 5·3 per cent. This contrast was repeated in 1947–51 when profit in low barrier concentrated industries averaged 15·4 per cent, in the less concentrated, 10·1 per cent.

Thus a train of causation can be traced right from the nature of the work or product to price policy and other forms of behaviour, through the size of firm and other structural traits measured in the last two chapters. This ergological explanation of business policies is supported by the similarity of the concentration ratios for the same type of product or industry in different countries. More detailed research must be undertaken, but a prima facie case can be presented.

Among the twenty major groups of industry in the U.S., five of the seven with the highest concentration ratio are given (Table XIX) as tobacco, transport equipment, primary metals, chemicals and electrical machinery. In the United Kingdom among the fourteen trade groups those with the highest concentration ratio (in terms of employment) are given by Evely and Little (50) as chemical and allied trades, electrical engineering, vehicles, and the "primary" iron and steel and non-ferrous metals. If tobacco is separated out from drink it had the high ratio of 74 per cent.

4. THE ROLE OF NATIONAL OR STATE GOVERNMENT AND PLANNING

Over and above, and sometimes overriding the firm's government, stands the national Government (written for clarity's sake with a capital G). The role of Government in industry varies widely according to the country concerned. In communist countries its power is greatest and implies detailed State planning including (72, pp. 267–8) (i) an acknowledgement of intention, (ii) prearranged tasks or targets, (iii) knowledge of resources, and (iv) some organization to carry out or control the plan and check up on results. State planning with these four implications has also become important in underdeveloped countries as we shall see in Chapter VI, §6, particularly "pre-arranging in five year plans increases in exports, in investment and employment". Recently, Western countries, such as France, have on the basis of an input-output table planned the total production required from a given pattern of consumption.

Except during wars and their aftermath, however, planning in the developed Western countries is relatively complicated and controversial because the scarcity of obvious necessities for a bare living and efficiency, which we shall find in the under-developed countries, is not the main problem. In the developed countries, instead, controversy rages among planners on the priorities for, say, private or public welfare expenditure, for full employment or equality of distribution as against total pro-duction or income, on how much leisure to allow or in what special region, if any, to encourage development and what weight to give foreign balances. In short, the very first of the four ingredients of planning, the acknowledgement of intention, seems missing in a developed economy, though some inten-tion is usually expressed for further general development, as measured in an increase in the total national production and income, and in full or fuller employment in industry generally. But, as Edwards and Townsend say (47, p. 573), "industrial organization should provide for variety and change", not just for increased aggregates.

Though little real planning of industry is undertaken by the Governments of developed Western countries, they have nevertheless many other relations with industry which private industry is apt to regard as "interferences". It is usually thought that the country having the minimum of Government inter-ference with industry is the United States, but is it not the home of tariff protection, "trust-busting" and food and drug control, not to mention agricultural price supports?

The different types of relations of the State with industry are analysed in Chapter VII, §3, in dealing with underdeveloped countries. Each relation is represented by a different preposition. Here, dealing with decisions on developed business policy (and their preparation and implementation) we find Govern-ment information about industry, services for industry, direct operation of industry and control over industry. Information about industry is provided by the U.S. Census of Manufactures, by Senate inquiries, by periodical publications and the annual Statistical Abstract. It is given more systematically by the U.S. Federal Government than by the Government, probably, of any other country; certainly this present book could not have been written without such data. Information when used by industry is in itself a business service, but the U.S. Government also renders industry such services as mediating labour disputes and setting up employment exchanges.

It is in their operation of industry or control over industry, however, that national Governments have the largest impact on industrial behaviour. In the United States the Federal and the State Governments leave the direct operation in private hands of many economic activities which in other Western economies are operated publicly—that is, nationalized—mainly, as I put it, because of the "fact, likelihood or necessity of monopoly" (72, pp. 228–9). I list other causes of nationalization, many of them ergological and connected with the nature of the work, such as the need (but lack of) large capital equipment, common use, routine management and need of scientific experts. In fact the Government-operated or nationalized segment of these mixed economies includes such activities as mines, railroad transportation, telegraphs, telephone and broadcasting communication and the public utilities of gas, electricity and water. Even in the United States the Tennessee Valley Authority was formed under the New Deal to provide hydro-electric power, as well as irrigation and flood control. But generally speaking the United States Government rejects the direct operating of public utilities in favour of control over them.

Control is exercised either by the carrot of inducements such as tax differentiation (for instance, tax relief on profits ploughed back rather than paid out in dividends) or subsidies, as in agricultural price supports, or else by the stick of compulsion and absolute prohibition. Location of industry in certain city areas is, for instance, prohibited by zoning laws. But it is in the control by compulsion of the size of firm and of the scope of their activities that the U.S. Government has influenced the whole economy most strongly. The trend toward larger industrial firms traced in the last chapter is threatening to disrupt the market mechanism by establishing a monopoly or near monopoly, making it possible for one or a few firms to exploit the consumer or the supplier by "administered" pricing.

Here again, the type of work entailed makes a difference. Because of the intensity of capital investment and the increasing returns from large-scale production (and their use of city streets) it is wasteful to have rival telegraph and telephone systems and rival gas, electricity and water supplies in any one locality. These so-called "*natural*" monopolies are regulated by State or Federal Commissions and limits are placed on the price the private operators can charge. In other industries, such as railroads, usually nationalized in mixed economies, other policies have been applied. Instead of regulating monopoly, the United States Federal and State Governments have tried to abolish it; they have tried to bring about real competition, either by forbidding industrial structures certain types of conduct such as restrictive agreements, or by interfering with the very structures themselves.

Larger scale organization has certainly raised the problem of monopoly in manufactures though its incidence, depending on the nature of the work done, is less foreseeable than on the natural monopolies. Manufacturing is only seldom nationalized in mixed economies, and in America the solution attempted by United States Governments has been more radical than in other Western countries. Federal legislation, such as the Sherman Act of 1890, attaches penalties to behaviour in restraint of trade by nominally independent firms, and has resulted in a certain change in business conduct.

This type of statutory regulation with a possible reference to Courts of Law has since 1948 been adopted in Britain (238, Part 7, 1968 evidence of Florence) for restrictive practices between firms. But for investigating possible monopolizing practices by single firms or mergers of firms, a Monopoly Commission advisory to the Government is relied upon. British policy does not consider a monopolistic *structure* in itself illegal and encourages mergers if increasing returns are expected and thought to be needed for meeting large-scale competition of larger countries or common markets. This dilemma of *either* a danger of monopoly *or* small-scale inefficiency is only likely to occur in certain types of work, such as (Table XIX, Column ivd) transport equipment, petroleum, primary metals and chemicals, where, usually, a mass market is presented and large firms prevail.

United States policy goes further than mere regulation in the legally enforced breaking up (i.e. trust-busting) of manufacturing firms where monopoly behaviour could be proved. This proof is often difficult and has called for detailed statistics such as the concentration ratios in different industries referred to earlier. And the Federal Government now seeks not only to maintain competition, but to establish and enforce a certain plane of "fair" competition (228, pp. 249–362). For this purpose a Federal Trade Commission was created in 1914 which protects not only competitors from deceptive behaviour but also consumers. Legislation may go as far as prohibiting the sale of products of certain industries. The Food and Drug Acts are a leading example.

CHAPTER VI

INDUSTRIALIZATION OF THE
UNDERDEVELOPED COUNTRIES

1. Identification and Contrast of Countries
Developed and Underdeveloped

NINE trends in economic development were traced at the outset
of this book. Many countries—indeed whole continents—of
the world have even today hardly started on this development,
and to them the adjective *underdeveloped* is applied. The stage
in the trend toward mechanization that was achieved by some
underdeveloped countries or continents was given in Table IV;
but the only two trends measured by the U.N. for the majority
of countries are average income-a-head and (Table II) percentage of workers in agriculture. Both these measures appeared
in Table I for the ten least developed, the ten most developed,
and the remaining five other important countries.

In any one country the stage reached, whether early,
middling, or late, is probably roughly similar for each of the
trends. If the data were available most countries could probably
be placed as underdeveloped or developed by a regular
"syndrome" of tests such as low mechanization and staffing,
weak industrial differentiation and small organizations, on
the one hand, and high mechanization and staffing and strong
differentiation and large organizations, on the other. Certainly,
using the two tests almost universally available, there are
only marginal difficulties involved in classification. Countries
shown in Table I with low income-a-head can be seen to be
also countries with a high proportion of agriculturists.

The underdeveloped countries, in the early stages of the
various measurable trends of development, form a majority of
all countries, and it is not difficult to name the comparatively
few developed countries that appear in the *United Nations Year*

162

Book. Though homogeneous in having reached the later stages of the trends, the developed countries are heterogeneous in other respects, particularly in density of population. They fall into three distinct groups: older countries with the high density of populations of over eighty per square kilometre—in order of income-a-head in 1951, Switzerland, Britain, Belgium, Denmark, France, West Germany, the Netherlands, and Austria; older countries with the low density of under twenty—Sweden, Norway, and Finland; and the new countries, all with densities of twenty or under—the United States of America, Canada, New Zealand, and Australia. The low-density countries, particularly the new, could certainly all take more development with advantage. It is important to realize that "developed" does not mean *fully* developed. In fact, some *regions* of the developed countries show traits of the underdeveloped such as low income-a-head and are subject to development plans. Historical instances are the British depressed areas of South Wales and the North-East Coast, actually *called* "development areas", and in the United States, the Tennessee Valley, the Dust Bowl, and now the West Virginia mining area. Action taken by the developed countries to solve the problem of these underdeveloped or derelict parts and their degree of success will be found to form a useful object lesson for the underdeveloped countries.

We may take an income-a-head in 1957 of $500 as the dividing line (Austria had $543) between underdeveloped and developed countries, and 40 per cent in agriculture. In only two of the twenty-five countries of Table I are these two tests in conflict. Japan and Italy, though not highly agricultural, yet had an income-a-head less than $500: in both countries income-a-head has since 1957, however, been rapidly increasing. Venezuela, not quoted in the table, is another case of conflict, highly agricultural (49·6 per cent) but with income-a-head over $500 due largely to oil production. Four Western European countries, Portugal, Spain, Greece, and Ireland, appear as underdeveloped on both counts; all had in 1957 over 40 per cent in agriculture and income-a-head less than $500. It may at first seem surprising that Canada, New Zealand, Australia, Norway, Denmark, and Finland should pass the "non-agricultural" test, but in fact, owing mainly to labour-saving methods, they all had 20 per cent or less of their occupied population in agriculture, except Norway with 24·6 per cent and Finland with 34·2 per cent.

The developed countries are thus both enumerable and enumerated. In this chapter attention will be devoted to the remaining countries, for the reasons that they have a standard of living near starvation level and that most of them can be helped to increase their standards by industrialization or development of certain services, and that, if trade is likely to be insufficient even in the long run, the question of permanent aid must arise. Accordingly, aid will be considered in the final section of this chapter; but practical policies of industrialization will be considered immediately. First, however, come the questions (A) how low are the standards of living of the under-developed countries and how far their people are really on the verge of starvation and likely to remain so; and (B) how far, if at all, industrialization would be able to help raise those standards.

(A) Average income-a-head is, of course, very far from a satis-factory indicator of comparative welfare. An average American, though his income be over forty times that of an average Burmese, does not necessarily fare forty times as well. The differences in "welfare" are "over-indicated" by money in-comes for certain quite tangible reasons. The more important of these are—

(i) That most of the underdeveloped countries are in the warmer climates where less clothing, housing, and also food are physically required to keep warm.

(ii) That welfare and certainly happiness is obtained in simple social ways without the use of income—ways studied at home by sociologists and in the more primitive countries by anthropologists.

(iii) That the largely urban poverty of the developed countries is more unpleasant than rural poverty at a similar money income.

(iv) That much of the higher income-a-head of developed countries simply overcomes difficulties and costs created by development. A commuter owning a car to travel to work through a congested conurbation needs a large income compared with a villager walking to his work; but is he to that extent better off?

(v) That the wants satisfied by a small income will be the more urgent and the average American or Briton with forty or twenty times the income of the average Burmese will not spend it on goods and services of forty or twenty times the urgency. Assuming the Burmese is keeping alive, the average American or Briton will not eat forty or twenty times as much as he. After they have satisfied their hunger they will spend most of their many remaining dollars or pounds on goods and services that are of less urgency. This is an example of the economists' law of diminishing utility which is partly substantiated statistically by Engel's Law. Food is the most urgent demand and food forms a higher proportion of expenditure, the poorer the consumer. Countries will thus not differ in their food intake-a-head as much as in other forms of consumption. While in the United States and Britain food forms less than a third of consumer expenditure, in many underdeveloped countries it forms as much as 90 per cent.

Against these five considerations qualifying the apparent differences in standards of living must be set the fact, substantiated later (VII, §3), that the underdeveloped countries have distributions of income more unequal than have the developed countries and that their few rich men push the arithmetic mean average up unduly. On the whole, we may conclude that the average income-a-head forms a useful indication, at least, of the order or rank along the affluence-to-starvation scale.

Two-thirds of the world's population have, according to the warden of the Tombs prison, a standard of living below that of New York State jails. But a fuller comparison has been made with the austerity standards of war-time Britons at large (205, pp. 2–3)—

> Before the war, the British diet furnished an average of about 3,000 calories per head per day. But on two subsequent occasions, in the critical period of shipping shortage in 1940–1 and in the post-war supply and currency crises of 1946–7, the level fell to slightly below 2,800 calories. . . . In 1946–7 it was possible to secure a completely objective measure of inadequacy, since the results of an extensive survey of the body-weights of adults

showed a definite, if small, loss of body-weight during the period
when the calorie level was reduced to 2,800 per head per day—a
regression paralleled in the loss of weight of children throughout
the same period. . . . It appears that the food supplies of countries
representing only about 20 per cent of the world's population
exceed a calorie level of 2,800. On the other hand, the food supplies of countries representing no less than 60 per cent of the
world's population actually fall below 2,200, of which nearly half
are below 2,000. . . . Under such conditions there is not only
weight loss and reduction in physical activity but also characteristic behaviour symptoms such as lack of mental alertness and
coherent and creative thinking, apathy, depression and irritability.

These are the results only of *under*-nutrition. There is, besides
malnutrition—a shortage of protein and particularly of animal
protein, which falls (205, p. 5) from 66 grams per head per
day in North America to only 7 in the Far East. And the diets
of the less developed countries "also tend to lack adequate
quantities of vitamins and essential mineral constituents. This
in turn leads to the incidence of specific deficiency diseases."
These estimates are developed in detail by Dr. Sukhatme (178,
pp. 463–507). His broad conclusion (in italics) is that "should
population *grow according to the United Nations medium forecast*",
as early as 1980, "*the world's food supplies would have to be doubled
. . . to provide a reasonably adequate level of nutrition* to the peoples
of the world".

Are the underdeveloped countries likely to stay thus,
relatively and absolutely so very poor? In the answer to this
question lies the most vital reason for studying their development. For if the answer points to the danger of a vicious circle
of poverty leading to low productivity and thus to further
poverty, then the necessity must be faced of somewhere breaking the links in that circle. Once broken, there lies a possibility
of a take-off, setting the *virtuous circle* in train where well-fed,
well-educated people will have a high productivity and low
reproductivity, plough back savings to capital and thus invest
in still higher productivity, with high income-a-head and mass-
consumption as the final phase.

(B) To break the vicious circle of poverty and possibly condition a take-off, the practical question is the form which development should take.

Broadly, the policy to be discussed is one of increasing the number occupied in manufacturing industries and certain services—the secondary and tertiary industries that have been found increasing in the countries already developed. By concentrating on industrialization, however, I do not wish to imply that it will automatically bring higher standards of living, nor to maintain that developing agriculture cannot greatly help to increase income-a-head. Unfortunately, industrialization is unlikely to attain a successful economic take-off unless supported by a certain social discipline. Myrdal (232, e.g. pp. 895–900) refers constantly to "soft states". Agriculture in the underdeveloped countries is, moreover, particularly beset by sociological obstructions to its productivity. Higgins (223, p. 19) shows that (about 1953) the value of manufactures per worker was in the three chief underdeveloped regions of the world, Latin America, the Near East and S.E. Asia, as low as 19·8, 13·6 and 7·4 per cent of the North American region, and for services 28·5, 13·0 and 7·3 per cent. But their productivity was still lower—12·5, 9·8 and 5·9 per cent compared to the North American standard in the primary, mainly agricultural sector. In his thorough-going study of South Asia, Myrdal (232, p. 1157) may be said to sum up the sociological and economic limits to agricultural development in two sentences—

> In industry large and more rapid advances in productivity are possible partly because it is easier to circumvent attitudinal and institutional obstructions to effective utilization of labor. Moreover in industry there is no limiting factor analogous to the availability of land in agriculture to impede the realization of increasing returns.

Myrdal stresses also, on the economic side, the cost of irrigation and land reclamation schemes, and (pp. 1290 ff.) the difficulty of getting agriculturists to adopt new methods, such as the use of artificial fertilizers and improved seeds, in the correct combinations. This difficulty lies at the root of agricultural development in more advanced countries too. After a careful analysis of Australian experience, Emery and Oeser (213, pp. 63, 64) stress the importance of "practices that hang together" and conclude the function of experts such as Agricultural Officers is that of "discussing interrelations, planning of the whole farm, not of advising on the details of specific operations".

A further difficulty in agricultural development involving

N

both economics and sociology, concerns the size of holding. Small holdings are democratic but uneconomic, large holdings permit the efficient use of machines but maintain a status hierarchy and involve unemployment. Myrdal falls back on an "undoctrinaire" plan of combining large estates employing wage labour with the granting of small plots to each labourer.

Turning back to industrialization and bearing in mind the law of comparative costs in international trade, my object is to point out particular kinds of industry or services for which the underdeveloped country is comparatively fitted—work, though it may be, at which it is merely "least worst". A discriminating ergological analysis is thus called for.

Some industrialization will undoubtedly increase the living standards of most countries at present predominantly agricultural—a prophecy supported, though not necessarily proven, by the remarkable correlation of high income-a-head and a low proportion in agriculture. This correlation, already pointed out when comparing the countries of the world as a whole, also applies to the 48 states of the continental United States of America (215, Fig. 64). Of the twelve with the highest proportions occupied in agriculture, ten were among the poorest twelve, the remaining two among the next poorest twelve. At the other end of the scale ten of the least agriculturally occupied were among the twelve richest states and the remaining two among the next richest twelve.

Apart from exploitation by absentee landlords, sociological reasons for the lower income from agriculture are the presence of small-scale subsistence farming and, when the farmer owns the land, the attraction of independence compensating, as suggested earlier (II, §3), for a lower money income. Agriculture is a way of life, particularly in underdeveloped countries, and where food is the overwhelming concern, those fearing to take the risk of full unemployment in industrial towns may well remain immobile though under-employed on the land.

If agriculture must give place, a policy of industrial employment does not follow as the only alternative. The trend of employment in the developed countries was in fact found to be toward services rather than manufactures. When indicating activities that can with advantage be located, and even localized, in particular countries, certain services will not be neglected, especially not the tourist trade.

2. FITTING INDUSTRY TO THE RESOURCES OF UNDERDEVELOPED COUNTRIES

Accepting the need for some industrialization, we now tackle the practical question what particular industries to select for underdeveloped countries. This selection will rely heavily on the type of data illustrated in the Appendix and on the experience of the developed countries, in trying to revitalize depressed industrial areas and, still more to the point, to repopulate rural areas. Particular industries were specially selected for the British depressed "development" areas which would employ the high proportion of unoccupied women and unemployed older men. And in 1947 (68) I suggested measurable criteria in selecting industries for the rural areas. Consideration was given both to *desirable* traits, such as growth and stability, and to traits making a rural location *feasible*, such as linkage with agriculture and small scale of plant to fit populations of low density.

This desirability plus feasibility analysis can be applied to the underdeveloped countries. Desirability points to industries that are growing, or at least not diminishing, and that are not subject to cyclical fluctuations or to great uncertainty and risk. Industries subject to known high seasonal fluctuations (Table XIX) are, however, positively desirable if their fluctuation dovetails into and counterbalances the known fluctuation of existing activities.

Besides growing itself, many an industry will lead to growth in other industries which simply follow its leadership. The selection of these desirable leader industries has occasioned considerable controversy, not to say confusion. Confusion has resulted particularly from their being identified with exporting industries and named *basic* and the whole controversy named *the basic/non-basic issue*. If exporting industries really led to more general industrial growth, then Britain, with its "through-putting" economy and high export ratio, should be one of the fastest-growing countries on earth! The practically significant distinction is not between industries exporting from their country, region, or city, but that stressed repeatedly in this book, between industries with a low coefficient of localization tied to serving the local residents, i.e. residentiary industries, and the footloose industries. Instead of importing a product localized elsewhere a locality may itself start making it. This import substitution will employ people directly and indirectly increase custom for more residentiary industries, in fact will help development but is not "basic" in the sense of exporting.

Feasibility, however (particularly the economic possibility of trade eventually being set going without aid), depends not only upon the location pattern of the industry, but upon a country's natural and human resources and upon the size of its internal and external markets.

Location patterns of different industries were discussed in Chapter III, and the U.S. major groups of industries are ranked by localization coefficient in Table XIX. It must be remembered that many industries cannot be located at will, however desirable that location. Mainly by reason of cost of transport (though lack of storability and durability also count), some are restricted to being "rooted" near their materials, others "tied" near the scattered final consumers, and in yet others, plants must swarm together in close localization. On the whole, it is the industries with neither high nor low coefficients of localization that are footloose and "localizable". In selecting industries for location in underdeveloped countries economic restraints are thus put upon many industries, particularly those with a high or a low coefficient of localization. Tied industries of a low degree of localization must be dispersed near the consumers, particularly the manufacture of heavy and perishable foodstuffs that are in widespread demand, but of great weight per given value such as cattle-food or beer. On the other hand, the highly localized rooting of early process industries must occur, as we shall note, in those particular regions where heavy materials or produce are mined or grown.

Such resources and all other facilities that are relevant to industrialization that a country may or may not possess are surveyed in Table XVI, which is designed as a useful model for

TABLE XVI

SURVEY OF NATIONAL RESOURCES

A. MARKET POSITIONS: COMPOSITION OF DEMAND

 Size and type of internal market
  Total national income
 Foreign markets and sources (their accessibility)
  Types of exports and imports
 Linkage
  With source of material and power
  With other industries and agriculture

B. FACTORS OF PRODUCTION

1. *Land*
 (a) Natural resources; Acts of God
  Mineral and oil deposits; scatter and accessibility
  Soils; climate; freedom from pest and disease
  Water, rain, springs, rivers, harbours
  Forests; fishing
  Scenery, recreation areas
 (b) Quasi-natural: national parks, buildings, and art and antiquities

2. *Capital*
 (a) "Infrastructure" (public utilities, industrial aid)
  Power-stations, supply of electricity, gas, and water, transport and communication facilities
 (b) Agricultural equipment, irrigation, drainage
 (c) Mining and manufacturing equipment
 (d) Tourist facilities
 (e) Social capital, buildings, and installations
 (f) Capacity and willingness to save and *bear* risks

3. *Labour*
 (a) Present and future population and "economically active" proportion
  Mobilization of women; age-structure, migration
 (b) Distribution over agriculture and industry, and over occupations, skilled and unskilled; mobility
 (c) Literacy and numeracy, schools
 (d) Trade unionism
 (e) Capacity and willingness to work effectively

4. *Management (Enterprise and Expertise)*
 Staff ratio (clerical, technological, research staff)
 Size of plants and firms
 Capacity and willingness to plan, supervise, organize, and *take* risks
 The efficiency of factor use

C. ECONOMIC CONTEXT OF INDUSTRY

 Distribution and marketing network, industrial urbanization
 Business repair and maintenance services
 Financial intermediaries, banks, stock exchange
 Facilities for technical and vocational education and apprenticeship

D. LEGAL AND POLITICAL CONTEXT OF THE ECONOMY

 Company and commercial law; patents
 Land tenure
 Administrative efficiency, systems of taxation
 State aid for industry, tariffs, tax-remission, risk of confiscation
 State controls; planning
 Foreign aid

a preinvestment inventory or practical check-list. Resources are of four main types: the potential market position; the economist's four factors of production—land, capital, labour, and management; the economic context of industry; and the legal and sociological context of the whole economy.

The main task of selecting industries is one of fitting together Tables XIX and XVI, broadly of finding industries with the traits that fit the resources of the country. Putting it negatively, the task is to sieve out the industries with traits that demand resources the country lacks. Industries, even major industry groups (as Table XIX will always remind us), vary widely in the demand for their products and the resources they require in power, capital, staff, size of plant, and raw materials. Out of this wide choice, each country should select industries demanding the resources in which it has, or might have in the future, a comparative advantage. This task is the same as the vocational selection of personnel—finding the men to fit into the square and round holes—and is obvious enough. Yet many a country has put forward projects for establishing industries with little thought of their "fit" either for desirability or feasibility.

Since industrial traits and national resources are to be fitted, Tables XVI and XIX have some similar headings and often use the same measures. Markets appear in both tables, with the connected questions of capital and its intensity and of labour, e.g. the occupation of workers, and unemployment. The factor of management again has affinity with organization (Table XIX, ID, IV and V), particularly the staff-ratio, the size of plants and firms, and also their government.

Some resources are particular to certain undeveloped countries, others (or lack of them) are common to all.

3. RESOURCES PARTICULAR TO CERTAIN COUNTRIES

For the practical planning of development the key distinction is between resources that are given by nature, as "Acts of God", and those that have been, or must be, created by man. Economists include under *land* (129, p. 144) all "utilities over the supply of which (man) has no control; they are given as a fixed quantity by nature . . . the term *land* has been extended by economists so as to include the permanent sources of these utilities; whether they are found in land, as the term is commonly used, or in seas and rivers, in sunshine and rain, in winds and waterfalls".

The term may be extended further to include any quasi-natural resources not, like capital, originally formed deliberately to add to public or private income, but artefacts such as anti-quities and historical monuments. Cathedrals were not put up for earthly gain, but have subsequently become a source of national income from tourists. They may fitly rank with resources in land as Acts of God.

Now, land is the factor that includes most of the particular resources of particular countries. Underdeveloped countries differ especially in their mineral wealth such as natural gas, oil, coal, and metal deposits. Though less well endowed in known mineral resources per head of population than Europe and North America, Asia and Africa have (29, p. 264) con-siderable resources to build upon. And much exploration is still to be done. Within each underdeveloped continent, however, countries vary from no known mineral resources at all to countries like Kuwait with the highest petroleum resources in the world per head of population. Wide differences between underdeveloped countries are also found in the other natural resources besides minerals, and the quasi-natural resources listed in Table XVI. The international Land Survey initiated by Dudley Stamp is classifying soils, and water resources—not only essential to agriculture, but in mountainous country a possible source of power. Climate and scenery are of vital importance to the tourist trade.

Natural resources in minerals, soil, and climate, if they are demanded and accessible, result in mining and agricultural activity, and they often lead to some linked manufacturing, especially if the product mined or grown is costly to trans-port in its raw state. The earlier processes of metal-refining, cotton-ginning, bacon-curing, seed-crushing, sugar-refining, saw-milling, rice-milling, and tanning reduce transport costs and are thus economically rooted near their material supplies, as also is the whole process of cement- and brick-making.

Some agricultural demands, for example for fertilizer, may also form a link in the pattern of location. Indeed, next in im-portance to natural resources are the differences between countries in their market position, particularly the size of their internal and external demand. By definition, income-a-head is low in underdeveloped countries, so that if the population is small and heads few, total income will be particularly low, the home market small and with only rather elementary demands. The foreign market will be large if the underdeveloped country has a particular resource not found elsewhere and if it is naturally accessible and its products not obstructed by artificial barriers such as tariffs and quotas. It is hypocritical of developed countries to advocate trade not aid, and then put up such barriers. A small internal market and little chance of export is, unfortunately, the position of the majority of underdeveloped countries.

Fairly recently, in a book entitled *The Economic Consequences of the Size of Nations* (161), the conclusion was reached, on the basis mainly of a study of Belgium, Switzerland and Portugal, that a small size was little handicap to a country's efficiency and did not prevent sufficiently large plants being established in a variety of industries. The book was edited for the International Economic Association and contains contributions from some of the leading world economists. This is all the more unfortunate, as its conclusions are, as was likely, widely quoted and applied to the really small countries. For, after all, Belgium and Switzerland, if not Portugal, are, relatively to the great majority of underdeveloped countries, far from small. Belgium and Switzerland (Table I), had in 1957 an income-a-head of $920 and $1,223. With populations of about nine and five millions, their total national income was in fact $8,270 m. and $6,259 m.; that of Portugal without its colonies was $1,755 million. But, to quote only from the countries listed by Andic and Peacock (4), Jamaica had, that year, a total national income of only $410 million, Uganda $321, Honduras $320, Costa Rica $283, Ghana $273, Panama $246, Bolivia $222, and Paraguay $187. And many other countries not so listed (for instance, Liberia, Libya, Mauritania, and the other ex-French colonies of Africa) have equally low, if not lower, national incomes. In fact, of the countries usually counted as underdeveloped, only India, Turkey, Mexico, and Brazil had, in 1957, a larger total national income than either Switzerland or Belgium. Compared to the majority of underdeveloped countries, Switzerland and Belgium, if not Portugal, are not small but large economies.

Few, if any, underdeveloped countries export manufactures to the proportion of Belgium and Switzerland. The remainder, with neither an external market nor a large internal market, have too small a demand to organize plants of economically adequate size, except in those industries where even in developed economies small plants prevail or all sizes of plant are found. Examples appear in the low-ranked groups under heading IV in Table XIX. The selection of some of these industries is not a feasible project in countries where urbanization has not developed sufficiently to yield the external economies of localization. Other small-plant or cottage industries, however, are quite feasible in small-market underdeveloped countries. Some, such as milk-products and grain-milling, may be linked or rooted to the predominating agriculture; others make products in everyday low-income demand like bread. Others, again, like timber, wood containers, furniture, soft drinks make, out of materials in common supply, products costly to transport in relation to their value, and this relatively high transport cost applies to all repairing. Many small countries neglecting selection analysis, either import what they could make or, as with repairs, go without. Industrialization could often include more "import substitution".

It is largely because of the market limitations of small nations that political federations are advocated for many ex-colonies or, failing federation, some common market regions within which separate countries could specialize and produce some goods on a large scale. Unfortunately for standards of living, economic considerations, as the next chapter will tell, get submerged in the political and sociological excitements of independence.

4. RESOURCE PATTERNS COMMON TO UNDERDEVELOPED COUNTRIES

After prescribing the industries fitted to the particular natural and market resources, we are left with certain resources or lack of resources common to almost all underdeveloped countries before development trends have set in. Selection of industries must now be reviewed in relation to these common features, which mostly fall under the headings in Table XVI that follow market position and land, namely, capital, labour and management. The absence of capital has received by far the most attention, but the need for capital without distinction of type can be overstressed.

Among capital resources, a certain sector is now distinguished under the curious title of *infrastructure*. This sector comprises public utilities and the basic facilities which *aid* industry, and in distinguishing these industrial aids many years ago (60, pp. 371–5, p. 460), I noted they were often provided by the State, either free, or trading at a loss, at cost, or occasionally for a profit. The items I then listed as in the "industrial aid" class were comprised in transport and communications, provision of markets, supply of electricity, gas and water. No country can develop either industry or tourist services without these infrastructural facilities, and international aid has been channelled into this form of fixed capital as a preliminary "must" which is fairly certain to be relevant to a country's development.

It is when fixed capital for specific lines of manufacture has to be decided upon that selection becomes difficult, and that the careful analysis here being advocated becomes so necessary. The capital that can be supplied from the country itself is limited—mainly for sociological reasons discussed in the next chapter—and the capital that can be given or even lent as aid from abroad is not unlimited. So an agonizing choice has to be made between investment in various uses. Two schools of thought have been in open opposition. One assumes broadly that the return to successive doses of capital for any one use diminishes when other factors remain constant and advocates distribution among many uses so that the extra "marginal" return is equal in all uses. The other school believes with Rostow (167, 168) that take-off is not possible without massive development of some particular use, as textiles were developed in the English Industrial Revolution and railways were, later, in other countries. Apart from these early examples, it cannot be said that much empirical verification of the comparative advantages of these two policies is yet to hand, and it is even doubtful whether the conditions for a take-off after priming exist in many countries. Meanwhile, practical policy should pay attention to the particular resources of the underdeveloped country being planned for, as well as to resources common to most underdeveloped countries and, once they are surveyed, should invest in industries that fit these resources.

The short supply of capital resources in nearly all underdeveloped countries together with abundant labour points to priority for industries with a low intensity of capital compared to their labour content and supplying primary needs such as food. The extreme examples of low intensity judged by both indicators in Table XIX include apparel, leather (shoes) and furniture. Industries with high capital intensity, however, cannot always be avoided and a conflict of criteria does come up frequently between capital cost and the first-processing of underdeveloped countries' raw material. Heavy capital equipment is normally required to deal with the raw materials in such early process industries, cited in Table XIX, as primary metals, petroleum and some food and stone-glass-clay industries.

At this point we must meet the argument that the measurements of the characteristic traits obtained from a developed country such as Britain will not hold for the underdeveloped countries. This is undoubtedly true for the absolute measurements. We know already that power-a-worker is much lower *for the same industries* in Britain than in the United States and lower in certain underdeveloped countries than in Britain. But, relatively to one another, industries probably fall into much the same ranking in respect of capital intensity and other characteristics. We know this is true of Britain and the United States (69) in respect of power-a-worker. Bohr (20) shows similarity of ranking of twelve industry groups in respect of the ratio of fixed capital to value added in Australia, South Africa, and the United States. Exceptions to similar ranking may occur, however, where two quite different techniques are possible for the same industry, such as cottage hand-loom and mill power-loom weaving of cotton. Yet, even here, a certain uniformity of technique appears to be set when trading is the object. Cottage hand spinning could not exist in trade competition with power spinning in India unless it was (153, pp. 74 *et seq.*) subsidized and, *a fortiori*, could presumably not exist under world competition. In short, the techniques that result in the measures given for groups of industries in Table XIX are the result of internal and external trading competition over a long period, and the industries probably hold their relative rank fairly similarly in all countries. Observations, statistically recorded, have even shown that in spite of abundant cheap labour, the capital-intensive methods of performing particular industries may yet be economically the more efficient in the underdeveloped countries, as they are in developed countries. Labour-intensive techniques in these industries can then only be justified for reasons other than economic efficiency, such as absorbing labour that would otherwise be unemployed and which, in a welfare state, would be a cost, paid for by the tax-payer.

These theoretical expectations are confirmed when we look at the actual prevalence of various types of industry in under-developed countries as a whole, and at their level of capital to labour intensity. Industry groups in which Latin America and East and South East Asia employ over a third of world employment (185) are food, textiles and clothing, wood and furniture, all with low horse-power or assets per worker; but also include primary metals where heavy local materials are in the first stage of processing. But there are industry groups in which the total of these underdeveloped regions falls below a quarter of world employment: paper and printing, coal and petroleum products, and metal products in later stages of processing and assembly.

Proceeding with the survey of resources for the practical selection of industries according to fit, we now reach in Table XVI a country's human resources as factors of production. In fitting industries to the labour situation, policy must consider—

(i) The total of the available labour present and future and, in particular, how far a general economic mobilization would include women.

(ii) The present distribution of labour over agriculture, and industries, and among skilled and unskilled occupations and how far mobility allows change in distribution for the future.

(iii) The extent of literacy and numeracy.

(iv) The incidence of trade unions.

Most underdeveloped countries are short of skilled labour but have a plentiful supply of unskilled, illiterate, and willing though often ineffective men and boys, but (as Chapter II warned) only a limited mobilization of women. The reasons for this limitation and ineffectiveness are mainly sociological (including the low status of even skilled manual labour) and are discussed in the next chapter.

With insufficient resources in capital and skilled labour, management becomes particularly important. What capital exists must be utilized to the full, by standardization, shift-working, staggering hours, and stocking materials, to avoid machines waiting to be fed. Skill, often not fully discovered till after man-power surveys are undertaken, must be husbanded by dilution, work study and work planning, and the scientific management introduced by Frederick Taylor should not be despised. Unfortunately, underdeveloped countries as a whole are as short of persons fit for appointment to the management of large industrial firms as they are of capital. Sharing the English ruling-class disdain for a business career (63, pp. 245–8), particularly as a manufacturer rather than a merchant, the ex-British colonies have too many trained lawyers, too few trained engineers. They are short of potential for the type of manager now (following the trend) making the top decisions in the big industrial firms of the developed countries. Though thereby missing large-scale economies, industries may have to be preferred where high staff ratios or large size of plants or firms do *not* prevail. In fact, in India, 1956, two-thirds of the industrially employed were in plants employing under five (232, p. 524).

Finally, any survey of resources must include the general "context" of industry and of the whole economy. By the economic context of industry as a resource, I refer to auxiliary facilities in which underdeveloped countries are often deficient, facilities leading particularly to external economies. They include organization for the collection or procurement of material and for the distribution of products; the services to advise small businesses (for instance, on the purchase of machinery) or to repair and maintain machines; or financial intermediaries such as banks and the money market, the stock exchange and the financial journals that form, as we have put it, the entourage of industrial companies.

If industry has an immediate context in the general economic network, this whole network has a still wider political and sociological context in law and government. Most, if not all, underdeveloped countries suffer from a legal and political framework inadequate for economic development, often due to a colonial system where the government confined activity to keeping law and order. Many, for instance, have as yet no company law.

Much of a nation's basic facilities or infrastructure, in particular the roads, and also its education, are provided free, as well as a police and political administration adequate to maintain order and the rights to rewards for work. Facilities provided free require taxation, so that the fiscal system must come into the survey. This fiscal system should be ample and elastic enough for the State to be able to encourage industries to settle, less by protective tariff than by tax remissions, at least until the infant industries are on their feet and large enough to be capable of trading competitively.

To sum up: industries that are footloose and would fit the *common* features of underdeveloped countries, that is, their shortage of capital, managers, and skilled labour and immobilization of women but abundance of unskilled and illiterate male labour and their preoccupation with agriculture, are indicated in Table XIX mainly under five headings: sources (especially agriculture), capital intensity, labour composition, staff ratio, and size of plant. Industries to be selected should, in theory, not be capital- or staff-intensive, and not dependent on employing women. They should be linked with agriculture, have a low staff ratio and small need of skilled labour and make goods to meet the more elementary needs of food, clothing, housing, and furniture.

Do the industries that are now actually present or absent in underdeveloped countries bear out these hypotheses and prescriptions?

(i) Industries first-processing agricultural products, either industrial products or food products, are usually present in all underdeveloped countries.

(ii) Labour- not capital-intensive industries are found in the presence of hand-loom weaving of textiles, in the extent of the clothing industries and in the absence, in all but the largest underdeveloped countries of such capital-intensive industries (unless subsidized) as aircraft, electrical, iron and steel, and motor-car manufacturing.

(iii) The industries that appear to flourish, at least relatively, in underdeveloped countries can be found fairly exactly and comprehensively by comparing the "activity structures" of underdeveloped and developed countries. Classifications of industries are usually too different for different countries, but a chance of an exact comparison is presented in Puerto Rico, which answers the same census questions as the United States. Like other underdeveloped countries, the bulk of its workers is in agriculture. Of the twenty major industry groups, Puerto Rico has a higher proportion of all manufacturing workers than the United States in four groups—tobacco manufactures (largely exported), food, leather and clothing—and has more than half of the United States' proportion in clay and stone products, and furniture. In none of the other fourteen groups does the Puerto Rico proportion rise above a quarter of that of the United States.

(iv) Industries apparently requiring a high staff ratio though not a particularly high capital intensity, such as the electrical machinery and instruments group, are also absent or only found in a very rudimentary form in underdeveloped countries.

(v) Preliminary investigation of a number of countries suggests that some industries, like most food, clothing and woodworking, fit countries of all sizes of market and stages of development, that others, in particular textiles, pottery and glass, late-process chemicals (e.g. soap, paints, or starch), and simple machine-making, fit the middle stages and market sizes, others again, like the large-plant and intensely capitalized industries, fit only the later stages or larger market sizes. Much more research (and ergological interpretation) is required into the industries that are in fact flourishing at various stages of development and sizes of market, if the underdeveloped countries are to be wisely advised in their plans for industrialization.

5. THE CASE OF THE TOURIST TRADE

Few, if any, of the smaller underdeveloped countries export manufactures, and exportable products are hard to suggest. Yet one trade capable of employing many persons in some underdeveloped countries, small or large, is very acceptable to a certain category of foreigner—the tourist. For some underdeveloped countries with an unfavourable visible balance of trade, the tourist trade is capable of reversing the balance. Though invisible, tourism acts as an export. The countries where tourists go sell their attractions to the foreigner for his nation's currency, just as they sell the exported visible products of their industries. The characteristic of the exportability of products thus arises again. This time it is free of the fear of adverse tariffs (though not of a limit to the foreign exchange allowed to tourists). But there remains the possible drawback of an "import-content". If tourists have to be fed entirely with imported food and served by imported chefs, *garçons* and couriers, tourism will hardly contribute much to a country's national income.

Eire can be cited as a country benefiting greatly from the tourist trade. Its gross receipts in respect of tourism, travel, etc., were in 1958, for instance, £34·6m. or as much as 28 per cent of its visible merchandise exports and re-exports. As relatively few Irish became tourists abroad, the net receipts were not far below the gross, and as Ireland is not a great food importer, the import-content of the food provided for the tourist was low.

Export markets require careful research to find what merchandise the foreigner demands, what limits his country's tariffs or quotas impose, and what competing exporters can supply cheaper. Similarly to any industry, the demands of the tourist market and its hazards must be carefully analysed by the country planning to develop tourism, with a view to discovering the demands of the type of tourist being attracted and likely to be attracted and, in competition with other tourist centres, the kind of attractions and facilities to supply and to encourage by tax concessions or direct subsidy. Tourists may (if on a cruise or motor tour) be one-day trippers, may plan to stay a week or a month, or may be retiring for life in foreign parts, as they do in Cheltenham or the Channel Islands. The day trippers are, like the poorer hiker or pilgrim, less important economically to most underdeveloped countries. Among week-long or month-long tourists, who are growing rapidly in number, great diversity is found. The elderly will want rest and shopping facilities and possibly lectures on what they are seeing; the young, recreation. Moreover, the demands of all types of tourist often seem strange, if not primitive, to the inhabitants. The study of their habits and wants is anthropology in reverse. The "native" must analyse the "white man".

Often I have found the actual and potential demands of the tourist uncatered for, because unknown. A questionnaire issued in winter to local guests in Jamaican hotels (44), who mostly turned out to be elderly couples, elicited their dis-appointment with the shops available. In particular, the American habit of bringing back gifts to friends and relatives and, particularly, children (for the elderly couples had plenty of grandchildren) was not understood, and thousands of dollars were thus lost to the island economy and taken back to the American continent. Moreover, the hotels—dotted at intervals along the north coast, east of Montego Bay—were isolated, and residents of the different hotels could not easily mix. In the winter season the few young people who could afford the trip were "lost" among the many elderly couples and soon left. In a Jamaican broadcast in 1958, I suggested accordingly that a New Town should be planned, with cafés, recreation facilities, and public beaches where the young from different hotels could mix, and with large-scale shops where the older tourists could find the wares they missed in the small hotel gift-shops.

Failures to meet tourist demands should not be smiled at as part of the simple minds of underdeveloped people. Let us not forget the iron fixity of English meal (and drink) times—also the procrastination of English waiters in bringing the American his ice-water. Some rationalize this by contending that ice is bad for the stomach, but this is hardly the point. The customer, particularly the tourist customer, is always right.

The demand of the tourist is primarily for the particular scenery, climate, history, and art or recreation which he cannot find at home—demands which directly involve the services of travel agents, attendants at museums, guides, transport workers, maintenance men, and diggers at the sites. If he is at some

o

distance from his home and the tour takes longer than a few hours, he will demand, secondarily, refreshment during the day and accommodation for the night. And there are tertiary demands, such as obtaining souvenirs in shops.

Climate and scenery indeed are free enough. In Jamaica (44), where 95 per cent of tourist expenditure could be assigned, only 6 per cent went to transport and 4 per cent to entertainment, tourists paid roughly 50 per cent to hotels, 29 to shops, and another 6 to food and drink outside hotels. Once inside the country, the tourists' secondary or tertiary demands for accommodation and food or for shopping are thus the chief income raisers, but the real leverage *under* tourist spending are the primary net attractions of travel and entertainment. The word *net* points to certain drawbacks of travelling: the distance to be covered (and paid for) from home or from other countries likely to be visited, and certain worries of life abroad, including possible language barriers and the risk of being cheated. Table XVII lists the main considerations in eight columns. The main types of the original positive attractions, the resources for tourism, can be summed up as five: climate, scenery, recreation (e.g. ski-ing, swimming, fishing), local colour, and the various cultural interests which, avoiding sophistication, we shall call "art and history". All but local colour have appeared in Table XVI under Natural and Quasi-natural Resources. Three columns rate the drawbacks; those of distance may be measured in money or, for the rich, in mere time. To tourists able to afford it, air travel has brought islands, particularly, much "nearer" in time and convenience.

To test the rating of resources, a few countries, most now admitted tourist successes, are, in Table XVII, given marks under these heads based partly on measurable fact, partly on subjective valuation. Recreation has higher marks in the underdeveloped countries because beaches are not already overcrowded by the local inhabitants. Equal weight is assigned to each of the headings except distance from original market, i.e. home (e.g. the home of the largest tourist purchasing power, the United States of America), which is weighted double. To the average tourist, the distance away is no doubt more important than any other single consideration. Nearly 50 per cent more United States' citizens visited Canada, Mexico, Central

America, and the Caribbean than visited Europe and the Mediterranean. Less important, perhaps, and certainly less easily measured than distance, are the snags of language and behaviour such as spitting or wolf whistling. Honesty and consideration for tourists, even by customs officials, is important. If a country once gets a reputation, "has an image", of cheating taxi-drivers or shopkeepers or fierce officials, many tourists may well keep away.

TABLE XVII
ASSESSMENT BY RATING SCALE OF NATIONAL
RESOURCES FOR TOURISTS*

Country	Climate	Scenery	Recreation	Art and History	Local Colour §	No Language and Other Snags†	Small Distance from Market		Total Rating out of 9 (Minimum 4)
							Original e.g. U.S.A.‡	As By-product	
Switzerland	0	1	1	0	0	½	1	1	4½
France: Paris	½	0	0	1	1	½	1	1	5
France: Riviera	1	½	1	0	0	½	1	1	5
Italy	½	½	½	1	½	0	1	1	5
Britain (parts of)	0	½	½	1	½	1	1	1	5½
Canada (parts of)	0	1	1	0	0	1	2	0	5
Mexico	1	½	0	½	1	0	2	0	5
Jordan‖	1	1	0	1	½	1	0	½	5
Jamaica	1	1	1	0	½	1	1	0	5½
Israel‖	1	0	1	0	½	1	0	½	4
Ceylon	1	1	½	½	½	1	0	0	4½
Puerto Rico	1	½	1	0	½	0	1	0	4
Greece	1	1	1	1	½	0	0	½	5

* Particularly to United States tourists.
† e.g. Dishonesty, spitting on pavement, etc. High cost of living should also be taken into account but varies from year to year. If stay is long, it may become as important as cost of travel, i.e. distance from market.
‡ Maximum 2 points.
§ e.g. Calypsos, trooping, folk-dancing, bazaars, festivals.
‖ The assessment was made before the 1967 war.

Once market research establishes the type of potential tourist and the rating of tourist attractions, publicity can function more effectively. Advertisement can be concentrated on the organs read by the likely tourist—for instance, church periodicals for visitors to Jerusalem. Statements and pictures can tally with the real facts and developments. Some countries publicize what they have not got, others miss out telling points for the tourist. For instance, Jordan recorded its temperatures, humidity, and rainfall, but omitted hours of sunshine, and officials were surprised to learn that northern Europeans were interested in such a humdrum statistic.

So much for the demand side of the tourist trade and its stimulation. On the supply side, unlike most other services, such as retailing and transport, the tourist trade is localized and is not dispersed wherever the consumer-population is found. In fact, by very definition, it must be plied away from the consumers' home. Planning for the tourist trade, therefore, follows the same principles as planning for any manufacturing industry which is rooted and material-oriented, and must localize in the relatively few places in the world that possess tourist attractions. In wide regions—the Middle West and Great Plains of North America, the Steppes of Russia, the Midland and Northern coal-fields of England, there are few tourist attractions whatever. It happens, however, that many countries which suffer economically from being a small market (for instance, the Caribbean islands, Jordan, Greece, or Ceylon) possess the very resources that prove attractive to tourists throughout their entire area.

While extreme localization of the tourist trade favours certain areas and the trade is growing, it exhibits a concentrated *time* as well as *place* incidence of demand—in short, considerable seasonality. Seasonality is normally due to the weather cycle of the toured country and also the annual work-cycle of the tourists. It must always be the object of a country's tourist trade to fill in the off-season and get the maximum yearly occupancy of hotels and the other overhead facilities. Switzerland succeeded, thanks to the importation of ski-ing from Norway, and Jordan should succeed with its variety of climate, from the Jordan valley, almost a thousand feet below sea-level, to Amman, nearly four thousand feet above.

Besides its seasonal fluctuations, the tourist trade is uncertain and risky—in the economist's useful phrase, it is highly "income-elastic". For the British working-class (150, p. 107), holiday expenditure rates a higher elasticity than any product listed in family budgets. With rising incomes, people take avidly to tourism; with falling incomes, tourism is often the first form of expenditure to be cut out. And, in addition to depending on the prosperity of the tourists' own country, the trade is highly sensitive to possible crises and revolutions in the country to be toured.

Apart from extreme localization and seasonality, the characteristics of the tourist trade's demand for natural attractions, services, and facilities present generally a more favourable fit to the resources of underdeveloped countries than do most manufactures. The trade is labour- rather than capital-intensive, can employ women, older men and boys, and does not always have to be large-scale! The *bistro* can flourish side by side with Savoy grills. Though feasible in many countries, the trade cannot, however, be captured without effort. It requires basic transport facilities, a modicum of literacy, including foreign languages, skill in cooking, waiting, and guiding, and is management-intensive with high staff ratios.

A particular advantage to underdeveloped countries is the tourist trade's linkages with manufacturing industries, such as the metal craft work that can fashion souvenirs, always provided they are not imported from, say, Birmingham, England. These are the *by-demands* of tourism. Other industries, such as furniture-making and pottery, are helped by the adding of hotel to home demands. Thus this linkage brings us to the repercussions and percolation of the tourist trade over the whole economy and to the workings of two forces to which economists have for long drawn attention: external economies and the multiplier.

Internal economies, it will be remembered, arise with the growth in size of the plant or firm; external economies with the growth of a whole industry regardless of the size of its constituent units. Wherever the tourist trade grows many units may flourish, either in the same line of business or in co-operating lines, to meet the primary, secondary, and tertiary demands of the tourist. After disporting himself or being shown the sights and sites, he must be fed and rested, and in the afternoons and evenings sold souvenirs and entertained. All these lines of business co-operate to keep the tourist interested and happy, and, if possible, never bored. His pleasure should be unalloyed, and the external diseconomies of the sight and smell of gas-works or factory chimneys (reminding, perhaps, of toil back home) kept away, together with unsightly posters, slums and beggars. The Welfare State has its uses even here!

Making a civic survey for the planning of Worcester (85), my colleagues and I recommended this English country town, suffering from the loss of industry, as said earlier, for a tourist centre. Its resources were its own attractions as a cathedral city on a fine river and proximity to Stratford on Avon and the Malvern hills. But this selection involved the removal from the riverside of certain workshops and the zoning of noxious factories to leeward of the winds found to be prevailing over a ten-year period. The mere size of the resort is important. The external economies of the tourist trade will be greater the larger the resort up to a point, but after a certain size, scenery and recreational facilities will suffer from the diseconomies of urbanization. It is probably significant that no town founded on its tourist attraction, even if it has attracted "life" residents as well, contains more than 300,000 inhabitants. Miami is probably the largest, and numbered 292,000 in 1960. The largest British tourist resorts are Brighton, with Hove, and Bournemouth, with Poole, each just short of 250,000 inhabitants. Blackpool has about 150,000, but no other British resort has more than 90,000.

The multiplier was first used to estimate how investment in public works would give employment to the unemployed, indirectly, round by round, as well as directly; it can be applied to underdeveloped countries so long as they, too, have resources unemployed. Investment in *construction* of hotels and other capital facilities for tourists gives immediate employment to building workers. In this, the first round, greater advantage usually accrues to an underdeveloped country than in factory-building, because stone or brick and the skilled builders for hotels are usually available locally, whereas the machines, steel structure, and the construction workers for factories have usually to be imported. In the second round the workers building hotels and other facilities spend most of their earnings in retail shops on consumer goods. Similarly, in the third round the shop-assistants and shopkeepers, and wholesalers and producers of the goods sold, earn money and spend most of it on further goods and services. At each round there is, however, some money spent on materials which may be imported, and out of wages some saving, and spendings at home get less.

The conception of the multiplier arises in the original investment in hotels and other tourist facilities. A process of multiplication also occurs with a number of rounds in their operation. In selecting the hotel trade for investment, the relevant question is how far its operation compares in net benefit as against cost with operations after a similar investment in manufacturing or agriculture. Each round involves one of three patterns: a three-element pattern, as in selling souvenirs, where materials, wages, and profits are involved; a two-element pattern, where services such as transport and entertainment involve only payments to wages and profits; or a plain one-element pattern like tipping. Wages (including tips) and salaries are mainly paid over to retailers. Materials are mainly bought by payments to wholesalers or direct to producers. Local retailers, wholesalers, and producers then all repeat in the next round the threefold pattern of profits–wages–materials. Gross profits go in taxes, in plough-back, and depreciation, or else in dividends, and it is relevant to know how far dividends are distributed to citizens or to foreigners.

The benefits to national income and employment of the operations of tourism and hotel-keeping, in relation to costs, over most manufacturing lie—

(i) In the greater labour content of the services involved. Little material is used in transport and entertainment and much labour, often skilled, in waiting, guiding, and cooking.

(ii) In the high food content of the materials, much of which could be raised in underdeveloped countries with their high agricultural occupation.

(iii) In the by-demand of the hotel guests for mementoes and souvenirs, many of which could be made locally, in small craft shops.

Multiplier effects work so long as resources are unemployed; but, especially in a small country, importation of goods and services from foreign sources may soon have to occur and the multiplier stops. Resources for growing high-quality food will, if they do not exist, have to be built up if tourists are not to involve high food imports. The tourist trade should, indeed, stimulate agriculture.

If we are to go beyond mere theory, its empty boxes must be

filled with the actual proportions of the income and the workers employed. A realistic investigation of this sort was undertaken in Jamaica starting from a hotel-by-hotel, item-by-item analysis of the provenance of hotel purchases, whether from home or from foreign sources. The conclusion (44, p. 299) was that, even excluding tips, 60·7 per cent of tourists' expenditure remained in Jamaica. The import-content roughly of two-fifths is, for a small economy, low compared to the cost of machinery and raw-material imports required for all but first-stage manufactures rooted to local resources.

6. Aid, Trade, and Planning

However ideologically repugnant to the capitalist outlook, accustomed till recently only to annual budgets for *government* expenditure, most underdeveloped countries have been advised for practical reasons to adopt *national* plans extending over a period of years. National planning can be defined (72, pp. 267–8) by—

> pointing to its opposite, the market mechanism whereby, to quote Adam Smith (173, IV–2), "every individual . . . neither intends to promote the public interest, nor knows how much he is promoting it. . . . He intends only his own gain; and he is in this . . . led by an invisible hand to promote an end which was no part of his intention".

In contrast, national planning is an intention to promote the public interest by the more or less visible hand of the State. As said of communist economies (p. 157), it is an acknowledgement of intentions embodied in prearranged tasks based on knowledge of existing conditions and carried out by an organized structure which should include a review of the progress of the plan. The tasks must be logically co-ordinated and the *organized structure* State-controlled, either by nationalization or by offering private-enterprise incentives (tax remission, tariffs, cheap facilities) for the carrying out of the national plans. Applied to the underdeveloped countries *intention* is essentially to increase standards of living (as consciously stated in the Indian plan) by setting "targets" for national income, and the proportion to be invested, in hopes of a "take-off"; embodiment in prearranged *tasks* (the programme) includes industrialization and tourist facilities, which have just been discussed, on the basis of *knowledge* of existing resources. Facilities, both for industry and tourists, such as machines for factories, or plumbing equipment for hotels, can, in most underdeveloped countries, be obtained at present only from abroad, either by "trading" exports or by aid in loans or grants from state-governments or the United Nations, or else by loans from private capitalists.

The facts of international trade are tolerably well recorded; the total visible and invisible items of merchandise and service and the balance of payment are measured and these statistics available for many countries. The classical "colonial" pattern for underdeveloped countries is for their visible exports and imports to balance or even for their exports to exceed imports in a "favourable" balance. Their exports are normally raw materials, food or fuel of a few categories, such as coffee, tea, citrus fruits, rubber, copper, tin, iron ore or oil produced under the control of capitalist firms in the developed countries, and paying them dividends—hence the frequent "favourable" balance. The imports are manufactured goods, particularly metal capital goods. This type of trading is the opposite, but, since world exports and imports must be equal in value, it is the necessary counterpart of the highly developed British, Dutch, or Belgian through-put economy measured in the first chapter, and may indeed be part-cause of the colonial empires of those countries. Materials are extracted—pulled out—from the land for manufacture abroad and for feeding the manufacturers, and manufactures, normally capital goods, such as machinery and vehicles, or parts of them and tools of industry generally, are taken back in exchange for the products of the extractive industries. In contrast to the "through-put" it is a "pull-out take-back" economy, equally measurable statistically in its export and import structure. This "colonial" *economic* trading structure is likely to persist yet awhile, whatever *political* changes may occur.

In some underdeveloped, as in developed countries, there is an unfavourable international balance of payments on account of the visible items, due to the invisible items, including foreign grants, loans, and credits. Malta, for instance, imports many times the value of merchandise that she exports; but makes up some of the difference by the invisible items of service in ship repairing and maintenance, tourism, and remittances home of emigrants.

Other underdeveloped countries, Jordan for instance, have an unfavourable total balance of trade, visible and invisible, a gap that can be made up for only by aid in gifts or loans. Such aid cannot be indefinitely multiplied. The number of possible aiding countries is limited and the calls are heavy upon their resources for social welfare at home and for their own development. Underdeveloped countries must, therefore, increase their exports or substitute home production for imports. Though a high proportion of their workers are found in agriculture, many underdeveloped countries actually import more food than they export, and often there is an economic case worth research for increasing food production as import-substitution, rather than industrializing. Certainly, in underdeveloped countries, as Myrdal says (143, p. 227) "however rapidly industrialization proceeds, the great masses of their working populations will for decades and, perhaps, generations, be employed in agriculture, and the levels of living of the rural masses will mainly be determined by their productivity there".

To get back to the overall plan, targets, which must include trade and agriculture as well as mining, are measured statistically in money or employment and must be internally consistent. These measurements, not simply for government budgets, but for the nation as a whole, mark great progress in the application of statistics to economic and social affairs—mark in fact a new discipline of social accounting, not yet, unfortunately, appreciated or understood in some civil services. Often included in these targets are the proposed government expenditure or budget, and income ceilings for salaries, wages, and dividends, and some estimate by projection of the increase in population and the labour force. But the framework essential for development consists in planned changes in four statistical task or target aggregates which should combine satisfaction of intentions or goals with a realistic appreciation of what is feasible.

(i) *The Gross National Product*
When income from abroad is added and the excess of indirect taxation over subsidies subtracted, total domestic expenditure

becomes this **G.N.P.** It is the national income used for calculating the average income-a-head.

(ii) *The Total of Employment*

This aggregate, partly dependent on, partly independent of gross national product, is particularly important for underdeveloped countries because of their high unemployment and underemployment, and the liability of both to rise still higher with the fast increase in population. In some plans the employment target reckons only, in fact, to mop up the addition to unemployment due to population added.

The employment target is independent of gross product, particularly where investment saves labour and more is produced with less labour. And sometimes the total employment is kept up, uneconomically, with no greater product, by "feather-bedding" labour. The employment target will, of course, favour the selection of labour-intensive industries and thus often exclude the capital-intensive heavy industries which might eventually have greatly increased the national product.

(iii) *Exports*

The amount to be exported is not always stated in plans; indeed, for underdeveloped countries relying on agricultural or mining products, export values are extremely fluctuating and unpredictable. Recently, in fact, the prices of such raw commodities have fallen considerably and the "terms of trade" (export in relation to import prices) have, for the underdeveloped countries, worsened. This implies that, to import the necessary machines and capital equipment, underdeveloped countries must export more of their produce in volume.

(iv) *Capital Investment*

Total (gross including, net excluding, depreciation and maintenance) of capital and services for sectors, e.g.—

For *agriculture*.
For *industry* making capital or consumer goods.
For *infrastructure*, i.e. basic aids for industry and agriculture

(such as transport facilities, power generation, water supplies, communication, irrigation schemes).

For *education*, especially technical.

For *research* and exploration.

The second Indian plan (1956–61) had, for instance, the following key figures for its framework of target increases apart from exports over the previous period.

	Percentage
Total national product	+25
Total employment	+12

Capital investment increased from 7 per cent to 11 per cent of national product distributed as follows—

To agriculture and community development	11·8
To industry which may be divided into subsectors (e.g. capital or consumer goods) or into control segments (e.g. public, small crafts, companies)	18·5
To transport, shipping, roads, etc.	28·9
To irrigation and power	19·0
To social services, including education	19·7
To miscellaneous	2·1

India is more developed than most underdeveloped countries. Typical of planned investment programmes in countries relying more on plantations is that for Malaya, 1956–60. Here agriculture, especially rubber growing, was to increase 23·4 per cent, but industry and mining only 1·9 per cent. The same high proportion, however, goes to infrastructure: for India it was, as just shown, 28·9+19·0 = 47·9 per cent, for Malaya 41·4 per cent. Econometrics is now applied in planning. A useful example in a fast-developing country is that of Chenery and Bruno (37) applied to Israel. The investment ratio and the national product targets are quantitatively related and must be consistent. If capital investment is increased, it will subsequently increase national product, the precise extent depending upon the capital/output coefficient and the "multiplier", which may vary from time to time. Most underdeveloped countries have capital investment ratios considerably below that of developed countries, and if education is included as an investment, the distance between the two, as Kuznets suggests (111, 112), becomes still wider.

The knowledge of a country's resources (as surveyed in Table XVI) which is part of national planning often shows up the practical *economic* limits on plans, let alone the *sociological* limits to be discussed later.

To the factors important in plans for *all* countries mentioned in the last chapter, Chenery and Bruno add, apart from the inflow of foreign resources, two that are particularly important for the countries as yet underdeveloped: (*a*) the present and future composition of demand; and (*b*) ability to plan and carry out development activities.

(*a*) As for demand, when total invested is subtracted from the gross national product, together with direct taxation, then privately spendable income-a-head will not, if population is increasing fast, grow much, if at all. This, alas, has been the experience of many a planner. If a country is ultimately to be viable it will certainly not do to expect too rapid an increase in present private standards of living. Nehru put it bluntly (143, p. 354), "Self-help and self-reliance is the thing, and austerity is at present the prerequisite for future prosperity". Social contacts with the affluent world make austerity hard. Nurkse (145, p. 62) notes the "demonstration effect": "It is much easier to adopt superior consumption habits than improved production methods. . . . The temptation to copy United States consumption patterns tends to limit the supply of investible funds by inhibiting the willingness to save." Other economists have pointed, however, to the incentive to production presented by the desire to "keep up" with the Americans. On balance productivity is likely to go up; in any case the *proportion* "saved" as already said is not a useful concept where consumption is inadequate for efficiency.

(*b*) In view of increasing population and the sociological obstacles to production, saving and taxation set forth in the next chapter, the scope is limited for carrying out development activities, in order to raise standards of living. To do this by trade and home-based investment alone is not possible for the bulk of underdeveloped countries in the immediate future. Only a few, such as Japan certainly, and Israel or Puerto Rico probably, have achieved or are approaching a "take-off" when they can rely on their own resources. The practical question is thus at what points the necessary aid should now be applied with the prospect of building up trade in the long run. Part of the answer already given is selecting the specific industries and services to fit the specific markets and resources, material and human, of a country, bearing in mind the balance of payments. Priority in aid must be given to these particular "fit" industries and services, and to the particular bottleneck factors of production in short supply, whether it be capital, management, working skill, or research.

Our survey of markets and resources threw up, in particular, the need to develop the factor of management, at least in manufacturing for export or import substitution and in the tourist trade. Rostow (168, p. 50) has pointed to the need in any "take-off" of a group within any underdeveloped country which is prepared to accept innovations. But there is a scarcity, too, of routine managers and of research specialists and in fact, as our third trend of development indicated, of all persons educated enough to form an industrial staff. Whether in agriculture, manufacturing industry, tourism, or infrastructure, investment involving postponement of immediate consumption may be in material capital, or in services such as education and research, or both; and it would be useful always to set forth in plans a ratio of national product to be invested in education and training for management and also applied research, similar to the percentage usually given for capital investment. The type of investment is not independent of the industry invested in, since, as the Appendix shows, some industries are capital-intensive, others management and staff, or labour-intensive. But, in general, the supply of management, as of all staff and skilled workers, is short in the underdeveloped countries.

In the countries now developed the art of management was, in the early years of their industrial revolutions, mainly picked up by experience in small-scale entrepreneurship. The system had its inefficiencies, notably nepotism, which, in the wide kinship sociology of underdeveloped countries, might be carried to even greater breadths. If development is not to take the whole century it did in most of the developed countries, education for management must play a large part. Wherever markets and the location of materials permit, large plants have already been set up (and are likely to be set up faster)—many of them nationalized. Successful large-scale managers are thus less likely to be of the ex-entrepreneur and more of the trained administrator type.

Sociological obstacles are probably less formidable, as we shall see, in education and research than in the necessary local saving and capital investment. If aid is eventually to promote trade, investment in education may well, in the long run, lead to more net export or import substitution per unit of aid expenditure than investment in capital. Whatever education and research is invested in may take place either at home in the aided, or abroad in the aiding country; and in either location education may be either in school or else in learning on the job. When at home, in fact, nationals are quite often attached as apprentices or "fellows" in a United Nations technical assistance project.

Much less has been written about investment in human capital, in education and research, than in material capital; for the underdeveloped countries, we may conclude with pointers to the practical directions of such investment—

(i) The scarcity of management and skill is mainly the result of past restriction of the higher appointments and even of skilled workmanship to the colonizers. A local *élite* of skilled technicians, experts, and managers must be educated and trained to fill the more responsible posts now at last open to the ex-colonials. Many authorities have asserted that this training must, if funds are limited, be instituted at all costs, even that of postponing universal primary education and risking a mandarin class of superior intellectuals.

(ii) In higher education a practical turn must be encouraged and nationals sent abroad to read for University degrees in engineering and management or, probably better value for money, similar courses established at home. Models are to hand in the courses for the B.Com. degree, introduced into modern British Universities beginning with Birmingham in 1900, and in the first and higher degrees in Business Administration found in American Universities and Institutes of Technology.

(iii) Industrial Management and tourist catering follow certain principles common to all branches of business, and all students in commerce or administration can be taught certain tool-subjects, such as accounting, commercial law, statistics, and econometrics, and the use of English, as well as

market research and economics. Sir William Ashley, first
dean of the Faculty of Commerce at Birmingham, considered
these subjects capable of forming a liberal education provided
that the *rationale* or (as I should say) the *logic* of their procedures was made clear.

Other, more specialized subjects could be added to the
curriculum according to the special career envisaged. For
manufacturing, elementary engineering; for hotel management, foreign languages and some sociology to explain and
cope with foreign behaviour, also, perhaps, elementary
plumbing!

(iv) Training its citizens abroad, either in Technological
Colleges and Universities or in the field, or both, will be
necessary till a country has sufficient training facilities and
staff at home. This points to the high priority of training
students abroad who will be willing to return home as
teachers, eventually to train industrial staff or further
teachers at home.

(v) Many of the natural conditions and resources of underdeveloped countries in climate, soil, oil, minerals, and, above
all, water are not yet known and require geological and
meteorological survey and research. Until experts can complete surveys, only a temporary plan can be laid down as to
which of the "rooted" industrial, agricultural, mining, and
tourist activities depending immediately on these resources
should be developed, and to what extent. In the course of
the surveys nationals can be trained as experts.

(vi) Before costly investment is undertaken in industry,
staff, foreign and national, is required for "preinvestment"
"feasibility" studies. To attract tourists, preinvestment surveys are also required of possible sites for national parks and
recreation facilities and for archaeological excavations. A
further research might well examine what monuments and
scenery are worth protection from hoardings, bill-boards, and
other tourist deterrents.

CHAPTER VII

SOCIOLOGICAL LIMITS TO ECONOMIC DEVELOPMENT

1. CONDITIONS FOR ECONOMIC SUCCESS: THE TRIPOD FOR HIGHER LIVING STANDARDS

PLANS were outlined in the last chapter to develop industries and some services in hitherto underdeveloped countries so that the higher standards of living which these countries desired could be attained. These plans looked toward trade rather than aid for the long-run solution and were mainly economic in selecting as likely to be successful industries and services with characteristics fitting the characteristic resources of the country.

Man is not a purely economic creature, and the question must now be raised how far his total nature and circumstances will allow these plans to come to fruition. The question is particularly pertinent when, returning to Table I, we realize that in many underdeveloped countries average income is rising less fast than in developed countries and that, instead of narrowing, the gap between the two groups is widening.

As stated by Andic and Peacock (4) "the *relative* position of the less developed countries has worsened considerably". While the 40 per cent poorest nations had, in 1949, 6·5 per cent of the aggregate world income, in 1957 they had only 5·0 per cent.

Owing to the fall in the value of money, it is difficult to reckon the absolute change in the real income-a-head of individual countries. But Table I measured, as explained, the relative changes between 1949 and 1957 compared to total world change. By 1964 the gap, we saw (I, §1), had widened. Why, in spite of aid, did the gap between the underdeveloped and developed countries widen instead of narrowing?

The most obvious check to the success of aid and other plans for raising standards of living is the standard of living itself. A high proportion of people in underdeveloped lands are physically on the verge of starvation and thus incapacitated from working full out. Even though sufficiently fed, once they obtain employment, semi-starvation in childhood may leave its mark. To quote a Colonial Office survey (144, p. 119), "the listless, apathetic and ineffective Africans of farm and field, of shamba and street corners, bear upon them the brand of malignant malnutrition".

This conclusion is important for practical policy of aid or trade. If underdeveloped countries increase exports by turning from subsistence farming to specialized agricultural products, their own nutrition may suffer. In any case the productivity of labour might often be raised and trade helped in its competition with other countries by aid for feeding workers quite as much as by equipping them with machines or other capital. Thus, if investment is defined not just as a possible result of saving out of consumption but as any spending, including consumption of food, for the sake of greater capacity to produce in the future, then, paradoxically, such consumption would count as investment, just as would technical education. Certainly investment in capital and education may have little effect on the worker's productivity, if, however well educated and equipped, he is going hungry.

Another physical circumstance possibly limiting productive capacity is climate. Some underdeveloped countries are certainly enervating, particularly in their low-lying tropical areas. Other underdeveloped regions, however, such as the fertile Middle East and Northern Africa, set in the midst of desert, are stimulating. Climate may explain the low income-a-head of some underdeveloped countries but not of all of them. And with the gradual elimination of tropical diseases, physical geography is likely to play a less important role in limiting development. The main causes for limitation must then be sought *behind* incapacitation by semi-starvation and enervation.

Why should men be starving? Colin Clark tells us (41, pp. 503–4) that the Dutch return in product per square mile is six times the Indian, and if all the cultivable land in the world were farmed at Dutch standards of skill and hard work, the world could support at least four times its present population.

This, obviously, is a big *if,* but calls for an answer to the question why Indians and other underdeveloped peoples do not in fact exhibit the hard work and skill which developed people do. The basic obstacles in the path are neither natural, physical, technological, nor economic, but sociological. This point was put clearly by many physical scientists at the special Plenary Session on Food and Population of the British Association for the Advancement of Science at Cardiff in 1960.

H. D. Kay, an Emeritus Professor of Biochemistry, may be quoted (104, pp. 58–9)—

> Sociology and social psychology have for some time been accepted as sciences, and it is perhaps in these growing regions of knowledge that scientific research and the application of existing techniques and of future findings is going to be most fruitful in solving some of the more stubborn, long-term problems of many of the hungry countries. There is as much need, in my view, to lessen the psychological and social handicaps which harass these countries as there is to remedy shortage of capital and the almost complete absence of modern agricultural technique. . . . It is *not* shortage of basic scientific knowledge nor of sound and practical methods for applying it to agriculture or dietetics that is the major obstacle to fairly speedy improvement of nutrition in most of the hungry countries. . . . It is rather the extreme slowness of implementation of that knowledge, a slowness caused by political, sociological and psychological obstacles, to overcome which effective techniques have still to be found.

In the content of this present book, political and social psychological are included in the title *sociological*; and in the last chapter greater integration will be urged for these social sciences with economics and with natural sciences. In the present context of the underdeveloped countries the need will become particularly obvious of integrating social anthropology, human geography, demography, social psychology, and even political science.

Before setting forth sociological factors, as an explanation of *continued* low standards of living, we must, however, call to mind what exactly has to be explained. The standard of living refers to a *minimum stable income per head below which no one* (or at most only a small fraction of the population) *will fall.* The standard of living is thus a tripod standing upon three legs: the total national income; the number of heads; and the form of distribution of income among those heads. Standards of living may fail of achievement because the total national production and income is too small, heads too many, or forces making for more equal distribution too weak. Each of these three legs of the tripod will, in the following sections, be examined in turn for sociological causes of failure.

2. SOCIOLOGICAL OBSTACLES TO GROWTH
OF PRODUCTION

The first leg on which a high standard of living rests is high national production analysed (in Chapter II) into three elements: productivity, proportion occupied among the population, and structure of occupations or industries. Plans for raising national production were discussed in the previous chapter, but in spite of aid from abroad, only slow progress was noted in most underdeveloped countries. They were in fact so far behind the developed countries in their production that it seems too optimistic to assert that they are in the stage just previous to the Industrial Revolution—that of England, for instance, in the early eighteenth century. Judging from the standards of living of the bulk of their population, their economy is more like that of England in the Middle Ages, if not the Dark Ages. What hope exists, then, of any substantial raising of productivity in the course of, say, a century instead of a millennium?

The main hope held out in the previous chapter was the experience and knowledge already acquired by the developed countries which can be handed on immediately through the direct advice and action by citizens of the developed countries, and, in the longer run, through the education of the local inhabitants. Lack of knowledge appears at first sight the easiest obstacle to overcome, since knowledge can be taught and teaching is labour- not capital-intensive. Most underdeveloped people are eager for education and for training as teachers, and do in fact readily learn and teach. The only obstacle appears to be insufficient financial aid to education.

But, looking below the surface, obstacles to education often have a deeper sociological foundation than the purely financial. Even when funds are available, it is often not the most suitable candidates who are trained as teachers. In many a country, particularly where the Mohammedan religion prevails, women, the most suitable teachers for younger children, are likely to be barred, whether educated or not, from leaving the shelter of their home after attaining marriageable age. Furthermore, if finance and teachers are available, the teaching curriculum is often unsuitable. In Mohammedan countries much of the time in elementary school is spent reciting the Koran, a mere feat of verbal memory. At later stages the prestige value of universities teaching law and "cultural" subjects (particularly where Oxbridge influence is still strong) takes precedence over faculties of commerce, technology, and, of course, over the secondary schools that would prepare candidates for universities, whatever they teach. In consequence, universities are handicapped by the poorly prepared material they receive and do not make the contribution they might to economic development.

Let us, however, suppose the obstacles to have been surmounted which check the education in technology and management of at least some inhabitants of underdeveloped countries. Can these "key" men, or *élite*, rapidly change the economy of their countries and lead them toward a take-off?

Underdeveloped economies are not all, of course, at the same sociological stage, particularly in their organization of agriculture. Two types of general economy are usually distinguished, that of a price system centred on a market and that of State authority. Much of the economy of the underdeveloped countries follows, however, neither system, but is ordered by social tradition and custom in broadly speaking one of three subsystems: the feudal estate with landlord (often an absentee) and serfs or peons as still prevalent in Latin America; the independent peasant; and the primitive community. In the last two there is little differentiation of employer and employed in production, and all three subsystems subsist on their own. Whole communities, or single peasant families or feudal estates, produce wholly or mainly for their own consumption. There is little cash crop and exchange of goods or services is exceptional.

Compared to that for sociology, particularly social anthropology, traditional systems offer little scope for economic theory. Obstacles to production can usefully be considered under the standard four "factors of production" only if the effects are noted of the different sociological subsystems, particularly, in contrast to the market economy, the traditional and communal organization. In virtually all underdeveloped countries sociological obstacles check (A) labour productivity, (B) land productivity; and also (C) capital, and (D) management formation as well as productivity.

A. Obstacles to labour productivity take at least five forms—

(i) In the primitive communal organization the product of the individual worker is submerged in the group. The labour situation is indeed the prototype of that which Mayo found in the Hawthorne factory. Lewis (121, p. 59) puts forward two definite limits to what can be achieved by communal organization. There must be *local* benefit, "the villagers will build a minor road connecting their village to a main road but they will not build a main road for all and sundry, without payment"; and *general* benefit, the work "must not be obviously of much greater advantage to some than the rest". Communal action, he considers also, is limited to "stable economic situations where routine action is all that is required and no industrial initiative". Emerging from the primitive community to be employed in industry is far from an easy transition. Clark Kerr (105) distinguishes the early stages as that of the uncommitted worker who earns money in industry for a single specific purpose, such as the price of a bride, and then returns to his community; and that of the semi-committed worker whose wife and family remain on the tribal land and to whom the worker returns periodically to help in cultivation. In terms of "labour cohesion" used earlier (IV, §8) for developed countries, the uncommitted will have a high labour turnover, the semi-committed a high absence rate. Both such relapses increase industrial cost and, moreover, make any long training of workers not worth while.

(ii) Under all social forms of organization the most obvious example of an obstacle to the contribution of labour is its deliberate *in*capacitation during the periods of fasting, often followed by all-out feasting, as commanded by certain religions. During Ramadan, which lasts over a month, for instance, true Mohammedans do not eat during daylight and all have to wake long before dawn to partake of breakfast.

They do not eat again till sunset. The loss of food and sleep and the irregularity of meal-times combine to lower physical productivity and increase irritability. Nor do the days of feasting that follow help to make up the output lost.

(iii) Not only may the work of the given labour force be restricted but industrial work may, for certain classes of people, absolutely be taboo. The outstanding case is that of women, in not only Mohammedan but other cultures, and the proportion of women to men occupied in industry has been shown as far lower in most underdeveloped than in developed countries. Economists would expect logically that poverty would stimulate more women to work in industry and thus help with the family income in the poorer than in the richer countries. But where so many men are unemployed or underemployed, this is sociologically "unthinkable".

(iv) Loss of industrial labour and a lower mobilization also occurs where idleness has respectability if not positive prestige, and fit persons must be carried by the economy as passengers. The beggars of India come to mind and those monks of many lands who do not engage in production, directly or indirectly.

(v) Finally, obstacles to labour mobility such as caste-systems tend to restrict output, since the worker potentially best able to tackle a particular job may be tied to another for which he is not fitted and demand for workers unsatisfied in one job cannot be supplied from another. Immobility affects equality of incomes still more than total income and will be further considered later.

(B) The productivity of land affects agriculture rather than industry, but agriculture occupies the majority of the workers in underdeveloped countries, and we cannot, when discussing the general standard of living of any country, omit consideration of its major economic activity. Moreover, industrialization and tourism may fail to bring a higher net standard of living, if agriculture is not developed and any addition to gross income from industry and tourism has to be spent on importing raw materials and food.

Now, it is precisely in agricultural development and the productivity of land that sociological obstacles are strongest,

The traditional communal system of holding and working the land Lewis (121, p. 121) considers to be now far from allowing the land to yield its potential product. "Communal tenures worked passably in Africa so long as populations were very small in relation to land, but population pressure everywhere causes such tenures to . . . handicap innovation. Livestock cannot be bred selectively unless they are segregated and their mating controlled; neither is it convenient to experiment with new agricultural methods."

Under less primitive organization, where individual peasant subsistence-farming prevails, the legal system of land tenures often fails to give an incentive to work the land or to invest in improvements; and usually results in relatively unproductive sizes of holding. Religious practices play a part here also; notable are the sacred cows that graze the land of India, so lacking in water anyhow, without giving return to man in food value or even leather. And now a sacred cow population explosion is reported.

In Indonesia too, much of the land is said to be ideal for pig-raising. Unfortunately, the prevailing Mohammedanism forbids the eating of pork.

(C) Unlike labour and land, the existence of industrial *capital* cannot be taken for granted and obstacles occur to its very formation.

Apart from the economic difficulty of poor people saving any part of their income, there is the psychology of those who are rich enough to save, but who do not invest their savings in productive capital and instead buy jewellery, build temples or their own palaces, or just hoard money. Here the under-developed countries are behaving very much as the older countries now developed did in their middle age. The medieval cathedrals are a lasting (and, aesthetically, a happy) example of a high proportion of savings that did *not* go into helping further production.

In answer, however, to the poorer countries' own desire for higher standards of living we are discussing not aesthetics, but economics. Investment (i.e. capital formation) is insufficient and when formed is often not as productive as it might be.

Discussing companies, we found three distinct steps in capital formation—

(a) saving;
(b) entrusting savings to certain financial institutions such as industrial companies;
(c) those institutions in turn equipping industries.

The original source of capital in most of the underdeveloped countries, most of which were then colonies, involved entrusting savings to private capitalist bodies, largely companies, in the developed colonizing countries. The thrifty Victorian empire-builders placed their savings into companies which equipped tea and rubber plantations or copper, tin, diamond or gold mines, or public utilities. In fact, companies were at first far more frequent in the colonial than in the home industrial field. This capitalist company method of providing capital for the underdeveloped countries got a bad name because of gun-boat diplomacy, and more important today, because profits were often not reinvested in the underdeveloped country and much of the salaries paid to the staff from the colonizing country were spent on imported goods or saved and sent back home. In short, the economic multiplier was low.

Whether their image of colonization really applies today or not, the ex-colonies and present independent underdeveloped countries have taken an almost immovable dislike to foreign "capitalist exploitation". Many of them have lately nationalized the equipment capitalists provided for them, for instance in refineries. This hardly encourages the others. The original "capitalist" source of capital must, in some countries perhaps, be left out of account for the future. The first obstacle to capital formation is thus often political.

If foreign capitalism is not acceptable, and finance by foreign governmental loan or gift is insufficient, as it may well be for long-run development, underdeveloped countries are thrown back on their own resources for capital. Can they save, invest (i.e. entrust) and equip for industry on a sufficient scale? The obstacles are formidable at each of these three stages. Saving is checked by poverty, and a changing age-structure with more children to feed will increase poverty and in particular hold down savings, and, anyway, incomes are so low that saving would only be at the cost of working capacity. Entrustment is checked by the lack of intermediaries operating in the country itself. Savings in underdeveloped countries are, indeed, sometimes entrusted through intermediaries in developed, often neutral countries, such as Switzerland; but though this helps individuals in underdeveloped countries, it does not necessarily help the country as a whole. The final, capital equipment, stage of investment is handicapped by investors' excessive fear of taking risks in particular ventures, and by the high interest that can be got by lending for some purpose other than equipping industry or development generally.

Once formed, the equipment must be fully utilized and maintained. The tendency has been noticed to equip underdeveloped countries with the latest capital-intensive, automatic machinery, as a psychological matter of prestige, rather than economic calculation. But often there is no adequately trained maintenance and repair staff and the expensive equipment remains idle for long periods.

(D) Management, like capital, does not exist in sufficient quantities in the underdeveloped countries, and we must look at the obstacles to its very formation as well as to its productivity. Since this formation must be by education rather than "picking it up" through experience, the most obvious obstacles will be economic—the financing of schools and universities. But economic policy will not by itself overcome the sociological obstacles to education already indicated in unsuitable curriculum; dearth of women teachers; low prestige of an industrial career; or class immobility—any more than it can overcome the lack of will to innovation and taking risks.

3. INEQUALITY AND LIMITS TO THE STABILITY AND MORE EQUAL DISTRIBUTION OF INCOME

The standard of living toward which underdeveloped countries strive includes, with a certain average income-a-head, the notion of less inequality, particularly of no one below a certain minimum of poverty. A further aim is usually included in the notion of a standard, that of stability or security, which may first be examined. How do the underdeveloped countries fare, compared with the developed countries, in the economic security of their nationals and of the nation as a whole?

In the more primitive societies the sociological set-up (prevalence of caste and extended family or kinship and sense of community) makes for the greater security or, at least, the greater feeling of security of the individual. On the other hand, dependence upon primitive agricultural technique makes the economy vulnerable to periodic natural catastrophes, such as droughts or floods. On entering the world market, a developing nation is at a further comparative disadvantage. Exports of the primary agricultural or mineral commodities in which it normally specializes are subject to violent price changes, largely due to fluctuation in supply and inelastic supply and demand. Even the tourist trade, we have seen, suffers both when political upheavals in the country to be visited engender fears and when, in the visitors' own country, there is a business slump and few can afford the luxury of holiday travel. Thus, conditions natural and sociological as well as economic limit and upset the stability of underdeveloped economics. The stability and security of labour in *developed* countries since 1945 form a telling contrast; and even before that, in spite of industrial slumps, unemployment insurance smoothed out incomes. In the depression of 1929–35, for instance, the real total income of the working-class in Britain did not, measurably (65), fall.

We now turn from the distribution of incomes through time to their distribution at any one time among persons and classes. A simple measure of the inequality of incomes within any country is the percentage of the total income accruing to the richest 10 per cent of income-receivers. After subtraction of income tax, Morgan found this index of inequality (141, pp. 821–33) was, around 1947–50, 40·8 per cent in Puerto Rico but in the United States of America 27·0 per cent. In Ceylon 9·7 per cent of families received as much as 32·5 per cent of income, but in the United Kingdom 13·1 per cent of incomes received 30·2 per cent and, in 1952, Lydall and Lansing (124) give the top 10 per cent 26 per cent. Pareto has attempted to establish a general law (149, pp. 693–700) of the form of distribution of incomes within a nation. Whether it is universal or not, his formula can be used as a yardstick to measure which countries have a greater, which a less degree of equality in incomes. Colin Clark (39, p. 538) thus found that while the older developed countries varied within the middle degrees—the newly developed countries had the least degree of inequality, the underdeveloped the most—

> The greatest degree of equalization of incomes is found in Australia and New Zealand and the Prairie Provinces of Canada. These are developing communities where access to economic opportunity seems to be open to many. On the other hand, Argentine, Brazil, and India appear to be developing a very high degree of income concentration.

The United States had a highly unequal income distribution in the 1870s and again round about 1929. In recent years this inequality has been reduced. France for the last fifty years has gained a more equal income distribution, and also Britain.

Extreme poverty has been the lot of sections of the population of developed countries in the past, and their statistically recorded experience in overcoming primary poverty may prove useful in estimating the breaking point of obstacles in the underdeveloped countries. Primary poverty was defined in 1899 as income insufficient for the bare physical subsistence of a family even when the utmost economy is exercised by husband and wife. At that date Seebohm Rowntree found in York 15·5 per cent of families in primary poverty. Subsequent events in England point the lesson (73, p. 185)—

> Between 1899 and 1936 when wages boards, national insurance and pensions were being introduced, the percentage of all families whose income was below that necessary for bare subsistence had dropped from 15·5 to 6·8 per cent. This insufficiency was due to low wages for 8 per cent of all families in 1899, but only for 0·6 per cent in 1936. Comparing 1936 and 1950 Rowntree used as his poverty line a higher standard than bare subsistence. Individuals whose income was below this standard fell from 14·2 to 0·37 per cent of all individuals surveyed, a change due mainly to a composite of full employment, family allowances and food subsidies.

Previous to their development, the countries at present developed suffered the consequence of poverty, not excluding premature death. Even as late as 1900 (57, p. 309), general labourers, the poorest paid of all occupations, suffered in England over twice the average occupational mortality rate. Extremes of poverty amidst plenty were due to very low incomes of persons even when fully employed; no income from the chief bread-winner when unemployed; and no income from other (often numerous) unoccupied members of the family. All of these immediate causes of extreme poverty are to be found in the underdeveloped countries, though not easily distinguished owing (154) to a further cause looming larger—the situation of *under*employment.

Some of the roots of inequality—low wages, unemployment, unoccupation and underemployment—are *economic* and have already been mentioned as early stages in the trend of development, for example—

(i) The high proportion of persons engaged in primitive agriculture and thus with a very low income. In a plantation economy the disparity between the wealth of planters and labourers is particularly obvious but it is not so extreme as between landlord and peasant.

(ii) The absence of mechanization and, therefore, the low productivity of the bulk even of *industrial* labour doing the heavy mechanical labouring that is performed by machines in the developed countries.

(iii) The low staff ratio in industry and the absence of any large middle-class.

But the main roots of inequality are *sociological* in the wide sense of sociology, including demography and political science.

(iv) A differential birth-rate. Fifty years ago (58, p. 36) the birth-rate of English working-class families was almost twice that of the upper or middle class, and evidence of a similar differential today has been found (212, pp. 136, 280) in underdeveloped countries such as Lebanon and Chile.

(v) The social immobility imposed by custom, often with a religious sanction. The extreme case is the untouchables caste of India—a segregation difficult, apparently, to change.

(vi) The mass of illiterates. This situation is not deeply sociological and is easier to change, given financial resources for education.

(vii) Political power in the hands of the educated *élite*—small in numbers because of the restriction in education, and becoming almost a mandarin class. Here, probably, lies the main cause of failure in several underdeveloped countries to use and enforce "progressive" income taxes as a means of redressing inequality.

(viii) Weak State and trade-union action.

Trade unions' main objective and one of the State's has been to increase labour's wages and particularly to institute minimum wages and measures for economic security. This action has been followed by diminishing inequality and often, too, by increasing productivity via, as I have put it (73, p. 65), six routes: the physiological and psychological conditioning of workers, more inter-industry and inter-firm mobility, and the spread of mechanization, directly or indirectly.

In many underdeveloped countries trade unions apparently have a large membership though not always paid-up. But they are often political machines rather than organizations giving thought primarily to the possibility of permanent economic advancement and security of their members. The danger lies in overdoing claims and raising wages too high in relation to labour productivity. Economists have held that wages equal marginal productivity, but we need not stress the finer points. It is enough to assert that wages cannot in the long run exceed labour productivity, i.e. the average output-a-worker minus raw materials, fuel and depreciation of capital equipment and the cost of management and risk-bearing. The productivity of labour is lower in underdeveloped than developed countries, and wages cannot be on the same level. Efforts to make them so, with no prospect of raising productivity, would simply drive the country out of trade in the competitive export market owing to its higher labour cost per unit of production. Unfortunately, this truism (however platitudinous it appears to economists) is not always accepted by labour in underdeveloped countries— indeed, a certain proportion of labour in developed countries does not appear to accept it either.

In all developed countries individual *laissez faire* has been modified and the State has intervened in industry for the purpose of making distribution more equal and providing security in a number of ways which I have distinguished (73, *passim*) by appropriate prepositions. The State has defended labour FROM exploitation, overfatigue, and ill-health by Maximum Hours and Minimum Wage Acts or acts to set up machinery for that purpose, and by participation WITH employers and trade unions in wage negotiations; it has provided services FOR industry, such as employment exchanges, or technical colleges to further mobility, and has provided direct palliatives and security AGAINST the hazards of life and work from the womb to the tomb by providing benefits for childbirth, children, sickness, injury by accidents, unemployment, and old age and death of bread-winners through national insurance schemes. Finally, in its direct operation OF nationalized industries and in its planning, taxation, or control OVER private industry, the State itself has often set a certain standard of fair shares between wages and other forms of income.

Attempts have been made to carry these various roles of the State in developed countries over to the underdeveloped by the agency of the International Labour Organization. Allowing enough time for full consideration (and omitting Communist and recently created states), we find that conventions drawn up before 1939 had by 1962 been signed by a fair proportion of underdeveloped countries on accident compensation and minimum wage fixing machinery, by a small proportion on insurance against sickness, by a very few on old age pensions, and on invalidity and survivors' (e.g. widows and orphans of bread-winner) insurance. Only one underdeveloped country had agreed to perhaps the most direct "equalizer and stabilizer", provision for unemployment, partly, no doubt, because of the difficulty in distinguishing full unemployment from chronic underemployment. On the whole, the governments of the underdeveloped countries do not seem to have gone far in trying to equalize or to stabilize the incomes of their citizens.

Will industrialization of these countries or developments of the tourist trade increase inequality still further? To judge from the more recent development of the countries already industrialized, development should tend to equalize incomes, and living and working conditions, if the stubborn sociological and antagonistic political forces can be overcome. The older developed countries of Europe had, after all, to overcome medieval feudalism, and then the aristocratic set-up of the eighteenth century. A revolution did this in France, but in Britain almost feudal sociological forces were recently still potent, as Tawney has pointed out (179, pp. 74–5).

In short, sociological forces may check equality and security for the poorer classes, as they check production, if industrialization keeps, or increases, power and the wealth created in the hands of a few, without effective opposition from labour or the State. Indeed, the State itself, in the hands of the rich and the traditionalists, may not be particularly enamoured of a more equal distribution.

4. THE POPULATION EXPLOSION

The third leg of the tripod upon which rests the future standard of living is the number of "heads". Population is now said to be "exploding", and the expression is well taken. Coale has calculated (42) that world population doubled in the two centuries between 1650 and 1850. It increased on average 50 per cent a century. But instead of a similar 50 per cent rise between 1850 and 1950 the rise was 100 per cent, and population is now increasing at a rate of 500 per cent a century and shows little sign of abating. Population, moreover, is particularly "explosive" in those very countries, identified as under-developed, which can least sustain this explosion. A projection for the half-century from 1950 to 2000 is given by Glass (87, p. 17)—

Population Projection for A.D. *2000; 1950 being 100*

Developed Regions	170	
Africa	250	
Asia	280	
Latin America	350	(Doubling in 28 years)
All Regions	244	(Doubling in 41 years or fivefold a century)

Though all the nine trends outlined in the first chapter should take place except the last, that particular trend—increase in the standard of living—may not, as a result of population increase, ever take place. If the principal object of industrial development is higher standards of living, this population explosion which offsets the effects of industrial development must certainly be examined, particularly to discover the reason why increased supplies of labour cannot increase production proportionately. At the present low world level of income-a-head the immediate production needed is mainly food raised by agriculture, and beyond a certain point agriculture cannot, in the long run, increase production at the decreasing or constant cost that manufacturing can. Together with labour, capital, and management, agriculture requires, unlike manufactures, an extent of more-or-less fertile land, and such land is, in fact, scarce.

Diminishing returns are, of course, delayed when new capital in irrigation schemes or fertilizers or more capable and knowledgeable management and labour are applied to the land. But these new factors do not have the same open horizons that they have in manufacture. Natural resources—the land factor —still present a limit and, unless new fertile lands can extensively be opened up (as the Middle-West of America was in the nineteenth century), the new input of labour, capital or management has to be piled on intensively to more or less fixed land.

The law of diminishing return is that with successive "doses" of expenditure or "inputs", the additions to the total output diminish; not necessarily that the absolute *total* return diminishes. But more and more frequently in countries where labour is plentiful, doses of labour are applied to a fixed supply of land in such intensity that output eventually does diminish absolutely. If, as in India, cow-dung has to be used for fuel to cook with, the cattle will not be fertilizing the land, and if there is over-grazing and wholesale tree-felling, erosion of the soil will diminish the productivity of the land, absolutely. And the more the number of workers who need to cook with dung and the cattle who need to graze, the less, absolutely, will be the return. In Africa agriculturists cannot, after exhausting resources, move on to fresh pastures as they used to do, since all possible pastures are getting settled. There is not just a diminishing but a devastating return. The result is often that population moves off to the cities, though industry offers no increase in productive jobs. Indeed, of all the trends mentioned in the first chapter, urbanization is being realized the fastest in some underdeveloped countries, particularly in Latin America.

Minerals are included by the economist in "land", and they are obviously wasting assets. Prophets have recently been inclined to optimism about the length of life of the resources at present in demand. But if a population increase of 1½ per cent annually is combined with a standard of living and similar demands, say, only two-thirds that of the United States today, then Villard shows (194, pp. 189–95) that by the year 2100 total demand will increase eightyfold, and not many years' supply of coal, petroleum, steel, or copper will be available—in fact, not one of the last three commodities would have more than thirteen years supply.

The immediate cause of the population explosion is not an increase in the birth-rate, but the maintenance of birth-rates in the underdeveloped countries, with a spectacular decrease in their death-rates. India, with Pakistan, had in 1910–14 an annual crude death-rate of 31 per thousand population. In 1951 the rates were 14·4 for India and just above 11·9 for Pakistan, and they have been falling since. In Mexico the death-rate was 16·7 in 1948, 9·5 in 1965. This decrease can be reasonably imputed to biological and medical knowledge applied in controlling (often to the point of eradication) the killer diseases, such as malaria, smallpox, sleeping sickness, and yellow fever. In any realistic model of the balance of forces affecting changes of population, such as I have presented (58, p. 19) for Malthus's argument, this factor (then summed up as Public Hygiene) must be brought into account. The point of practical importance is that this *death control*, whether by immunization of persons or destruction of disease-carriers, can be, and has been, effected by a few expert *élite*; but effective birth control depends on acceptance by large numbers—a much more difficult operation. Two significant diagrams in the United Nations *Demographic Yearbook* for 1955 (183) compare changes in birth- and in death-rates for some seventy nations. Between 1945–9 and 1950–4 all nations but one show a fall in death-rates, but in their birth-rates the nations are evenly split between those rising and those falling.

Many underdeveloped countries have now a crude death-rate as low as the developed countries. This rate is due, however, to the age-structure of their population. With their birth-rates maintained, underdeveloped countries contain a much higher proportion of young people. A more exact and comparable indicator of health is the expectation of life at birth given in Table I. The men of *all* the ten countries of highest income-a-head, except Belgium with 62·0, show an average expectation of over 66 years. None of the seven most underdeveloped countries where data was available, except Ceylon (with 60·3 years), had an average expectation over 50. But life expectation is rapidly rising. Linton (122) has drawn maps showing the rise between 1920 (when average expectations of less than 40 years occurred in almost all South and Central America, Africa, and Asia) and 1950 when life expectations shorter than 40 occurred only in Central Africa, India, and China.

We do not want, presumably, to put death-rates back up again. So if production cannot be exploded faster than population—quintupling a century—the only way to increase production-*a-head* is to reduce the birth-rate. Recent birth-rates are given for all the twenty-five countries listed in Table I wherever they are available. At a glance, it can be seen that all the ten countries with the lowest average income-a-head have birth-rates clearly above the rates in any of the ten most developed countries. They range from 34·2 to 50·0 compared with 16·5 to 28·3. What are the factors accounting for this maintenance of high birth-rates?

For practical purposes I have referred to the "human factor", as analysable, broadly speaking, into human ability and human willingness. In the maintenance of high birth-rates the double reference, as also the distinction, proves again of practical importance.

Most writers seem to have plumped for unwillingness to control births as the determing element. Economists say much about the willingness—nay, the positive desire—to have children for work in agriculture at an early age, and for props to the old age of the parents. Sociologists stress religious beliefs about the importance of multiplying, the ritual of ancestor worship, and the lack of any will to maintain or acquire a standard of living. But to interpret the difference in birth-rates between countries, *more* weight than at present should, in view of the evidence, be placed on people's knowledge of methods and ability in controlling births; *less* on motives and will. After all, unless couples know that there are means of preventing births, they may not think contraception possible and may not will it because they don't think about it. As Himes says in his *Medical History of Contraception* (95, p. 392)—

> It is bad sociology to overlook the means or mechanism by which the Vital Revolution has been and is being achieved.

Economics has been guilty of this error in emphasizing almost exclusively the rising standard of living to account for small families.

But sociology need not fall into the same trap. Unwillingness to have more than a certain number is probably not such a new phenomenon, confined to developed countries, as all that. It may have been present, at least among the wives, in the countries now developed long before their birth-rates fell; it was latent because the capacity to prevent births was not known. This may be the situation at this very moment in the still underdeveloped countries. Queen Victoria's plaint is well known of the "great inconvenience a large family would be", yet she had nine children. In a Puerto Rican inquiry (177, p. 159) 63 per cent of women mentioned less than four children and 91 per cent four or less as their ideal number. This number is corroborated in the United States, where women have high status and where knowledge of birth control is almost universal.

Where, through lack of knowledge or facilities, couples are unable to practise birth control, the course of events has followed the three propositions of Malthus (127), particularly the bald second. The first was that "population is necessarily limited by the means of subsistence"; the second that "population invariably increases where the means of subsistence increase, unless prevented by some very powerful and obvious check".

Just after Malthus died, means of subsistence increased dramatically owing to the effects of the Industrial Revolution, England becoming the sole "workshop of the world", and the opening up of the American Middle-West. The population of the areas affected, before birth control took effect, increased rapidly, but not as rapidly as the means of subsistence and standards of living rose. Malthus's third principle was that "the checks which repress the superior power of population and keep its effect on a level with the means of subsistence are all resolved into moral restraint, vice and misery". Malthus was a clergyman and would undoubtedly have classed birth-control methods, as abortion, under "vice". Elsewhere he classed checks to population more neutrally as positive (e.g. death) and preventive. Subsequently the latter proved powerful. The differential effect of birth control as a *preventive check* on population is evident in the fall of English birth-rates since 1880, when wide publicity followed the Bradlaugh–Besant trials of 1877–9. It is also evident when comparing Catholic and Protestant regions in the same period and in the same country, for instance (58, pp. 38–9; 36, pp. 67–77) in Holland and Canada. In Asia, Africa, and Central and South America, containing the bulk of the world's population, the standard of living remains, with little or no birth control and fast-increasing population, at or below subsistence level. Though he is critical of some of Malthus's wording, Flew (55) best sums up the practical applicability of his central argument—

> For the rough and practically vital understanding of the populations explosions now occurring in so many of the underdeveloped countries, Malthus's simple model of an enormous power of increase opposed by various counteracting forces is perhaps both necessary and sufficient. For it can bring out that, in these countries, the application of modern medical knowledge is weakening the positive check, while nothing is occurring to produce a proportionate strengthening of the preventive check.

Indeed, in his combination of probable economic and sociological (58, pp. 23–5) hypotheses with attempts to verify by statistical induction, Malthus's methods form a model, unfortunately not followed by subsequent generations of economists.

The practical importance of considering ability no less than willingness as factors in the birth-rate is that so many authorities believe willingness to control births will arise automatically as standards of living rise and families "aspire" to yet higher standards. Till then they see no point in worrying about spreading knowledge of birth control and studying its acceptability. Unfortunately in many underdeveloped and all too slowly developing countries standards of living may never rise and few have shown, up to the present, much evidence of any spread in "aspiration" effect. Though few precedents existed then in developed, in some underdeveloped countries efforts have been actively encouraged by the State-government, to set up family-planning clinics, or otherwise to teach "know-how", to sterilize or even, as in Japan, to allow abortion. Elsewhere only a few signs have appeared currently of lowered country-wide birth-rates. Other factors besides higher incomes were probably necessary in the past experience of countries now developed.

Allocating points to different occupations for likely degrees of ignorance, low "informability", and women's status, as well as lower income, it became evident to me that, in the England of the early twentieth century, access to and acceptability of knowledge strongly influenced the size of families. Doctors, teachers, cotton operatives, and other urban factory workers had families much smaller (58, Table C) than miners or farmers living in relative isolation.

Other surveys have found other limits to know-how. Extreme poverty and grinding toil induce ignorance and fecklessness, and even moderate poverty will keep up the birth-rate because of the expense of appliances and chemicals, and the lack of privacy in inadequate housing. Lella Florence (56, p. 199) has shown the extent of the distaste of wives, rich or poor, for pre-pill birth-control methods. Know-how, not in itself technically difficult to master, must thus in practice be supported by enabling facilities and acceptability.

High production, but low reproduction, is the main formula for raising standards of living. Research is continuing, looking for the most suitable appliances, technologically, for high yet economic *production* in underdeveloped countries where capital is scarce and labour plentiful. So also, research and laboratory and clinical testing are beginning (225, *passim*) for a reliable yet accessible and acceptable method of lowering *reproduction*. The contraceptive pill received in 1960 its first European clinical testing in Birmingham, but with developments in plastic devices, more and even simpler and cheaper foolproof methods have been invented. However, the birth-control leg of the tripod, so necessary if industry is to lead to higher standards of living, is not likely to be firmly and widely established if the censorship continues such as that imposed on early discussion at the United Nations. In that case, the return likely to be obtained from international aid toward development is just more and more people at the old level of bare subsistence.

5. SUMMARY OF FEARS AND HOPES FOR STANDARDS OF LIVING

To sum up the practical possibilities and sociological limits to rising standards of living in the underdeveloped countries, the grounds for optimism may first be stated. They apply either to some particular countries or fairly generally.

Several underdeveloped countries have particular resources —comparative advantages—as the basis of trade: minerals such as oil or iron ore; scenery, a winter climate or artefacts to attract the tourists; or harbours to facilitate trading. Several are large enough to form a market sufficient for mass-production. All, or nearly all, underdeveloped countries have a tropical or sub-tropical climate where products, such as coffee, tea, cocoa, and cotton, can be grown, which are far more costly or even impossible to grow in developed countries, and have a plentiful labour supply that can be trained. Moreover, the know-how for higher production, if not for more equal distribution and lower birth-rates, which has only gradually been acquired by developed countries, could, some think, be rapidly transferred. Know-how for equalizing wealth is specially important where particular resources exist, since, like oil, they may at present be in only a few hands.

Grounds for pessimism are also particular and general. Several underdeveloped countries form only a small market, and have few minerals or convenient harbours, or little natural scenery or few artefacts to attract the tourist. And all, or nearly all, suffer from the violent price fluctuations of primary products and find export earnings growing slower than the necessary import demand for capital goods. Sociological obstacles (including political and psychological) block the effective adoption of productive, equalizing, and birth-controlling know-how. And even if productivity rises, this is likely to be achieved by a lower level of employment. The bulk of the effort must come from within, and even considerable external aid may fail to pump-prime their trade. Grounds for pessimism seem to me to prevail for most of the underdeveloped countries.

A summary of the practical feasibility of and yet sociological limits to rising standards of living must stress the present abject poverty of underdeveloped countries and the vicious circle from poverty to poverty. It can be represented graphically (p. 222).

The practical question is where to break the chain of events in the circle. If certain sociological traditions are broken, as they are being broken by contacts with the developed world, some writers believe that saving and initiative may eventually

appear automatically, indeed, that they are already appearing
and raising productivity; and that with rising productivity and
standards of living birth control, too, will appear automatically.
But this process, if it occurs at all, will be slow and probably
only sporadic; and meanwhile the highly successful death control will most likely overwhelm any possibility of a rise in pro-
duct-a-head of total population.

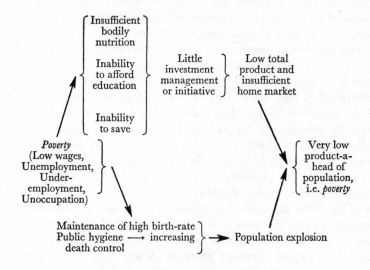

The most hopeful solution is an attack on several fronts.
Productivity must be raised by better nutrition and by education, saving increased by checking any consumption which is
unnecessary to higher productivity, and at the same time a
check put on birth-rates. One of the unfortunate features of
the birth-control controversy is the claim that raising productivity is to be preferred to checking population. The two are,
however, not alternatives, but, if a high standard of living is
to be achieved, are both essential in coping with the otherwise
desperate situation, together with the third leg of the tripod—
equalization of incomes. This is the point of my tripod meta-
phor. Each leg is required if the tripod is not to topple over.

The several fronts to be attacked are not, however, equally
vulnerable. The most tractable front is education, since mainly
finance and the planning of a useful type of education of a

limited number of people are required. This, of course, may seem a tall enough order. But the barriers against education are weak compared to those checking payments high enough to assure nutrition for all and yet checking unnecessary consumption. Since the co-operation of all couples is involved, the strongest barriers of all are those which stop birth control matching the existing death control. In only a few countries, probably, can this all-front attack be successful with the finite means at the disposal of the countries able and willing to provide aid. As Ritchie Calder has said (31), the growth of population makes planning aid "like running up the down escalator". He substantiates his simile—

In the decade which followed President Truman's call for a bold new policy, some $30,000,000,000 went into the 100 countries and territories we call "underdeveloped"; that is, from all sources —multilateral, and bilateral and private investment. The over-all effect was to raise the per capita income from $90 to $100— an average increase of a dollar a year during the decade. The annual income grew at the rate of 3 per cent but their population grew at the rate of 2 per cent per year.

A real take-off into sufficiency does not, at this rate of progress, appear likely in many underdeveloped countries. The prime-pumping success of Marshall Aid supplied to the developed countries of Europe in 1947 is not being repeated. A practical example—a real object lesson—is the most effective persuader. Economic aid on any large enough scale to be effective may have to be confined to a few key countries that show some hope of co-operating—for their own benefit—in the attack *on all fronts*.

Underdeveloped countries differ widely in their chances of effective development. Unfortunately, many of the countries which have the particular economic advantages of climate and mineral resources are countries where the sociological obstacles to education, saving, income equalization, and birth control are strong. Since the obstacles to birth control and legal abortion appear the strongest, the underdeveloped countries likely to prove the most effective object lesson in raising standards of living by an all-front attack are those whose birth-rates are already falling. Among these are Japan, with a fall in crude birth-rates per thousand from 28·2 in 1950 to 16·8 in 1961 and

in the same period, Israel, with a fall from 34·7 to 24·9, and
Puerto Rico, with a fall from 39·0 to 31·0.

Obviously more research is called for, if the balance of
economic and sociological forces is to be correctly assessed that
will raise standards of living. My final chapter sets out practical
policies for development and the methods and fields of research
that have proved, and are likely to prove, fruitful.

SOCIAL RESEARCH FOR INDUSTRIAL
DEVELOPMENT

1. THE NEED FOR SOCIOLOGY IN DEVELOPMENT

THE social sciences are, by definition, sciences about society, that is, about groups of persons, or relations between them, not about single isolated individuals. Social psychologists and social anthropologists certainly draw this distinction in segregating themselves from *individual* psychologists and anthropologists; and a committee of the British Association for the Advancement of Science (22), basing conclusions in 1944 on the practice of the Royal Society, met no demarcation dispute. The recognized *natural* sciences were found to investigate "those attributes of man which are common to other species. . . . They do not deal with . . . facts arising from the contact of man with man."

The sciences that do deal with the "contact of man with man" are, like the natural sciences, many in number; though for brevity but not to imply restrictions this book bears only the two titles: economics and sociology.

Of all the social sciences, economics has in the twentieth century attained the greatest systematization. This does not mean that economists are agreed on the definition of their science. Between those who focus on exchange and those who, like Lord Robbins, focus on scarcity, Cairncross (30, p. 8) offers a "compromise" definition—

> Economics is a social science studying how people attempt to accommodate scarcity to their wants and how these attempts interact through exchange.

He brings in the scarcity that Lord Robbins has favoured because it "is more fundamental than exchange". But it is too fundamental. Lord Robbins considered economics "the study of human behaviour as a relationship between ends and scarce means which have alternative uses". This definition could include the study of almost all rational action by human beings—in politics, the arts, games, or military strategy and tactics. Scarcity is certainly one very critical problem in economics, as we have learned when observing the less-affluent countries with natural resources insufficient for their population. But scarcity, as R. L. Smyth has pointed out (174), is not the only economic problem, and in an affluent society not a very obvious one.

When the classical textbooks of economics are examined they will in fact be found to centre upon terms of exchange in a market, that is, upon the quantities exchanged of goods, services, money, titles to money, and factors of production, and upon the prices and costs at which these quantities change hands, thus forming people's incomes.

These terms may appear (59, pp. 90–4) on any one of three levels, monetary, physical, or as Marshall's "real costs" psychological. The monetary terms are the easiest to measure, and *economic* is frequently defined, for instance by Pigou in *The Economics of Welfare* (149, p. 11), as the part "that can be brought directly or indirectly into relation with the measuring-rod of money".

The national income is the point from which most modern textbooks start out—a macro- rather than a micro-economic approach—thus reviving Adam Smith's concern with the *Wealth of Nations*. This national income from which the calculation of standards of living derives, is the sum of all incomes derived from values exchanged. It excludes goods and services not exchanged and hence all gifts.

Cairncross (30, pp. 7–8) is clear that in societies where there is no exchange there is no economics. Primitive communities, before any development has taken place, are such societies, and it is significant that all their activities—industrial, family, religious—are studied by the social anthropologist. These communities do not, in fact, differentiate their economic from any other part of their social life. In Table XVIII social anthropology is thus placed above and across the social sciences such as economics and politics, studying later and more differentiated societies.

In developed societies exchanging, though a very distinct part of life, is not the whole of social life or even the whole of industry, and the coupling of sociology with economics in the title of this book is meant to indicate the co-existence of many other socially important factors in the world of industry. Sociology, as said already, is used broadly to refer to all the social sciences, excluding only economics. The exclusion is not a matter of principle, and certainly there should be a supersociology covering all the social sciences. But it is a matter of convenience to distinguish economics and sociology, both because economics is a fairly well-defined discipline and because the sociology of industry has hitherto been sadly neglected.

Industrial development has been accepted mainly as an economic phenomenon, and the nine measurable trends in development which were traced in the first chapter ending with higher incomes-a-head are mostly economic. Yet, in analysing the cause and limits of industrial development, we have repeatedly come up against social relationships, "contacts of man with man" that are not economic. It will be useful to bring together and review chapter by chapter the sorts of contacts they proved to be.

Many of the economic trends adumbrated in the first chapter had prominent sociological aspects, particularly urbanization, the emergence of a management staff, large organizations, and their government by the management. And few trends ran uninterrupted. Economic systems have to face up in fact to twists and changes in the conditions of supply and demand—conditions that are partly technological, but partly psychological or sociological and are rooted in the changing patterns of consumption.

The second chapter, dealing with the mobilization and mobility required for adaptation to the trends in development, was shot through with necessary references to sociology. Full mobilization of economies was found checked by the family roles and conventions restricting women's industrial occupation, not to mention the facts of life—in short, biology. Social biology, though from 1930 to 1937 recognized by the chair at the London School of Economics held by Professor Lancelot Hogben, is now merged in demography dealing with the population of individuals grouped by sex, age, locality, marital status, social class, and so on, all of them factors that affect the economics of labour in industry. Social class was found a particularly strong obstacle to the fulfilment of the economist's hypothesis of mobility by differential net advantage—an obstacle recognized in his "non-competing groups". And his conception of net advantages itself recognized many psychological motives other than differential wages, security and prospects, for instance, status, independence, respectability, and sociability. Sociological traditions and attitudes were found opposing adjustment to economic trends strongly enough to be recognized by economists as "friction" or a "lag".

Chapter III, on industrial location, brought in the geography of human and natural resources and was largely concerned with measuring the extent and causes—the social ecology—of urbanization. The modern conurbations are mainly economic in origin, but the problems of the town and country pattern which they raise have greatly exercised sociologists, notably Lewis Mumford. Chapter IV dealt directly with the size of organized associations such as the industrial plant and firm and with the motives, if any, of an entrepreneur or a salaried manager for expansion. Indirectly, psychological problems of morale and motivation arise when labour is employed in large numbers within one organization and the relative strength of economic and other incentives to productivity comes into question. Here, again, though factories and firms are economic in origin, famous contributions to the understanding of their functioning have been made by industrial psychologists, sociologists, and anthropologists, such as Elton Mayo.

The title of Chapter V was the economics and sociology of industrial government. Appeal to sociology, particularly the political science branch, was shown to be necessary when the unit of organization was large and dominant in a market, required a division of labour in financing and ruling it, and, so often, exhibited conflicting interests among its rulers.

Chapters VI and VII dealt with the underdeveloped countries, and in their investigation the distinctive approach and mutual help of economics and sociology was made explicit. Chapter VI concentrated on the economic aspect; the fitting of industries and the tourist trade to natural and human resources so as to produce, by trading, maximum national income. Chapter VII concentrated on the sociological limits to this economic development. Limits were set, not only on the aggregate of income, but on its stability and equal distribution, and on the average per head of population. The limits include traditional attitudes and values, and also customs and taboos affecting the will and ability to work, save, think, or plan. They have been laid bare by social anthropologists and have emphatically to be taken into account when predicting future development. Limits were also found to be set by forms of political government and by the small size of many states, affecting the size of the market.

2. TYPES OF SOCIAL SCIENCES REQUIRED

References to social relationships beyond economics have been found necessary in the course of this book for elucidating the events of industrial development. Their study will be seen, when analysed, to fall into two main categories. In the one are studies of groupings of persons in families, cities, factories, firms, companies, trade unions, and states; in the other are studies of the behaviour, activities, performance, attitudes, beliefs, motives, and their own values, of these groups. Using Talcott Parsons's words (147, *passim*) one may, for short, distinguish the study of actors and that of their acts.

Since the focus of economics is the act of exchanging and the ensuing values, and performance in production, consumption, and distribution of exchangeable goods and services, the second category—social behaviour—is its main field of interest. Most textbooks in fact deal even less than Marshall's *Principles of Economics* (where five chapters (129, Chapters VIII–XII) are devoted to Industrial Organization) with the nature of the actual groups engaged in exchange activities.

An objective test of the main interest of any science is to look at the index of its standard textbooks and to rank the number of references of the different words. If, for economics, we pick Cairncross's *Introduction to Economics* (30), the fourteen words in the index with the greatest number (eight or more) of subheads carrying references are: Money, 18; Costs, Margin (and Marginal), 17; Wages, 16; Unemployment, Capital, 15;

Profit, 12; Firm, Banks, Monopoly, Trade, 11; Rent, Market, 9; Prices, 8. If, for sociology, we pick McIver and Page's *Society* (135), the fourteen words in the index with the greatest number (again eight or more) of subheads carrying references are: Class, 28; Culture (and Cultural), 26; the State, 20; the Family, 18; Society, 17; Association, Environment, 16; Community, 15; Technology, 14; City (or Town), 12; Heredity, 11, Attitudes, Customs, 10; Authority, 8.

It is clear that the interests of the two main social sciences are very different. Economics is interested chiefly in money and money payments in exchange for things: costs, wages, profit, rent; and in the relation of man to his paid work or its absence—unemployment. And if we concentrate on *industrial* economics we find the same types of interest. Taking a period of years, articles in the *Journal of Industrial Economics* concerned with costs and prices outnumbered those concerned with structure three to one. Sociology, on the other hand, is interested in groups of persons: class, the State, the family, society, associations, communities, the city. Besides motivation (as in the top right-hand box of Table XVIII) the "concern" of sociology has been defined by Parker in a recent work by four industrial sociologists (233, p. 22) as "groups and social processes".

Nevertheless, when all the social sciences are surveyed, certain interests emerge that are common to them all, or to most of them. Among the most frequent references in economics, for instance, were those to *firms*, *banks*, and *markets*. These are all groups of persons, the main interest of sociology. And among the most frequent references in sociology several were not groups so much as the system of acts, thoughts, powers, or behaviour of groups; *technology*, *attitudes*, *authority*, *customs*. This overlapping of interests is an important point in the argument for the greater integration to be urged later.

The social science most clearly defined, next to economics, is political science when it is separated from the ethics of political philosophy. It has the same concern as economics with behaviour, but is also concerned with the behaving groups, and the emphasis is not concentrated on behaviour. Instead of exchange, the behaviour studied by Machiavelli and Hobbes was the exercise of control, of influence, and, more formally, of power: "all politics", writes Catlin (35, p. 79), "is, by its nature, power politics". But the emphasis, particularly if the work of Stubbs and Maitland and other constitutional lawyers be included, is as much on the groups exercising power, particularly the State, as on the terms of power—on actors, as on acts. Catlin devotes two main chapters to the "Power Hypothesis" and "Freedom and Authority"; and two to the "Forms of Government; Democracy and Tyranny" and "Aristocracy and Oligarchy." Laski, in his *Grammar of Politics* (1925), has two parts: one dealing with sovereignty, rights, liberty and equality, property, and authority; the other with institutions, the judicial process, and international organization. Henry Sidgwick wrote in the first chapter of his *Elements of Politics* (1891) the inquiry "has two main divisions (1) one relating to the Work or Functions of Government, and (2) the other to its Structure or Constitution".

This equal emphasis on structure, actors, forms and institutions of government, as on functions, acts, and behaviour is understandable, since the procedure and organization of groups armed with compulsory power are more important than those of small economic groups voluntarily exchanging goods and services and usually in competition. Where competition is displaced by oligopoly or monopoly of large firms, however, economists should certainly pay more attention to the nature of the groups exercising this economic power.

Economics and political science thus both study, though with different emphasis, behaviour and the behaving groups and there emerges a fourfold division of inquiry into (1) political behaviour, (2) economic behaviour, (3) political groups, and (4) economic groups. These cross-divisions are shown as four areas numbered 1 to 4 at the core of Table XVIII. Their position is irrespective of any theory and indicates, vertically, the established conventional division between the two parts, structural and functional, of political science and between economic behaviour and economic organization. The position in the table also indicates, horizontally, the less conventional affinity between political and economic behaviour and between political and economic structure. Catlin (35, pp. 144 and 148) has stressed in at least two of his propositions the analogy between the two types of behaviour. "Democracy conforms, in theory, to the type of a consumers' market, with freedom maximized"; the "law of the

R

(political) market . . . that all security involves an exchange of some general freedom in return for some security which we value more as assuring a particular liberty to realize what we wish".

The affinity with political structure and the use of terms and conceptions of political science has already (V, §3) been noted in studying large-scale industrial organizations' delegation of power (amounting often to a federal, even a confederate constitution), their use of cabinets and committees such as the Board of Directors, and their methods of appointment and dismissal, of promotion and demotion, and of pecuniary and other incentives to work and to stay within the organization. In both areas the question arises of the degree of member "commitment", including the cohesion of an organization, measured by the turnover of its members and of the degree of apathy measured in politics by the percentage of constituents polling, in industry by absenteeism. It is significant of their lack of interest in power that company shareholders have a high turnover and that absenteeism at their general meeting is usually well over 99 per cent.

Political science is, in fact, often extended to include, in an L-shaped area, box (4) in Table XVIII as well as boxes (1) and (3). Catlin, for instance (35, p. 43), considers "the study of trade-union structure and of personnel management essentially political in character". The area (2) which economics analyses is thus quite restricted and even so, part of it, 2x, is studied by industrial psychology. Realistic economics, however, often extends to areas (4), (6) and (10). These quasi-political and psychological questions are becoming more and more important as economic organizations grow. What goes on inside the large organization overshadows the unorganized market forces acting within the industry. Galbraith (219) has put this point strongly, but its validity depends on the particular industry's structure. A high concentration ratio is likely to make it more valid than a low. As we know, many manufacturing industries have a low market concentration and, still more so, the whole growing sector of services which are less capital-intensive and less subject to economies of scale than manufacturing.

Where concentration is high the outstanding question is *who*, within the firm, makes the top decisions as to what to make and in what amounts, at what price and by what investment, and why. Political science, which has dealt with similar problems of who? by what acts? and why? in connexion with State government, is perhaps a more appropriate discipline than economics to elucidate the relationships and development within large industrial organization.

TABLE XVIII

AREAS OF THE SOCIAL SCIENCES

UNDER-DEVELOPED AND UNDIFFERENTIATED COUNTRIES	Archaeology; Social Anthropology; General History; Human Geography; Ecology		
Differentiation	Power Sanction (Political Science Column)	Exchange Sanction (Economics Column)	Tradition and Other Sanctions (Sociological Column)
DEVELOPED AND DIFFERENTIATED COUNTRIES A: Own values and behaviour	(1) Relation of state government and the individual Authority and liberty Bargaining power "Command and reply" analysis	(2) Terms of exchange of goods, services and factors of production (value and distribution) (2x) Incentives to work, move, save, risk "Demand and supply" analysis	(7) Traditions Social codes Crime Religious practices (7x) Attitudes, motivation
B: Group structure and government 1. Associations (a) Close	(3) Legislature, and other "bodies" The state constitution		(8) Church congregations Clubs
		(4) Factories	
(b) Scattered	Political parties The electorate	Trade unions Companies or other firms	Church organization
2. Communities a) Close	(5) Pressure groups	(6) Industrial conurbations and localizations Informal small factory groups	(9) The family Small groups
(b) Scattered		(10) Industrial and occupational activity-structure Markets	Social Classes (11) Population, vital statistics and age grouping

Sciences for separate Areas in Developed and Differentiated Countries
(1), (3), (4)?, and (5) Political Science
(2), (4)?, (6)?, and (10) Economics; Sub-area 2x, Industrial Psychology
(6) Industrial Sociology
(7), (8), and (9) Sociology
Sub-area 7x, Social Psychology
(11) Demography or Social Biology

Even when the organization and exercise of power and control are added to exchanging, they do not constitute the whole of man's industrial life and cannot wholly explain or foretell the course of development. Table XVIII allows room, therefore, at its foot and in a third column for groupings (and their

types of behaviour) other than political and economic—for
unorganized groups which must be studied in forecasting the
industrial future, and in planning realistically.

Before development and differentiation start it is hard, as
already said, to distinguish economic, political, or other human
activities, and social anthropology has evolved, to study primitive man's undifferentiated social life as a whole. Here the
sanction for acts is often neither power nor exchange but tradition and social duty. As Firth (51, pp. 142–3) puts it, "powerful
incentives to work lie in the individual's membership of a
social group". Though "in the long run contributions and rewards may be assumed to even out", . . . "in the short run it is
the impact of the social obligation that is most marked, the
frequent rendering of the service with no apparent equivalent
return".

Development is a dynamic process and its study extends
from the primitive to the present. One task of history is to
connect the primitive with the developed society and to follow
development through from the past in each or in all of the
activities involved. While anthropology and archaeology are
put at the head of Table XVIII as studying the past, general
history and ecology are placed with geography in the next row
as studying past and present, near and far.

For the later stages of development, sociologists, though they
differ in their thinking, agree, as mentioned earlier (p. 25), in
distinguishing two types of group, the *association* expressly organized for the pursuit of an interest or group of interests in common
and the *community*, like a family or a town, whose members
(135, pp. 8–15) "live together in such a way that they share not
this or that particular interest but the basic conditions of a
common life". Members of these communities may live close
together, as in cities, or, to widen the concept, may be more or
less scattered, as a market. Political science, like economics, is
clearly more interested in organized association than in
communities. But other social sciences have grown up (such as
industrial psychology and industrial sociology) to explore the
unorganized *communities*.

A few economists and sociologists have joined with geographers and demographers to inquire, as related in Chapter
III, into the large-scale communities resulting from industrial

urbanization, known in America as metropolitan areas, and more expressively in Britain as conurbations. No recognized name has yet been conferred upon this study of the (external) relation of industry to place, though a widely conceived "human ecology" might fit. On the other hand, the terms *industrial psychology* and *industrial sociology* have been coined to identify studies exploring the internal functioning of industrial production. At present this field of exploration has largely been confined to one factor of production—labour.

Industrial psychology sprang to life and flourished during and after the First World War and dealt with the selection of workers for jobs and the reactions of individual workers to the long hours that then prevailed and to various physical working conditions and incentives. It was quite as much industrial physiology as psychology. The switch to industrial sociology came when factory hours were reduced to a normal forty-eight-hour week and when Elton Mayo (133) drew attention to the importance of studying informal face-to-face *groups* rather than a rabble of unrelated individual workers. Some of these groups had a scale of values, described earlier (IV, §8), in ludicrous contrast to the management values. Industrial sociology, like psychology, still concentrated on the obstacles presented by *labour* to efficient production.

It is now time that psychological and sociological inquiries turned to the obstacles checking the factors of production, other than labour, in their co-operation to supply the individual and the corporate consumers' demands; obstacles checking effective organization, management, investment and saving, risk-taking and risk-bearing. Psychology must also be brought in to analyse the present demands of the consumer and his change in demands that makes labour mobility so necessary, and to forecast future demands. Economists stimulated by Keynes have been constructing their own models of "consumption-functions" assuming (118, pp. 343–8) an automatic, purely economic, relation between the proportion consumed or saved and total income. This certainly requires modification by sociologists. Veblen (191) with his conception of conspicuous consumption had already stressed the importance of emulation of families with higher by families with lower incomes, and "keeping up with the Joneses" in affluent, highly developed, countries has its counterpart in the peoples of the underdeveloped wanting to keep up with people in the developed countries—in the "demonstration effect" stressed by Nurkse (145, pp. 62–5).

Moving down Table XVIII from behaviour to structure and government, the groups and societies involved in industry present a bewildering variety; but they have analogues already being studied in other than economic walks of life. At one end of the scale are those "associations" which may be distinguished as *bodies* where people are together in close proximity, for instance a factory, and under more or less ordered discipline with rules of procedure and a drill. At the other end of the scale are loose, imperfect, communities such as the market, varying in membership from day to day according to variations in prices and consumers' tastes and such, too, as an industry itself, containing factories varying in their integration or specialization and with different degrees of localization. The plants that are members of the same industry may have no formal relations unless there are trade associations or agreements for restrictive (or other) practices. Between these extremes of coherence and incoherence comes the firm, often owning several plants, sometimes in different industries, and also trade unions, both of them in scattered locations but both with organized government. Both have close affinities in structure with the State government, on which political science concentrates. The Webbs' classic study of trade unions, *Industrial Democracy*, is divided, in fact, into the two parts that are standard in political science: structure and function.

The distinction drawn between behaviour and structure, whether political or economic, is of considerable practical importance because the tools of research used upon each facet are very different, and workers using different tools are inclined to draw apart instead of combining to see industry and industrial development whole. In thinking out probable behaviour, the economist uses cost and demand curves to show how the cost of production and the demand-price might vary with amounts produced or demanded. On the other hand, social *structure* is probably understood most easily by starting out with organization charts or with some kind of formal pattern or matrix. These forms can show graphically, by spacing of area and mutual position, how persons or groups of persons (communities, boards, general meetings) are subordinate, co-ordinate, or superordinate to one another inside a hierarchy or may overlap, or may act outside the hierarchy.

In my *Logic of British and American Industry* (72, pp. 56–7) I found it useful to picture the interrelations of lines of product or processes with plants and with the firms owning those plants by patterns of structures showing squares for plants, circles for the firms, and letters for the lines. To represent the government of a firm that is a company, we found (Chapter V) the hour-glass a more realistic pattern than just a circle. The whole hour-glass may further be pictured with many other hour-glasses of various sizes as forming industries each placed in a market. This anatomical model of structures within structures should then make clear one of the main complications in the use of sociological terms such as *function*. The function of a company in the external market may be to make shoes, but inside the company the function of the annual shareholders' meeting is to elect directors, and the function of the directors, besides appointing managers, includes making a profit and declaring a dividend for the shareholders. In short, the function of a company is very different if it is a relation between the company and its consumers in the market *outside* the company, or between the shareholders and directors or the manager and workers *inside* the company, or between the directors and the managers of its separate factories. Economists contrast the external economies of a large-scale industry with the internal economies of a large firm *or* large plant (*above* p. 104). But practical decision-makers wanting to enlarge their business would dearly like to know whether it is in enlarging existing plants or in building more of the same size that the economies will arise.

The external functions of subgroups like plants are many of them the internal functions or functioning of a superordinate, such as a multi-plant form. Functions cannot in fact be usefully discussed without a realization of the complex structure often involved, and I have consistently urged (72, pp. 1–4) the importance to economists of some structural approach—putting the question *who* as well as how and why. Economists are too prone to discuss scale, demand, supply, savings investment, without specifying whose scale; or who are the demanders, suppliers, and investors and savers, and even whether they are organizations (possibly with conflicting interests within them) or, as so often assumed, unorganized individuals. This abstraction becomes ridiculous when incentives or mobility are discussed without reference to whom incentives are addressed or who is supposed to be moving, or even whether it is everybody or just a sufficient few. And when economists do make a reference to the actual persons involved, quoting perhaps Lord Keynes's view that "the decisions which determine savings and investment respectively are made by different people" (108, p. 175), they do not always take account of all the facts. In every year from 1950 to 1960, though not in 1961–2, British company savings considerably exceeded personal savings (in five of the years they were over double), and as we saw (V, §3), company directors decide *both* how much to save by ploughing back profit and also how much capital to invest. Here in inquiring what structures or organs perform what functions the anatomical chart is particularly apt. An example is the hierarchy of cities presented in Table IX to answer the question in what functions if any do cities of various sizes specialize.

3. INDUCTION, ISOLATION, AND INDICATION

The last two sections have stressed the need for sociology in observing "in the round" industrial development and have described the parts which economics and each of the other social sciences, such as political science and social psychology, can most effectively play. In this and the next sections we shall sum up briefly the methods by which economics and sociology in its various branches have reached conclusions as exact as possible, particularly conclusions of practical value.

In primitive societies where taboo and custom prevail no one does what is "not done". But in developing or developed societies, in order to be exact in summing up so variable an element as human behaviour and organization, methods must, wherever possible, be statistical. Thanks to a spate of manuals, I need no longer explain, as I had to do in 1929 (60, Chapters V–IX), the elementary measures whereby statistics tries to sum up frequency distributions by averages and deviations, and to find correlations and measures of their reliability or uncertainty. On the contrary, the danger is of too slick a use of statistical measures such as (79, pp. 29–31) striking an average size of plants of any industry when there is in fact no representative typical size.

To avoid thus riding "smooth-shod" over the facts and riding, too, into pitfalls, certain rules of procedure are needed for pursuing industrial development (to practical purposes) and not just describing the facts. Following the distinction in the Cambridge Economics Tripos, when first set up, between Analytical and Realistic papers, these procedures might be referred to by three Rs, as rubrics for realistic research. The definition in basic English of realistic as "thinking in a way which takes the facts into account" is certainly the type of research required. But we will be more specific as applied to Industry and help the reader memorize the procedures as the five Is: induction, isolation, indication, integration, and interpretation. The last two procedures are closely related, and the first three (now to be discussed under A, B, and C) are part of the normal method of research used by the Natural Sciences.

(A) Induction refers to the attempt "empirically" to discover probable general regularities or laws from the observation of the available facts, not from presumptions. As a heading, I prefer "induction" to empirical because, to quote the *Concise Oxford Dictionary*, empirical carries the sense of "relying solely on experiment; quack". Facts are observed and recorded not usually at random but to test some working hypothesis. Russell contrasts an hypothesis (169, p. 194) with a theory. "The investigator believes the theory, whereas he only thinks the hypothesis sufficiently plausible to be worth testing." *Some* studies claim to be realistic merely if their propositions can be illustrated from a few actual cases, but a true test must take account comprehensively of *all* cases covered by the hypothesis or else a truly representative sample of them.

Most so-called economic laws are theories and were not discovered by observation of facts, but by deduction from empirically untested and usually untestable, "unfalsifiable" assumptions. As Hutchison puts it (99, pp. 63–4)—

> The prevailing tendency to call propositions of pure theory "laws" is misleading and inappropriate, and appears to be a survival from eighteenth-century rationalist philosophy and theology. . . . We suggest that the term law should be reserved only for

those empirical generalizations such as Pareto's or Gresham's law or the law of diminishing returns or diminishing marginal utility. It is such laws as these that it is the central object of science to discover.

To the empirical generalizations cited by Hutchison should perhaps be added, as of interest to industrial development, the classical Law of Increasing Return in manufactures (but emphatically not the short-run U-shaped "law" of diminishing return). Since, to quote Dr. J. N. Keynes (107, p. 206), Malthus, in the second and later editions of his *Essay*, pursues an inductive method of inquiry and his reasoning is directly based on historical and statistical data, we can add Malthus's law of population. Engel's Law, confirmed repeatedly, affecting the market for food products, may also be added, and Zipf's Law (III, §3) particularly affecting urbanization and the relative size of transport, marketing, and industrial centres. Though needing further confirmation besides the British experience of 1930–5 and 1951 and that of the United States of 1929 and 1941–5 (69 and 79) and the Italian of 1951 (26), laws might emerge out of the frequent identity, described in Chapters III and IV, of industries with larger sizes of plant and industries with (*a*) the more intensive capitalization and (*b*) the higher localization of industries. Modern econometrics may well be on the eve of inducing *wide* generalizations on industrial economics, and certainly H. L. Moore in his *Laws of Wages* and *Synthetic Economics* and (Senator) Paul Douglas, of Cobb–Douglas formula fame, may be counted as pioneers. Empirically discovered laws are formed from the less general to the more general and can, therefore, only be expected slowly to emerge.

In addition to laws that state more or less uniform "relationships", sequences can be empirically discovered and measured as the trends listed in our first chapter. The less general relationships called *effects* could also be empirically tested. They are special cases, and often special exceptions to a general proposition whether it is an empirical law or not. The best known is the *Ricardo Effect* that (155, Chapter XXXI) "every rise of wages will have a tendency to determine the saved capital in a greater proportion than before to the employment of machinery. Machinery and labour are in constant competition, and the former can frequently not be employed until labour rises."

This special application of the "principle of substitution" has recently been empirically tested and verified by Seymour Melman (138).

Again, the "effect" attributed by Marshall (129, III, vi, 4) to Sir R. Giffen, that a rise in the price of bread may result in more bread being consumed by the poor because they are forced by the rise "to curtail their consumption of meat and the more expensive farinaceous foods" is definitely an *exception* to the general proposition that a rise in price diminishes the demand. The Sargant Effect (129, IV, vii, 9) is an exception to the general proposition that a rise in the price of anything increases its supply. When only a fixed amount of interest is wanted, then if the rate of interest is raised, not more, but less is saved. When applied to labour the Sargant Effect has often been demonstrated. Where labourers want only a fixed income, then the "effect" is that the greater the rate of wages per piece or per hour, the less the pieces made or the hours worked—the higher in fact, as shown, among others, by Vernon (70, p. 99), the absenteeism. Again, the Florence Effect described earlier is an empirically discovered exception to the general empirical law that the more concentrated the location of an industry, the larger its plants. The special circumstance associated with this effect is the existence of a large town or conurbation in which medium or small plants of an industry are often found highly localized.

Few empirical laws or effects have been worked out, largely, perhaps, because of the prestige attached within the economics establishment to the propositions of pure theory. As Hutchison writes (99, p. 60), "empirical laws are obviously regarded as inferior and unsatisfactory and even denied the dignity of the term law altogether".

In his Valedictory Address to the London School of Economics (17, pp. 464–5) Lord Beveridge drew attention to the strange reactions of leading economists to Lord Keynes's "General Theory" when (109) it appeared in 1936—

> It is the duty of the propounder of every new theory, if he has not himself the equipment for observation, to indicate where verification of his theory is to be sought in facts—what may be expected to happen or to have happened if his theory is true, what will not happen if it is false.

That is the demand that would be made of the propounder of a new theory in every natural science. It is not the demand that has been made of Mr. Keynes by his fellow economists. I have read with some care . . . the reviews of Mr. Keynes' book in the three leading organs of economics in the English speaking world—the *Economic Journal*, *Economica*, and the *Quarterly Journal of Economics*. Each review is written by an acknowledged leader among professional economists. None of them takes the point that the truth or falsehood of Mr. Keynes' theory cannot be established except by appeal to facts; none of them tests it by facts himself. (The only reference (in all three reviews) to observation of facts as having any bearing on the subject under discussion appears to be a single sentence ending Part I of Mr. Knight's review.) The distinguishing mark of economic science, as illustrated by this debate, is that it is a science in which verification of generalizations by reference to facts is neglected as irrelevant.

The very assumptions from which pure theory deduces its propositions (instead of inducing them from facts) are coming more and more into question. As Kuznets puts it (112), "much of the work of economists in the field of economic growth suffers from excessive timidity in attempting empirical coverage, with an almost insufferable boldness in drawing unlimited generalizations from a mere handful of facts". Marshall himself thought (129, Appendix B) economists argued as though all mankind had the same habits of mind as city men, and since his day psychologists and sociologists, not to mention political scientists like Graham Wallas (197), have shown most of mankind most of the time to be acting irrationally. Even top industrial managers, according to Katona (103), we may recall (IV, §7), cannot be assumed to aim at maximum profit. Yet, following the synthesis I put forward in Chapter II, man is not completely irrational and it is up to realistic economics and sociology to find his degree of rationality—the amount of Economic Man within him.

(B) With observation and hypothesis, Russell (169, p. 194) joins experiment, and he describes experiment as differing from observation by deliberate control of conditions or isolation of factors. Like natural scientists, social scientists are confronted by multiple causation, but disclaim experiment on the effects of one isolated factor at a time as in a laboratory. In the design of their research they can, however, select times, places, or persons where the factors they are studying are isolated from other disturbing factors, or they can study the effect of changing one isolated condition at a time, as, for instance, methods (IV, §9) of wage-payment on the same group of persons, at the same job. This is often feasible in a factory, where conditions generally are standardized.

Many fallacies or pitfalls have to be avoided that are due to neglect of isolation, and in my *Statistical Method* (60, pp. 205, 209) I gave an example each of fallacies of "mal-selection" and of "mal-control", one rather obvious, the other less so, but often committed—

> Some health resorts have higher death-rates than industrial districts. The moribund tend to go to health resorts and before condemning these health resorts as fraudulent, one should *select* invalids, if possible of similar degree of invalidity, and find whether they do not die off at a more rapid rate in industrial purlieus.

> If persons know they are being experimented with they may, according to circumstances, be inordinately enthusiastic, sullen or self-conscious, and may thus render generalization and application to conditions of ordinary life impossible. Though it sounds the right and noble thing to do and is generally advocated, it is for this reason unscientific to "enlist the workers' co-operation" when carrying out any new industrial policy.

Though this caution about the isolation of factors and policies was written before the publication of Elton Mayo's observations of the relay assembly girls at the Hawthorne Works (164, p. 181), it is very relevant to any practical policy arising therefrom. The practical question is whether the self-consciousness and keenness (resulting in higher output) engendered among the operatives by the investigators consulting and "questioning (them) sympathetically about their reactions" was likely to last when the policies were applied in the ordinary routine of the factory.

The purpose of isolating two, or a few, characteristics or events is to find whether coincidences of certain of the events, but not others, are repeated in a pattern relatively frequently enough to be significant of some causal relation. The fallacy of "coincidence" lies in insufficient recurrences being observed and also in insufficiently exact coincidence in time or place, and here I took even Dr. Freud to task (60, pp. 196–7) for interpreting losses of gifts from relatives critical of the recipient as a wish to forget them, before the frequency, incidence, and closeness of timing of criticisms and loss were established exactly.

This test by the isolation of certain events in recurrent coincidence when all other events vary has been applied notably (28) in the statistical analysis of industrial fluctuations. Here Wesley Mitchell's *Business Cycles*, published in 1913, discovered certain uniformities occurring during major cycles lasting throughout the nineteenth and early twentieth century. As Mitchell summed up (140, p. 5) his own discoveries—

> Longer experience, wider knowledge of business in other countries and better statistical data have gradually discredited the view that crises are abnormal events, each due to a special cause. The modern view is that crises are but one feature of recurrent "business cycles". Instead of a "normal" state of business interrupted by occasional crises, men look for a continually changing state of business—continually changing in a fairly regular way.

Lord Beveridge (18, p. 286) found, in fact, four uniformities repeated in the cycle of the British economy, so dependent, as we have seen, on international trade: "the parallel movement of prices and production; the greater range of fluctuation in certain industries either as making durable goods or producer's goods; the greater range of fluctuation in British export industries; and the earlier incidence of fluctuation in British export industries".

(C) The procedure of indication has not been given as much attention as induction or isolation. But it is quite as important now that so many more statistical data relevant to the social sciences are being presented officially or otherwise. The question is how far available statistics can be found to measure or "indicate" the real issue under discussion, including ultimate aims. Economics and sociology are presented with certain practical problems, but the really relevant facts required to solve these problems may not tally with the available measured data. To meet this sort of dilemma between relevancy and availability I have distinguished (71) the real but often not directly measurable issue from the measurable index, or several alternative indices which are available in the statistics, or which can be derived from them, and which are more or less nearly related to the real issue. Thus the issue of capital intensity, so important for development, is measured in Table XIX by several indices or as they are now coming to be named "indicators", and the size of plants is indicated by number of persons employed, though this takes no account of the difference in material equipment. Critical articles such as Winsten and Margaret Hall's "Measurement of Economies of Scale" (202) should be appearing side by side with the growth in statistical data, not only to design indicators for hitherto unmeasured characteristics, for instance, the degree of vertical or other integration, but to set forth the pros and cons of the various indicators already available. Recently, for instance, the market value of their shares and debentures was used as an index of the size of companies, and it seemed to me a duty to my fellow researchers to warn them off this index (75) because it might, and often did, measure the opposite of what was intended. Market values of ordinary shares would *rise* if, out of a given profit, more were paid in dividends, but this would result in less being ploughed back—that is, in a lower total of assets, which is the usual index of the size of firm. Again, an indicator which this book has repeatedly used is the national income, and it has proved of the greatest value for the internal control of a nation's economy. However, if national income-a-head is used externally as an index of welfare compared to that of other countries more thought is needed (as already indicated, pp. 164-5) on the different sociological circumstances, and the available statistics of the countries being compared. Unfortunately, most economists, and sociologists too, are engaged in higher and more abstract things than scrutinizing and evaluating the mundane produce of official statistical departments. Thus data often promising enough for realistic research go unused, or misused. Yet this critique of statistical indices, for instance, our questioning in Chapter II of the comparability of the definition of "occupied" in the statistics of different countries, should be quite respectable. It is similar to the critical scholarship exercised by the historian and the editor of literary texts to establish the credentials of their data.

Finally it should be said that the process of indication sometimes serves a still higher purpose than finding measures for important concepts; no less than defining more clearly and concretely the concepts themselves. Sir John Clapham's simile of the empty boxes (38) of economic theory in which no phenomena can be filed, is valid, not only because the economist provides no measurable indicator of qualifications for admission to boxes but sometimes because the very thing to be measured is not specified. Scale of production (72, p. 4), may refer to the size of the output of a particular product or process, the size of the plant, or the size of the firm, and this ambiguity may not be noticed till the data have to be measured and classified according to some indicator. Ambiguity also haunts such concepts as capital-intensity, which few economists (T. Barna, with his use of fire-insurance valuations (9, pp. 1–36) is an honourable exception) have tried to measure or compare for particular industries by any accurate indicator.

4. INTEGRATION AND INTERPRETATION

To integrate is, basically, to "complete by addition of parts; combine (parts) into a whole". Research for industrial development calls for adding together and combining the different social sciences, and sometimes the natural sciences, too. Myrdal's *Asian Drama* is a fine example. But usually these sciences are cultivated and taught as special disciplines, largely with their own special tools of research.

The social sciences have already been surveyed, so here discussion can be confined to instances of three useful lines of integration, two of which involve interpretation too: (i) the same terms, conceptions, and tools of research could, with advantage to clarity and understanding, be used in discussing the interests the several social sciences have in common; (ii) reference is useful for interpretation from one social science to another, and so also is (iii) some cross-reference from social sciences generally to the natural sciences.

(i) A *common interest* for most social sciences is that of the structure (including the government) of the societies involved. Economic behaviour is different from political or social behaviour, but the associations involved all have some sort of constitution, rules of procedure, methods of appointment, sanctions, and so on. The government of large industrial firms and companies, analysed in Chapter V, now has devoted to it a vast bibliography. Outstanding authors (some of whose books I quote and number in my bibliography) include J. C. Baker, Chester Barnard, Wilfred Brown (25), Henri Fayol, Mary Follett, David Granick (221), E. Jaques (102), Herbert Simon (128), and L. Urwick. Many have their own individual terminology, but in describing his own firms' organization and management, Wilfred Brown found terms of political science, such as the Representative, Legislative, and Executive Systems, and the Appeals Procedure, quite natural as chapter headings. *Executive* has, in fact, long ago been taken over by big American business from political science. Under the editorship of Milward (139) large-scale organizations in central and local government, in nationalized undertakings, in banks, insurance, and manufacturing companies are all discussed, using similar concepts, such as centralization, delegation, co-ordination, executive committees, functional management, and speed of decision. The details of organization depended upon the work performed, but, and this is the point, their details though different could be described in similar terms, compared as to similar needs of organization and analysed with the same tools.

It is high time that, at least on the structural level, political scientists of the State broadened their outlook to integrate what is essentially a political science of large-scale industrial firms. They would then have many more cases from which to generalize.

For practical purposes the study of industry is no more confined than political science to questions of structure, but reaches for the interrelation of structure and activity. It is interested, for instance, in the effect of a single-firm industry—a monopoly—upon price or output behaviour; in managerial rather than capitalist control of a large company upon investment and dividend policy; or in the effect of nationalization or consumer co-operation upon costs, quality of production, and the use of resources. The structure and government of industrial organization must be analysed more systematically, and along political lines. I put three "categories" to the Aristotelian Society (64)—

State government and the government of large firms have many characters in common and the same three vital political processes: the process of sharing work among the persons and groups in a society, the process of selecting persons to do each work-share and,

S

most essential of all, the process of ruling (including training and
incentives). Every organized society has some (alternative)
variety of structure and also some (alternative) variety of selection,
of work-sharing and of ruling process as between the persons or
sub-societies composing it.

Integration of political science and economics should thus
test what particular combination or syndrome of varieties of
selection, work-sharing, and ruling process are "viable" and
are associated with success in development.

(ii) Interpretation is, indeed, joined to integration in the
heading of this section because a fact or trend observed purely
in one special discipline can often be explained (but usually is
not) by *cross-reference to another social discipline*. Weber and
Tawney's attribution of capitalism and the Industrial Revolution to Protestant forms of Christianity is the classic case, though
its validity is still under discussion. And most classical economists, particularly Adam Smith and Malthus, were by no
means "purists". Malthus (127, Vol. II, Chapter VIII) discusses at some length how decisions are reached about postponement of marriage by men (women are omitted) in the
different English social classes: gentlemen; tradesmen and
farmers; labourers and servants. Recently, to interpret wage-
rates, Lady Wootton (204, pp. 100–6) has drawn in sociology
and "dealing in ethical currency". Collective bargaining between trade unions and employers' associations is in fact based
upon tradition and precedent on the reasonable relation between rates for various grades, occupations, and industries. In
this realm of *laissez collectives faire*, as I have suggested, the
"reasonable" wage-rates settled for are often the opposite of
economically rational.

Other instances were cited earlier where the facts normally
studied in sociology strongly affect those studied in economics.
The reader may be reminded of the effect of the institution of
the English public schools and the ancient universities, and
their scale of values, upon the management efficiency of their
alumni in industry; and of the institution of the family upon
women's wages and employment. In general, economics and,
as Graham Wallas brought out in *Human Nature in Politics*
(197), political science, too, assume too readily man's rationality. Both should make more room for such anthropological

notions as sentiment, snobbery, taboo, myth, fetish, ritual, herd-instinct, or the "gentleman-ideal". They must accept man's irrationality, but study irrational behaviour rationally. Conversely, in predicting a fall in Britain's population by 1950, demographers underrated economic motivation and, basing their prediction on the slump year of 1933, failed to integrate the economists' knowledge of business cycles and man's rationality in having fewer children when he has suddenly become poorer.

(iii) Economists cut off their possible cross-reference to the physical sciences when they assumed, for purposes of argument, the state of the industrial arts to be stationary, and confined their studies to long or short "normal" periods, not secular movements (129, p. 379). Thus they missed the Marxian, or any other interpretation, of development based on the progress of science. Apart from growth, integration with the natural sciences has proved most useful in interpreting many another statistically observed economic phenomenon. Obvious instances are the observed correlations of a fall in output and a rise in accidents with longer hours interpreted by reference to the physiology of fatigue, or disparities in economic reward and the size of firms interpreted by reference to the wide distribution of innate psychological ability as between individuals in a population. Again the connexion of biology (16) with the food resources to meet the population explosion strengthens Malthus's theory, and reference to physical traits is implicit in the quasi-Marxian social relations of science such as my ergological interpretation of different industries' structure and government, including their possible nationalization.

For useful research, in short, too little cross-reference has so far occurred. Economists, still under the spell of the invisible hand, have not, as we have noticed, looked sufficiently into the structure and government of the visible hands, bodies, and organizations, the results of whose behaviour they study; and this behaviour is too often described impersonally in the passive voice. A structure of larger firms governed by managers may, for instance, make quite a difference to prices and output in any industry, as compared with a structure of many small-scale entrepreneurs.

Interpretation through integration of the social and natural sciences has been advocated, particularly by economists, over and over again, but the difficulty is to get anyone to practise what he preaches, or to practise integration without preaching. Historians and to some extent regional and human geographers are, however, natural integrators. They bring together for their particular period and their particular regions all types of relevant knowledge. In fact, integration has been achieved for past historical epochs and for the more distant regions more extensively than for events here and now.

The word interpretation rather than explanation has been used because, defined basically as "to make clear the sense of words, writing, etc." (presumably including statistics), it suggests a closer follow-up, as practised by the natural sciences, of the duly established statistical trends and correlations, and not just speculation from fancy assumptions. Examples of this close follow-up occur in my comparison (II, §4) of women's with men's wages and in my interpretation (IV, §1) of an increase, but a slow increase, in the size of factories. Here, interpretation is a matter of filling up the gaps in the statistical correlation by various non-statistical lines of argument.

This brings up the second use of interpret as "take (behaviour, etc) as having a certain purpose, cause". Statistical correlation, however high, of two traits does not tell us which is cause, which effect. They may both be the effect of a common cause or, as I have illustrated by genealogical trees (60, pp. 178–83), hold some other relationship. Interpretation non-statistically, or by further statistics, must make a "canvass" of possible causal relations. In my *Statistical Method* (60, Chapter XIV), from which I have quoted, the frequent applicability of the Laws of Evidence was pointed out, and (in addition to arguments derived from allied sciences, already discussed) three further lines of interpretation: mathematical deduction, step-by-step reasoning on certain general presumptions, and the common-sense experience and introspection, on which economists rely so much. In this reliance a grave risk of error lies in the economists being purposeful and relatively affluent while many they write about are neither. Yet purpose certainly enters, among other causes, into human affairs. Useful, too, is the Aristotelian distinction between this "final" type of cause and three others: the "material", the formal, and the efficient cause. To natural (material) causes there is added in human affairs the deliberate (formal) implementation by an (efficient) body of persons of some (final) purpose.

5. PRACTICAL DEVELOPMENT POLICY, VIRTUOUS AND VICIOUS CIRCLES

For the practical application of our economic and socio-logical diagnosis the first consideration is whether any supposed ills disclosed are part of a vicious circle and not likely to be pre-vented or cured without "breaking" action; or whether these ills are part of a self-rectifying process and simply one phase of an eventually virtuous circle.

The economists' conception of a stable equilibrium is the classic example of a supposedly virtuous circle. The pendulum that deviates out of the perpendicular to left or to right is bound to swing back again to normal. Thus if supply falls short of demand, prices will, under competition, rise and thus provide an incentive to suppliers; if demand fails to take off supplies, prices will, under competition, fall and thus provide a deterrent to suppliers. Many virtuous circles, not so universal as the classi-cal economists assumed, exist, as admitted of the "take-off", only to some degree. This view repeats our early conclusion (II, §6) that industrial development cannot be expressed in monolithic, perfect, thesis or antithesis, but in syntheses only measurable, statistically if possible, as matters of degree. Competition or monopoly is seldom perfect, and there are various degrees of imperfection in markets and sources of supply.

A thesis of virtuous economic circles was the philosophy underlying the *laissez-faire* policy of the nineteenth century; and an antithesis, of vicious circles to be planned against, forms part of much present-day philosophy. But we must still continually discover and rediscover what to let alone and what not to. Contrary to present "enlightened" opinion, but much to the benefit of freeing resources for planning elsewhere, there are directions in which *laissez faire* could be (and often, un-observed, has been) reintroduced because, in Galbraith's phrase (84), of some "countervailing power". Railways, as my colleague Gilbert Walker pointed out in 1933 (196) (though his view has only gradually been officially recognized and acted upon) no longer held a monopoly of inland transport. The competition between rail and road, if recognized earlier, might have left the railways much more free of government regulation in rate structure, without risk of exploiting their customers. Again, the growth in the extent and strength of trade unions which the higher subscriptions due to higher wages permit, and the possibility of collective bargaining based on equal bargaining power, has made State protection of the worker against lower wages less necessary. To use my phrase, *laissez collectives faire* (73, pp. 89, 163) has in several industries taken the place of the State-enforced minimum wages of the wages councils.

With virtuous circles may be classed behaviour that is necessary to the economy and which the community can obtain cheaply because psychologically and sociologically it runs harmoniously "with the grain" of natural human proclivities. One example is the love of the peasant owner-farmer for his land and for the independence it gives him. Other examples are the taste for certain types of work, such as fishing, which, as Adam Smith remarked (173, I, Chapter 10), "natural taste . . . makes more people follow than can live comfortably by them". Marriage of risks is relevant here and, generally, people's taste for gambling, so that a small chance of a large profit may induce the often necessary risk to the community to be taken at, *on average*, a lower cost than otherwise.

Released from paying out heavily where natural proclivities can be harnessed to the economy, or from interfering where competition or non-government collective bargaining will do, the State can concentrate on attacking by its various powers the permanently vicious circles. Some of these powers, distinguished by prepositions, were cited (VII, §3) as breaking circles making for greater economic inequality in both the developed and the underdeveloped countries. Equality is generally accepted as a virtue; what other circles are considered vicious or virtuous must, of course, depend on the general ethical orientation.

Economics, sociology or any social science, as I maintain elsewhere (61, *passim*; 73, pp. 11–16), work in the indicative not the ethical, optative mood. As sciences, they cannot lay down the ultimate aims or ends of society, however measurable these aims may be. Joan Robinson (163, p. 147) quotes Popper urging economists "to combat, not foster the ideology which pretends that values which can be measured in terms of money are the only ones that ought to count".

To be practical, the social sciences, though they cannot as sciences determine what is welfare, must take account of the public opinion which, in a democratic country, will be needed to implement their conclusions. They must recognize, if not the aims, at least the aversions of the people with whom they are concerned and if possible find their measurable indicator or indicators—for instance, rates of unemployment, or (accepting the Barlow Commission Report of 1940) city congestion, or low living or working standards. In short, the vicious circles which are most usefully and scientifically tackled by the social sciences, in the manner of operational research, are those where public opinion admits a specific ill such as unemployment, inequality, instability, ill-health, or illiteracy and where that illfare can be measurably indicated.

In the present poverty-stricken condition of underdeveloped countries the world's "number-one" vicious circle, recognized by most economists, for example Nurkse (145, pp. 4–5) and put in diagram form at the end of the last chapter, is that starvation begets starvation, ill-health ill-health, poverty poverty.

Economists and sociologists do not agree among themselves, however, whether this vicious circle will be broken more or less automatically or not. Some maintain, as noted earlier (p. 291), that if standards rise among part of the population, this *élite* will then, to maintain their standards, learn to control their birth-rate and thus cumulatively raise standards further. A precedent is often claimed in the English industrial revolution. Unfortunately, the new accessibility of food resources in the American Middle West and the then unique position of England as the workshop of the world, is not likely to be repeated elsewhere. My own view, shared by many others, is that this quasi-automatic reduction of the birth-rate cannot be relied upon to act, or at least to act quickly enough (English birth-rates did not start falling until after 1870); and that a vicious circle, continuing a low income for many heads, must be broken by positive action. This action must take the "tripod" form of controlling the number of heads, distributing aggregate incomes more equally among the heads, and increasing that income from the given resources. The attempt to increase the ratio or surplus of output and income in exchange for a given cost of all "inputs"—the striving for efficiency as usually defined—is peculiarly the economic means of achieving higher living standards. It involves not just more investment but increasing the productivity of each of the separate factors of production, labour, capital, management, and land, while giving full consideration to their sociological setting. Chapters IV and V were largely concerned with industrial efficiency in developed, Chapters VI and VII with industrial efficiency in underdeveloped countries.

The starvation-begets-inefficiency-begets-starvation circle apparently endemic in underdeveloped countries was, till recently, epidemic in the countries now developed, occurring during the slump of their trade cycle, and the slump areas of their location pattern. Lack of employment in these phases and areas led to increasing incapacity of the worker, increasing incapacity to greater unemployability. Accordingly, the State organized insurance as a palliative against the hazard of unemployment. But as the fully developed countries learn to smooth out temporary and local slumps, and as preventives are added to palliatives, these countries approach general affluence. Other aims are then put forward that can be attended to beside higher standards of living and security, and more equality— aims that are less easily indicated by statistical measures.

Equality (as among consumers) is now extended to cover, among producers, the aims of Jeffersonian democracy and the diffusion of ownership advocated by Belloc and Chesterton in opposition to highly centralized decision-making. A circular trend has developed in which large plants and firms with measurably more concentrated management have increased mechanization and the application of science (an application that will certainly continue, unless the final application occurs in an atom bomb), whereupon mechanization tends to result in turn in larger plants and larger plants facilitate the further use of more machines. This circle is considered vicious by many people because concentration centralizes authority, reduces the number of small, independent industrialists and increases that of organization man. Here, a clash may well occur between efficiency and democracy similar to the dilemma in under-developed countries between large federations and many small independent states with small markets.

Trying to find a balance of net advantages between industrial democracy and efficiency certainly involves integration of sociological and economic research and will probably result in a compromise degree of democracy and of efficiency. Democratic aims in industry seem to have gone too far for purposes of efficiency, for instance, in the constitution of the Co-operative Wholesale Society, where twenty-eight full-time paid directors are appointed by election, and in the practice of most Co-operative Societies of not appointing university graduates for management posts (32, pp. 312–16). On the other hand, most big capitalist businesses will, for the sake of democracy as well as amenity, have to allow considerable negotiation and consultation at an early stage about making changes in the working conditions of their employees, either at plant, at firm, or (as in development councils) industry level. Workers and management must, in particular, agree on adjustments, as a consequence of technological development, in the workers' social life—on the working of shifts, for instance, or mobility between industries.

A circle (considered vicious by many), in which conurbation breeds larger conurbation, arises by two processes. People migrating to large cities to man expanding industries, form, with their resultant income, a market for the city's services, which in turn attracts more people as workers. And once land outside the conurbation is occupied by a smoky factory, a dump, or ribbon development, the amenity value of neighbouring land falls, and it can be bought for further industrial development.

This circling or spiralling from big to bigger business and big to bigger urbanization does not occur in all circumstances, and it is part of the task of practical research to find where it does or needs to, and where it does not or need not occur. Large-scale linked industries may be needed for industries where firms are specialized and small. In sectors, such as house-building, retailing, and agriculture, owing to ergological factors, few plants, farms or shops are big, but bigness may, perhaps, be necessary, as already said (IV, §5) somewhere (e.g. whole-salers) in the whole process of which they are a part. Nor do most building or retailing operations require bigger cities. But in the activities where ergological circumstances (technology and sources of supply and markets) foster large size, as particularly in manufacturing, the trend will probably be cumulatively toward larger urbanization, unless deliberate policy intervenes (80, pp. 22–4), say to discourage the aggregation of footloose industries not linked to the main industries of the locality.

In the policy for breaking cumulative circles, of big breeding bigger (and analogous circles if thought vicious), the State has relations with industry similar to those, distinguished by different prepositions (VII, §3), for dealing with poverty, inequality, and insecurity. The differences in relationship indicated by different prepositions (73, pp. 47–50) are of practical importance, since very different attitudes and forms of administration are required in the government departments or agencies concerned, according as they form a third, second, or primary party. Political structure, in short, will differ with the kind of relationship required. It is as a third party that the State defends the small trader, as well as the consumer, *from* monopolistic agreements between big businesses by means of the Restrictive Practices Act administered semi-legally; and participates *with* industry informally to establish democratic negotiation and some joint consultation within industrial plants, such as occur when piece-rates were introduced (IV, §9), so that the stronger party will not accumulate further strength. As a primary party the State publishes information compulsorily collected *about* industry and provides services *for* industry such as economic, technical, and management education. This can be seen as an attempt to make the democracy more knowledgeable and not cumulatively weakened by ignorance as against the expensively educated, and also as an attempt to introduce more mobility and to stop certain highly respectable but not necessarily (marginally) useful professions attracting the most intelligent supplies of young people and thus becoming cumulatively still more respectable. The State, as a primary party, also undertakes through nationalization the operation *of* monopolies largely in order to check cumulative exploitation.

This primary operation calls for initiative and enterprise and requires a structure of government quite different from the requirements for a legislating and mediating third-party relationship. And as a second party directly facing industry the State requires yet a different organization, including a technically expert civil service, and a different procedure. As a second party the State exercises various controls (including tax and subsidy policies) *over* industry not only to develop it but to avoid spirals in stability (e.g. against inflation). In zoning industrial areas and town-and-country planning generally (including the building of new industrial towns), to defend living conditions and amenities *against* industrial and housing sprawl, the State must employ economists competent in industrial location because families must live where (80, Annex B) the chief *male* income-earner works.

In the practical procedure for breaking up vicious circles reliance must be placed either on compulsion or inducements to voluntary action or in some degree to both. In Western civilization the stress is on voluntary inducement; but it is often forgotten that it is easier to induce persons to act in a particular way if they are provided with the proper capacity and facilities for doing so. Recent sociology has in its diagnosis laid, in my view, too much stress on psychological willingness and motivation, too little on "capacitation" and on the facilities for greater capacity, including information, education, and "enlightenment". This conclusion was reached in such diverse directions as the stimulus to wider economic mobilization and mobility between industries, and to the checking of the birthrate.

The practical policy indicated by this conclusion is that more effort should be devoted to providing the required capacities and facilities, such as workers' housing and the means of moving, or access to birth-control appliances, medicaments, and clinics, and more effort in making people accept the facilities provided by breaking down traditions through education or "object lessons".

Furthermore, where willingness and motivation was not overstressed compared with capacity and facilities, as in the stimulus to labour productivity, my conclusion was that *economic* incentives had, in the modern literature, been overmuch despised, if not forgotten. Men in underdeveloped as in developed countries appear up to a point to react strongly to rates of pay,

and more should be discovered by integration between economists and psychologists as to the critical points involved.

As part of the policy of making people more capable of
industrial development in the underdeveloped countries and
also among the working- and voting-masses of the developed
countries must come the realistic teaching of the economics
and sociology of their industrial systems. A realistic treatment,
down to earth but up to date, must begin with the trends and
the trains of causation in each country and follow through to the
latest developments. It should stress the anthropology of the
less-developed countries, and not stop short of the sociology of
company development and managerial revolution in the developed countries. But, more than that, communication must be
widespread, intelligible, persuasive, and acceptable. Economic
development based on knowledge in the natural sciences has
been lop-sided, not so much because knowledge has advanced
unevenly, but because sometimes, as in death control, its social
application depends on only a few experts operating on nature
or on a population that need be only passive, while in other
fields, as birth control or agricultural productivity, implementation depends on the widespread active co-operation of the
population—a co-operation seldom achieved. Industrial and
agricultural technical development halts, as we know, not because of lack of scientific knowledge in the world, but because
the people who have to co-operate do not accept and apply to
their particular business the sufficient science that already exists.
Similarly, considerable economic and political knowledge exists
of financing and management of the State and of industrial
organization. But this knowledge has not been successfully
communicated and has not always been accepted.

An important factor in accepting a new technique is the
vehicle of communication being used, and here a common
world language, a lingua franca, and visual aids are almost
essential. An obvious lingua franca for the world generally is
English, which, in the form of Basic English, is easily learned
and easily adapted for the natural and the social sciences (82).
Indeed, both Basic English and visual aids may, by avoiding
the ambiguities that beset the language of the social sciences,
make existing knowledge clearer both in developed, as well as
underdeveloped societies, and I have made a point in this book

of defining many of my terms according to the *Basic Dictionary*.

A last word. I was careful, just above, to write not that "sufficient" knowledge existed in the social as perhaps in the natural sciences, but merely "considerable" knowledge. The laws and effects enumerated in this chapter, even if accepted as fairly scientifically established, admittedly do not cover much ground. It is in the hope of pushing from existing to further conclusions based on the realistic analysis of the facts of industry that this book has been written.

DIFFERENTIATION AND RANKING OF U.S. MAJOR INDUSTRY GROUPS BY MEASURABLE CHARACTERISTICS AND ASSOCIATION OF THOSE CHARACTERISTICS

REFERENCES have been made throughout the text to the wide range of characteristics or "traits" shown by different industries, even by different manufacturing industries. These differences are of direct practical importance, we saw, in framing a policy for the location of industries in depressed areas or in underdeveloped countries. In fact industrialization as a policy is somewhat meaningless and likely to be hit-or-miss unless the particular traits are known of the industries that are proposed to be introduced. Most of these traits are measurable, and with progress in census-taking some have been measured and correlated. All the summary measurements for all industries cannot, however, be found in any one document, and though such a document would certainly help practical research into industries, there is no space here for a comprehensive tabulation. While waiting for such perfection, Table XIX gives the ranking (lowest first) of all the twenty U.S. Census "Major Industry Groups" (covering all manufactures) in respect of as many of the "traits" as are measurable and relevant to industrial organization and development.

In contrast to this comprehensive and, I hope, comprehensible tabulation I gave, in my original British edition, the relatively few extreme individual industries only. The British Census of Production groups the individual 145 manufacturing industries that it distinguishes into fourteen "orders", but these orders were neither numerous enough nor relevantly enough distinguished to make them of analytical value. For instance, it is important, as repeatedly said in my text, to distinguish the early (usually processing) stage of manufacture from the later (usually assembling) stage. This distinction is made in the American twenty-fold two-digit grouping, notably in separating a primary metal, a paper, a textile, and a lumber group from a fabricated metal and machinery group, a printing and publishing group, and an apparel and a furniture group. The American "major" grouping is far from perfect, particularly in lumping together early processing food and chemical industries (such as grain-milling and sugar-refining, or *basic* chemicals) with later-stage assembly industries (such as baking and toilet preparations). But the grouping is sufficiently relevant to justify its use in summary tables aiming to cover all manufacturing industries.

The twenty major groups are named in the first column of Table XIX, and subsequent columns give their ranking in respect of each variable measure. The order in which the columns (I, II, III, IV and V) set forth these measures follows that of Chapters I to V and thus as far as possible expounds the "ergological" hypothesis advanced in my text, that organization is largely the consequence of structure, and structure of technology and the type and context of the work being undertaken. The possibilities of exposition depend, of course, upon the availability of the quantitative measures and their relevance to, and clear indication of, the point at issue. Many an easily available statistic is ambiguous. The proportion cost of material bears to total value of product is easily, and often, quoted. But it is ambiguous because it may not only indicate the importance of raw material and presumably a material-oriented location, but also a later-stage, not integrated manufacture using purchased materials already processed and thus expensive.

Ranking in one aspect of the type and context of the work is indicated by the first columns grouped under I Sources, Markets and Linkages (with other industries); and ranking in one aspect of technology in columns under IC, Capital Intensity.

Most of the measures, with their formulae at the head of the columns and their sources set forth at the foot of the table, are self-explanatory but a few points need further elucidation.

1. *Sources, Markets and Linkages:* The difference between direct and indirect percentage of personal consumption expenditure is perhaps puzzling. An example may be quoted from the official explanation.

> Furniture bought by persons is direct demand on the furniture industry. The lumber and upholstery fabrics used in the manufacture of the furniture are indirect demands of consumer expenditures on the lumber and textile industries. These two industries in turn require the products of other industries, for instance the lumber industry, chemicals and plastics, the textile industry requires cotton and wool and so on. The cumulative effect on each industry of all the indirect flows generated by personal consumption expenditures is called the indirect demand attributable to Personal Consumption Expenditure.

The requirement of the products of one industry by another is one aspect of the linkage between industries and the difference between total and direct personal consumption often shows up important linkages.

The test used in assigning (in Column IB) industry groups according to the weight of material or to processing or assembling operations was developed in my *Investment, Location and Size of Plant* (69) where the significance also was stressed of the geographical dispersion of materials (see pp. 9–10, 114–5 Table vE). A further indication of weight and, more relevantly, the industry's cost of transport is the percentage of goods given by the U.S. Census of Transport as carried fifty miles or less, only. The distinction between assembly and processing originated with Professor John C. Duncan in his *Principles of Industrial Management* (69, *passim*).

2. *Capital Intensity:* Several statistical indicators are available but none of them is completely satisfactory. Three of these indicators: (*a*) fixed assets, (*b*) capital expenditure for the year (the capital expenditure per employee for 1964 was found fairly typical of the preceding years, 1954 onwards), (*c*) added value of output not due to payroll, each expressed as a ratio per employee, were ranked 1 to 20. These three rankings were then averaged and the averages ranked 1 to 20 to form a combined accounting indicator. A further indicator, the horse-power capacity of machines to production worker, is given separately but, as explained in Chapter I, §3, is influenced by the sheer toughness of the materials being machined.

3. *Size of Plant.* Two indicators are given as measures of size of plant. The more obvious but often too "slick" rank by (arithmetic mean) average in Column iva is balanced by a measure (ivb) of the distribution of employees in plants of different size. The two measures do not always agree, for which there is a good reason.

My continued criticism of the simple arithmetic mean average as a measure of representative size (79, pp. 28–31) is particularly confirmed in comparing the apparel and the printing groups. The alternative measure of size of plant structure that I have put forward is a classification into five main size grades depending on the distribution of employees as between the ranges of plant size recognized by the Census (see above, pp. 89–91). Column ivb bases its ranking on an abridged form of this alternative. Now the printing group with the *second* lowest *average* plant size is only *ninth* lowest in the percentage (namely 29) of all employees in plants employing 500 or more; while the apparel group with a higher *average* plant size (eighth in rank) is second lowest in the percentage (14) of workers in the plants employing 500 or more. The printing group is in fact a clear example of a spread of employees into all sizes of plant yielding a quite unrepresentative average. Other major groups with rather unrepresentative average sizes are paper and textiles. Though in average size of plant they rank as high as fourteenth and fifteenth, the groups rank only tenth and eleventh in percentages of employees in plants employing 500 or more.

4. Two indicators are given as measures for *localization*. This is partly because no up-to-date indicator is available for the U.S. and partly because the more recent of the two, which is also the more obvious average measure, may not bring out sufficiently the significant constituent industries within the group that have a high localization, i.e. have coefficients far above the median coefficient of 0·43. No very great incompatibility of rank occurs, however, between

the two indicators except for Groups 29 (petroleum), 30 (rubber and plastics) and 31 (leather, mainly shoes). Two of these groups suffer from a paucity of constituent industries quoted in the sources. In the National Resources Planning Board Report (Source (d)) only one rubber and one fabricated plastics industry appear, to represent group 30; and for group 29 only one petroleum industry (i.e. refining). In the Stanford Survey (Source (e)) only three rubber, one plastics and three petroleum industries appear. Too much reliance should not be placed, therefore, on the ranks of either of these major groups. In the leather group the N.R.P.B. report gives only one general leather *goods* industry, the Stanford Survey five, three of them with high location coefficients.

Table XIX, then, attempts to exhibit the measurable differentiation of manufacturing activity. It sets out the different characteristics of different industries at present as briefly yet comprehensively as possible. What are the conclusions that can be drawn?

In spite of grouping together so many individual industries into so few groups, it is remarkable how, for each trait, the major groups stand out one from another. The wide differentiation in measures between the groups is set forth by figures at the bottom of each column giving the range between the lower and upper extremes of the measure—that, namely, of the first and twentieth ranking major groups. In the very first column, for instance, the percentage of the output going in direct personal consumption expenditure varies from 0 in the primary metal group to 74·2 in the apparel group. Another wide differentiation is in the horse-power per production worker, ranging from 0·22 in the apparel group to 89·5 in the petroleum group.

Wide differentiation occurs also in size of plant. The average sizes for each group varied from 15·8 employees in the lumber to 225 in the transport equipment group or, by the alternative measure of percentages in plants employing over 500, from 9 to 84 per cent in these same two groups. If individual (four-digit) industries were used as illustration the range would of course be much wider than in the (two-digit) major groups. For instance, as a measure of size of plant, the percentage of employees in plants employing over 500 varied in 1963 from 0 in quite a number of individual industries (employing as many as 10,000) such as creamery butter or condensed and evaporated milk, to 99 in aircraft.

This wide variation in characteristics shown by the different industry groups supports the differentiation listed as the fifth trend in Chapter I. The question now arises whether certain patterns of association can be discerned. Do some groups fall into broad categories with similar characteristics, based, perhaps on the effect of type of material, supply or market demand upon structure and organization; and, in particular, are some characteristics normally like a syndrome of symptoms, found in combination?

Looking across the board certain broad types may in fact be

T

distinguished and may be named after the processes or the materials involved.

I. *The Metal Assembly Type* of industry comprises major industry groups 35, 36, 37, and 38, making machinery, electrical goods, transport equipment, and instruments. All these four groups have (Column IA) on the marketing side a high personal consumption and on the material a low input from extractive industries. They have in addition (Column IC) medium capital intensity; (Column III) medium to high localization; (Column IB) durable product and (Column IIB) steep fluctuations; (Column ID) a high staff ratio; (Column IV) large plants owned by multiplant firms; and are (Column VA) mostly governed by corporations. Finally (Column VB), they have high concentration ratios. These assembly-type industries are all growing fast and becoming more and more important in the economy. In 1963 they employed one-third of all manufacturing employees.

II. It is conventional to speak of heavy and light industries but not actually easy to identify all of them. The heavy type would probably be accepted as including major groups 24, lumber; 29, petroleum; and 33, primary metals. It would also include some of 20, food; 26, paper; 28, chemicals; 30 rubber and plastics; 32, stone, clay and glass; and 35, machinery. Referring to Table XIX these industries have a high rank (Column IA iii) in input from extractive industry and (Column IB) in processing heavy materials. The U.S. major groups listed as heavy are also on the whole (Column IC) capital-intense. The average rank in horse-power per worker of the four grades of heavy or light material is H, $16\frac{1}{2}$; h, 12th; l, 6th; L, 3rd, their average rank in accounting tests is H, $15\frac{1}{2}$; h, 13; l, $5\frac{3}{4}$, L., $5\frac{1}{4}$. The heavy groups are not particularly distinctive in the more sociological characteristics except, as we shall show later, employing, not unexpectedly, a low proportion of women (Column IIA).

Much seems to depend on degree of localization. In primary metals, machinery, petroleum and chemicals, paper and pulp marked H in the table, the average size of plants is large. Other heavy industry groups such as food, lumber and stone, etc., clay or glass have, however, a small-plant structure. Food plants are often necessarily scattered where the consumer lives or the material is found, and similarly many industries in the stone, clay and glass group and particularly the lumber industry use heavy scattered materials. Thus the propensity of heavy and capital-intense industries for large plants is constrained by the very fact of the cost of transporting heavy goods to or from the plants. The influence of capital intensity (working on heavy material) upon large size of plant is then checked by the need of many scattered plants.

III. A further pattern appears in which measures of government seem to follow on from measures of sizes of plant structure. Five industry groups stand out characterized by large plants on both tests (Columns IVA and B)); tobacco, petroleum, primary metals, electrical machinery and transport equipment. The following summary table shows the ranking after averaging these two tests, and ranking also for percentage in multiple plants under a single firm, in corporations, and the concentration ratio.

SYNDROME: RANKING OUT OF TWENTY MAJOR GROUPS

Major Groups	Average of two rankings in Size of Plant	Percentage in Multi-Plant Firms	Percentage under Corpora-tion	Size of Firms	Concen-tration Ratios Percentage	Percentage in Merger Firms
21 Tobacco	18	19	$13\frac{1}{2}$	18	20	8
29 Petroleum	$15\frac{1}{2}$	20	13	19	19	10
33 Primary Metals	18	16	19	17	17	16
36 Electrical Machinery	18	15	17	15	16	18
37 Transport Equipment	20	18	20	20	18	20
Average Rank	18	18	16	18	18	14

All rankings are high and we may speak of a large-plant, large-firm, corporation-ruled, control-concentrated category of industry; or for short, a "big-business" syndrome of industry.

Does such a category behave in any particular way that can be measured? Statistics of mergers are published for each of the twenty major industry groups stating what percentage of their total employed were in firms which undertook mergers—that were, in short "mergerers". The major groups are ranked in respect of these percentages in Column vc of Table XIX. This ranking is entered in the last column of the table above. It will be seen that the ranks of the merging groups are all eighth or above and average fourteenth. In short, the big-business type of industry group is also the mergerer type.

It is possible to distinguish six more of the major groups that incline to this big-business "syndrome". They are groups coming next in rank on the score of size of plant (average of two rankings) from $11\frac{1}{2}$ to 14th with an average rank of 12.

FURTHER RANKING OUT OF TWENTY MAJOR GROUPS

Major Groups	Average of two rankings in Size of Plant	Percentage in Multi-Plant Firms	Percentage under Corpo-ration	Employees per Proprietor	Concen-tration Ratios Percentage	Percentage in Merger Firms
22 Textile	12	9	$13\frac{1}{2}$	10	13	9
26 Paper	12	14	17	12	11	14
28 Chemicals	$11\frac{1}{2}$	15	17	16	14	17
30 Rubber	$11\frac{1}{2}$	13	13	13	6	19
35 Machinery	$11\frac{1}{2}$	11	9	11	12	12
38 Instruments	14	12	11	14	15	15
Average Rank	12	12	13	12	12	14

Except for the rubber and plastics group's rank 6 in concentration ratio there is no rank less than 9. In mergers this set of major groups showed a very high ranking—all (except textile) 12 or over.

The percentages are also available for each group of the employed in firms that were merged—the merger*ees*. The ranking of groups in this respect appears in Column VD of Table XIX. Now rank-correlation of the mergeree ranking with that of size of plant is almost as high as that of mergerer. One may conclude that the big-business type of structure affects merging behaviour both ways, active and passive. In this type there is a propensity both to undertake mergers and to be merged.

In addition to the analysis of types of industry groups with a similar syndrome of characteristics, certain major industry groups can be seen to be definitely correlated in respect of two particular characteristics and also *not* correlated where correlation is often assumed. Several of these correlations or non-correlations were pointed out in the text—

1. Contrary to received opinion, high staff ratios are seen not to be correlated, industry by industry, to large-scale plants. The Spearman Rank Correlation (formulated below) between Columns ID and IVA was −·01.

2. Ranked within the nine assembly groups of industries, capital intensity measured by horse-power per production worker (Column IC) is correlated with large plant structure (Column IVB)—

Code and Name of Assembly Groups	Rank among nine Assembly Groups			Difference Squared (D^2)
	Size of Plant	HP/PW	Difference in rank	
23 Apparel	1	1	0	0
25 Furniture	4	5	1	1
27 Printing	5	3	2	4
31 Leather (mainly shoes)	2	2	0	0
35 Machinery, not electrical	6	8	2	4
36 Electrical Machinery	8	7	1	1
37 Transport Equipment	9	9	0	0
38 Instruments	7	4	3	9
39 Miscellaneous	3	6	3	9

Sum $\Sigma D^2 = 0.28$

The Spearman Rank Correlation

$$r = 1 - \frac{6\,(\Sigma D^2)}{N\,(N^2 - 1)} = 1 - \frac{168}{720} = 0.769.$$

A practical significance of this correlation, particularly in under-developed countries, is that large-plant assembly industries require an expensive equipment per production worker which cannot always be financed.

3. The percentage of women employed is correlated with the heavy nature of the materials. The average rank in the percentage of women employed in groups marked H or h in Column IB of Table XIX is 7th; in groups *not* so marked it is 15th.

This association may seem obvious but is often not borne in mind when planning the location of industry to balance deficiency in regional income. If not enough of the lighter industries are mixed in with heavier industries, there will be less chance of the relatively immobile women members of the family supplementing the men's earnings.

4. A relationship can be seen between major groups making durable products, as classified by the U.S. Census, and the wider fluctuations in employment. The groups marked D in Column IB rank 9th, 10th, 11th, 12th, 13th, 14th, 16th, 17th, 18th and 20th in the amplitude of fluctuation (Column IIc), yielding an average rank of 14·0, against an average rank for the remaining group of 7·0.

Among the officially classified non-durable product group are textiles, apparel, chemical, rubber and plastics, and leather. The products of these groups are certainly more durable in use than those of the food, tobacco, paper, printing and petroleum groups and accordingly I have ventured to mark them d in the table in order to subdivide them from the truly non-durable in use, marked ND. If these two sub-groups are distinguished the average rankings in fluctuation amplitude are—

Ten Durable (D) Groups	14·0	
Six Semi-durable (d) Groups }	7·0	{ 9·5
Four Non-durable (ND) Groups }		{ 3·3

indicating a consistent relation between durability and fluctuation in employment.

5. Some industry groups have in Column IB also been marked U for uniformity of material and/or product. They average high in capital intensity. In the two tests of capital intensity the six U groups have an average rank of 14·8 and 15·5 in a range between six-industry averages of 3½ (if all were in the lowest six ranks, 1st to 6th) to 17½ (if all were in the highest six, 15th to 20th).

6. Many other associations and non-association of characteristics can be worked out by readers from Table XIX, for instance a policy of merger in the industry group with a combination of growth and size, or growth with high staff ratios; and particularly relevant to Table III, a high correlation appears between size of plant and size of firm, Columns IVB and D.

In conclusion it may be stressed again that this and other correlations tend to confirm the model presented in Table III, in particular (working down the page) the connexion of uniformity of materials with mechanized industry, mechanization with larger factories, large factories (as already said) with larger firms, and large firms with company or corporation government.

TABLE XIX

RANKING OF MAJOR INDUSTRIAL GROUPS IN MEASURABLE CHARACTERS

U.S.A. Major Groups and Code Number	Total Employees	IA Sources, Markets and Linkages — % of Output in Personal Consumption Expenditure Direct (i)	IA — Total (ii)	IA — Input % from Extractive Industry** (iii)	IB Assembly, Process or Mixed — Heavy (H) or Light (L), h or l moderately so. SC = Sources of supply concentrated; Product (D) Durable, (d) Semi-durable, (ND) Non-durable; Material and/or Product Uniform	IC Capital Intensity — Horse-power per Production Worker 1962 (i)	IC — Three accounting tests combined 1958 (ii)	ID Staff Ratio — Total Employees—Production Workers 1963	IIA Women's Mobilization — % of Total Employed	IIB Growth — Added Value of Output % Increase 1947–65	IIC Flux — % amplitude. Peak to Trough of Production 1947–55
Sources of Data		(a)	(a)	(a)		(b)	(b)	(b)	(c)	(f)	(h)1
20 Food	1,644	17	19	19	h. Mix. ND	13	5	17	11	4	1
21 Tobacco	77	19	17	17	L.Proc. SC. ND U	6	2	3	18	3	2
22 Textiles	861	7	7	15	l.Proc. SC. d. U	9	7	2	16½	5	15
23 Apparel	1,278	20	18	0	L. Ass. d	1	1½	4	20	10	4
24 Lumber	563	4	2	16	H. Proc. SC. D	16	7	5	2	2	3
25 Furniture	374	16	12	0	l. Ass. D	5	3	7	8	14	16
26 Paper	589	6	4	14	H. Proc. d U	17	8	8	10	13	6
27 Printing	911	10	15	9½	L. Ass. ND	3	6	19	12	7	3
28 Chemicals	737	11	8	11	H. Mix. d U	19	9	18	9	20	5
29 Petroleum	153	14	14	20	H. Pro. ND U	20	9	20	3	8½	7
30 Rubber and Plastics	484	9	13	8	h. Mix. d	14	3	12	13	17	19
31 Leather (Shoes)	327	18	20	12	L. Ass. d	2	1½	1	19	1	8
32 Stone, Glass, Clay	574	5	6	13	H. Mix. D	15	6	9	6	8½	14
33 Primary Metals	1,127	1	1	18	H. Pro. D U	18	6	6	1	6	20
34 Fabricated Metals	1,079	3	3	0	h. Pro. D	11	10	10	7	12	12
35 Machinery	1,457	2	5	0	H. Ass. D	10	10	13½	5	15	17
36 Electrical	1,511	12	10	0	l. Ass. D	8	5	15	15	16	9
37 Transport Equipment	1,601	13	11	7	h. Ass. D	12	4	13½	4	19	18
38 Instruments	305	8	9	0	l. Ass. D	4	9	16	14	18	11
39 Miscellaneous	637	15	16	9½	l. Ass. D	7	4	11	6	11	10
All Manufacturing Range of	16,949	19·3* / 0	68·0* / 0·4	0·5 / 0		12·69 / 0·22	—	28 / 10·7	27 / 6	192 / 120	7·06 / 1·7

Major Groups and Code Number	Localization Coefficients % constituent Industries with Corporation Co-efficient 0·44 or more (d)	Localization Coefficients Average of Constituent Co-efficients 1957 (e)	Size of Plant Average Number Employed 1963 (b)	Size of Plant % in Plants employing 500+ 1963 (b)	Size of Plant % employed in Multi-Plant Firms 1963 (b)	Size of Firm % of Firms employing 2,500+ 1963 (b)	Diversification % employees in Primary Industry (h)2	% of employees in Corporations 1963 (b)	Four-company Concentration Ratio % of Groups Value of Shipments accounted for by industries with, in 1963 — Ratios 50% or more (k)	Ratios 26% or more (k)	Mergers 1959-62 (k)i	% of Employees in each Group Mergeres 1959-62 (k)ii
20 Food	9	8¼	7	6	8	8	2	3	11	7	13	8
21 Tobacco	20	15¼	19	17	20	18	1	18	20	20	8	9
22 Textiles	19	17	15	11	11	10	8	10	6	13	9	16½
23 Apparel	16	13	8	2	2	1	—	2	6	2	1	3
24 Lumber	15	18	1	1	1	2	—	1	1½	1	4	11
25 Furniture	6	6	4	5	3	4	—	6	1½	3	5	2
26 Paper	1	2	14	10	14	12	3	14	10	11	14	20
27 Printing	2	1	2	9	5	5	—	4	5	4	6	1
28 Chemicals	10	12	9	14	17	16	9	12	16	14	17	16½
29 Petroleum	7	15½	16	15	19	19	4	16	3	19	10½	10
30 Rubber and Plastics	12	3	11	12	12	13	11	15	14	6	19	4
31 Leather (Shoes)	17	10½	13	3	6	6	—	11	4	9	2	5
32 Stone, Glass, Clay	4½	4	5	8	10	9	5	7	13	10	10½	14
33 Primary Metals	4½	6	18	18	15	17	6	19½	18	17	16	7
34 Fabricated Metals	3	6	6	7	7	7	12	8	8	5	7	6
35 Machinery	13	10½	10	13	9	11	7	9½	12	12	12	12
36 Electrical	8	8¼	17	19	16	15	13	19½	15	16	18	19
37 Transport Equipment	14	13 4/10	20	20	18	20	10	17	19	18	20	15
38 Instruments	18	N.A.	12	16	3	14	—	13	17	15	15	18
39 Miscellaneous	11	N.A.	3	4	4	3	—	5	7	8	3	13
All manufacturing	46½	0·44	55·7	33·2	65·4	42·0	0·667	93·2	15·5	66·1	34·0	5·3
Range of Character	20 to 100	0·31 to 0·60	15·8 to 225	9 to 84	33·1 to 97·3	8·1 to 81·3	0·999	72·3 to 99·0	0 to 100	11·4 to 10·0	6·3 to 63·8	2·7 to 11·3

Sources (a) Input–Output Tables 1958, Survey of Current Business.
(b) U.S. Census of Manufactures 1958 and 1963.
(c) Census of Population 1961.
(d) U.S. National Resources Planning Board, *Industrial Location and National Resources 1943.*
(e) Stanford Research Institute, *The Role of Small Scale Manufacturing 1957.*
(f) *U.S. Statistical Abstracts*, Section on Manufactures.
(g) The distinction between durable and non-durable is drawn officially; between durable and semi-durable depends on "life" of product.
(h) M. GORT, *Diversification and Integration in American Industry* 1962, (1) p. 219; (2) p. 33.
(k) Evidence to U.S. Senate Sub-committee on Antitrust and Monopoly 1964–7.
    (i) Part 1, p. 335, Evidence of J. M. Blair, 6th October, 1967.
    (ii) Part 2, pp. 1022–4, Evidence of U.S. Bureau of the Census.
    * Median of groups 10½.
    ** Less than 0·2% = Rank of 0.

BIBLIOGRAPHY

In alphabetical order of authors' names except for additional references (208–42). Numbered references as in brackets in text. The page of the text where the reference occurs is given in the index under the name of the author.

Abbreviations

British Association: British Association for the Advancement of Science
E.J.: *Economic Journal*
I.L.R.: *International Labour Review*
J.I.E.: *Journal of Industrial Economics*
J.R.S.S.: *Journal of the Royal Statistical Society*

1. ACTON SOCIETY TRUST, *Size and Morale* (1953).
2. ACTON SOCIETY TRUST, *Management Succession* (1956).
3. ALLEN, G. C., *The Structure of Industry in Britain* (1961).
4. ANDIC, S. and PEACOCK, A. T., International Distribution of Incomes, *J.R.S.S.*, Part 2 (1961).
5. ANDREWS, P. W. S., *Manufacturing Business* (1949).
6. ANDREWS, P. W. S. and BRUNNER, ELIZABETH, Business Profits and the Quiet Life, *J.I.E.* (Nov., 1962).
7. BAIN, J. S., *Industrial Organization* (1959).
8. BALDAMUS, W., Type of Work and Motivation, *Brit. Jl. of Sociology* (March, 1951).
9. BARNA, T., Replacement Costs of Fixed Assets in British Manufacturing Industries, *J.R.S.S.* (Part I, 1957).
10. BARNA, T., *Investment and Growth Policies in British Industrial Firms* (1962).
11. BAUER, P. T. and YAMEY, B. S., *The Economics of Underdeveloped Countries* (1957).
12. BEESLEY, M., The Birth and Death of Industrial Establishments, *J.I.E.* (Oct., 1955).
13. BEHREND, HILDE, *Absence under Full Employment. Studies in Economics and Society*, University of Birmingham (1952).
14. BERLE, A. A., *The Twentieth-Century Capitalist Revolution* (1952).
15. BERLE, A. A. and MEANS, G., *The Modern Corporation and Private Property* (1934).
16. BERTRAM, G. C. L., *Population Trends and the World's Biological Resources*, Eugenics Society (1949).

271

17. BEVERIDGE, LORD, Valedictory Address, The Place of the Social Sciences in Human Knowledge, *Politica* (Sept., 1938).
18. BEVERIDGE, LORD, *Full Employment in a Free Society* (1944).
19. BLACKETT, P. M. S., Presidential Address, British Association (1957).
20. BOHR, K. A., Investment Criteria for Manufacturing Industries in Underdeveloped Countries, *The Review of Economics and Statistics* (May, 1954).
21. BOSWELL, J., *Life of Samuel Johnson* (1791).
22. BRITISH ASSOCIATION FOR THE ADVANCEMENT OF SCIENCE, *Report of Committee on Scientific Research on Human Institutions* (1943).
23. BROWN, A. J., Inflation and the British Economy, *E.J.* (Sept., 1958).
24. BROWN, J. A. C., *Social Psychology of Industry* (1954).
25. BROWN, W., *Exploration in Management* (Foreword by E. L. Trist) (1960).
26. BRUNI, L., *Aspetti Strutturali delle Industrie Italiane* (1961).
27. BURNHAM, J., *The Managerial Revolution* (1941).
28. BURNS, A. F., *The Frontiers of Economic Knowledge* (1954).
29. BURNS, A. R., *Comparative Economic Organization* (1955).
30. CAIRNCROSS, A., *Introduction to Economics* (1944).
31. CALDER, R., The Mathematics of Hunger, *J.R.S.S.*, Part 3 (1962).
32. CARR-SAUNDERS, Sir A., FLORENCE, P. S. and PEERS, A., *Consumers' Co-operation in Great Britain* (1938).
33. CARTER, C. F. and WILLIAMS, B. R., *Investment in Innovation* (1958).
34. CARTER, C. F. and WILLIAMS, B. R., The Characteristics of Technically Progressive Firms, *J.I.E.* (March, 1959).
35. CATLIN, G. E. G., Systematic Politics, *Elementa Politica et Sociologica* (1962).
36. CHARLES, ENID, *The Changing Size of the Family in Canada. Census of Canada* (1948).
37. CHENERY, H. B. and BRUNO, M., Development Alternatives in an Open Economy. The Case of Israel, *E.J.* (March, 1962).
38. CLAPHAM, Sir J., Of Empty Economic Boxes, *E.J.* (Sept., 1922).
39. CLARK, COLIN, *The Conditions of Economic Progress* (1951).
40. CLARK, COLIN, *The Economics of 1960* (1942).
41. CLARK, COLIN, New Light on Population, *Listener* (26th March, 1953).
42. COALE, A. J., Population Growth (A Review), *Science* (22nd Sept., 1961).
43. COPEMAN, G. H., *Leaders of British Industry* (1957).
44. CUMPER, G. E., Tourist Expenditure in Jamaica 1958, *Social and Economic Studies* (Sept., 1959).

45. Davison, J., Florence, P. S., Gray, Barbara, and Ross, N. S., *Productivity and Economic Incentives* (1958).
46. Dean, J., *Managerial Economics* (1950).
47. Edwards, R. S. and Townsend, H., *Business Enterprise* (1958).
48. England and Wales, *Preliminary Reports*, Census of Population (1951), (1961).
49. England and Wales, *Industry Tables*, Census of Population (1951).
50. Evely, R. and Little, I. M. D., *Concentration in British Industry* (1960).
51. Firth, R., *Elements of Social Organization* (1951).
52. Fisher, A. G. B., *The Clash of Progress and Security* (1935).
53. Fisher, G. R., Some Factors Influencing Share Prices, *E.J.* (March, 1961).
54. Fisher, R. M. (Ed.), *The Metropolis in Modern Life* (1955).
55. Flew, A., The Structure of Malthus's Population Theory, *Australian Journal of Philosophy* (May, 1957).
56. Florence, Lella S., *Progress Report on Birth Control* (1956).
57. Florence, P. S., *Economics of Fatigue and Unrest* (1924).
58. Florence, P. S., *Over-Population, Theory and Statistics* (1926).
59. Florence, P. S., *Economics and Human Behaviour* (1927).
60. Florence, P. S., *The Statistical Method in Economics and Political Science* (1929).
61. Florence, P. S., *Uplift in Economics* (American Edition, *Sin and Sociology*) (1929).
62. Florence, P. S., A Statistical Contribution to the Theory of Women's Wages, *E.J.* (March, 1931).
63. Florence, P. S., *Logic of Industrial Organization* (1933).
64. Florence, P. S., The Method and Content of Political Science, *Proceedings of the Aristotelian Society* (1934).
65. Florence, P. S., An Index of Working-Class Purchasing Power in Great Britain 1929–35, *Journal of Political Economy* (Oct., 1936).
66. Florence, P. S., Science and the Social Relations of Industry, *Sociological Review* (Jan., 1939).
67. Florence, P. S., The Selection of Industries suitable for Dispersion into Rural Areas, *J.R.S.S.*, Part II (1944).
68. Florence, P. S., The Statistical Analysis of Joint Stock Company Control, *J.R.S.S.*, Part I (1947).
69. Florence, P. S., *Investment, Location and Size of Plant* (1948).
70. Florence, P. S., *Labour* (1948).
71. Florence, P. S., Patterns in Recent Social Research, *The British Journal of Sociology* (Sept., 1950).
72. Florence, P. S., *Logic of British and American Industry* (1953).
73. Florence, P. S., *Industry and the State* (1957).
74. Florence, P. S., The Reward for Risk-bearing by Shareholders in Large Companies, *J.I.E.* (May, 1957).

75. FLORENCE, P. S., New Measures of the Growth of Firms, *E.J.* (June, 1957).
76. FLORENCE, P. S., A Note on the Ratio of Staff to Wage-earners *E.J.* (Sept., 1957).
77. FLORENCE, P. S., Tests of the Validity of Some Stock Exchange Folk-lore, *Three Banks Review* (March, 1958).
78. FLORENCE, P. S., *Ownership, Control and Success of Large Companies* (1961).
79. FLORENCE, P. S., *Post-war Investment, Location and Size of Plant* (1962).
80. FLORENCE, P. S., *The Future of the Conurbations* (Town-planning Institute, 1963).
81. FLORENCE, P. S., Economia Realistica e Problemi del-l'Industria Britannica attuale, *La Scuola in Azione* (1963).
82. FLORENCE, P. S., Basic English for the Social Sciences (in *Basic English as an International Language for Science*) (Evans Bros., 1963).
83. FREUD, S., *Group Psychology*, translated J. Strachey (1959).
84. GALBRAITH, K., *American Capitalism* (1952).
85. GLAISYER, JANET, BRENNAN, T., FLORENCE, P. S. and RITCHIE, W., *County Town* (*A Survey of Worcester*) (1946).
86. GLASS, D. V. How many can climb the Social Ladder? *Listener* (5th April, 1951).
87. GLASS, D. V., Population Prospects and their Implications (contributed to *Hunger*) (British Association, 1961).
88. GOODRICH, C. *et al.*, *Migration and Economic Opportunity* (1936).
89. GORDON, R. A., *Business Leadership in the Large Corporation* (1945).
90. GRAHAM, B. and DODD, D. L., *Security Analysis* (1951).
91. HAGUE, D., Economic Theory and Business Behaviour, *Review of Economic Studies* (May, 1949).
92. HALL, R. and HITCH, C. H., Price Theory and Business Behaviour, *Oxford Economic Papers* (1939).
93. HANEY, L. H., *Business Organization and Combination* (1913).
94. HENDERSON, SIR H., *Supply and Demand* (1922).
95. HIMES, N. E., *Medical History of Contraception* (1936).
96. HOBSON, J. A., *Evolution of Capitalism*, rev. ed. (1916).
97. HOOVER, E. M. and VERNON, P., *Anatomy of a Metropolis* (1959).
98. HOSELITZ, B. F., *Sociological Aspects of Economic Growth* (1960).
99. HUTCHISON, T. W., *The Significance and Basic Postulates of Economic Theory* (1938).
100. INTERNATIONAL LABOUR ORGANIZATION, The Size of Industrial Establishments, *I.L.R.* (Oct., 1955).
101. INTERNATIONAL LABOUR ORGANIZATION, Incidence of Industrial Disputes, *I.L.R.* (Sept., 1956).
102. JAQUES, E., *Measurement of Responsibility* (1956).
103. KATONA, G. T., *Psychological Analysis of Economic Behaviour* (1951).

104. KAY, H. D., What Limits Food Production, in *Hunger* (British Association, 1961).
105. KERR, C., Changing Social Structures, in Moore and Feldman, *Labor Commitment and Social Change in Developing Areas* (1960).
106. KERR, C. and SIEGEL, A., The Interindustry Propensity to Strike, in *Industrial Conflict*, Ed. Kornbaurer, Dubin and Ross (1954).
107. KEYNES, DR. J. N., *Scope and Method of Political Economy*, 4th ed. (1917).
108. KEYNES, LORD, *A Treatise on Money* (1930).
109. KEYNES, LORD, *The General Theory of Employment, Interest and Money* (1936).
110. KILBRIDGE, M. D., Statistical Indicators of the Continuing Effectiveness of Wage Incentives, *J.I.E.* (Nov., 1960).
111. KUZNETS, S., Toward a Theory of Economic Growth, in Lekachman, *National Policy for Economic Welfare at Home and Abroad* (1955).
112. KUZNETS, S., *Notes on the Study of Economic Growth*, "*Items*" (Social Science Research Council, 1959).
113. LABOUR, MINISTRY OF, Earnings of Administrative, etc. Employees, *Gazette* (Sept., 1960).
114. LABOUR, MINISTRY OF, Payments by Results, *Gazette* (Aug., 1961).
115. LABOUR, MINISTRY OF, *Gazette*, Monthly Estimates.
116. LABOUR, MINISTRY OF, Membership of Trade Unions—1960, *Gazette* (Dec., 1961).
117. LAVINGTON, F., *The English Capital Market* (1921).
118. LEKACHMAN, R., The Non-Economic Assumptions of J. M. Keynes, in *Common Frontiers of the Social Sciences*, ed. Komarovsky (1957).
119. LENIN, V. I., The Teachings of Karl Marx 1914, *A Handbook of Marxism* (1936).
120. LENIN, V. I., Imperialism 1917, *A Handbook of Marxism* (1936).
121. LEWIS, A., *The Theory of Economic Growth* (1955).
122. LINTON, D. L., Population and Food in the Tropical World, *The Advancement of Science* (Nov., 1961).
123. LONG, JOYCE, Labour Turnover under Full Employment, *Studies in Economics and Society* (University of Birmingham, 1951).
124. LYDALL, H. and LANSING, J. B., Distribution of Personal Income and Wealth, *American Economic Review* (March, 1959).
125. MACKINTOSH, A., *The Development of Firms* (1963).
126. MADGE, C., *War-Time Patterns of Saving and Spending* (1943).
127. MALTHUS, T. R., *Essay on the Principle of Population*, 2nd ed. (1803).
128. MARCH, J. G. and SIMON, H. A., *Organizations* (1958).
129. MARSHALL, A., *Principles of Economics*, 6th ed. (1910).

130. MARSHALL, A., *Industry and Trade* (1920).
131. MARX, K., *Capital* (English Translation ed. Engels) (1919).
132. MASON, E. (Ed.), *The Corporation in Modern Society* (1959).
133. MAYO, E., *The Social Problems of an Industrial Civilization* (1949).
134. McGREGOR, D. H., *Enterprise, Purpose and Profit* (1934).
135. McIVER, R. M. and PAGE, C. H., *Society* (1950).
136. MEANS, G., *Pricing Power and the Public Interest* (1962).
137. MEHTA, M. M., *Structure of Cotton-mill Industry of India* (1949).
138. MELMAN, S., *Dynamic Factors in Industrial Productivity* (1956).
139. MILWARD, G. E. (Ed.), *Large-scale Organization* (1950).
140. MITCHELL, W., Business Cycles, in *Business Cycles and Unemployment* (National Bureau of Economic Research, 1923).
141. MORGAN, T., Income Distribution in Ceylon, Puerto Rico, U.S., and U.K., *E.J.* (Dec., 1953).
142. MUMFORD, L., *The Culture of Cities* (1938).
143. MYRDAL, G., *An International Economy* (1956).
144. NORTHCOTT, C. H., *African Labour Efficiency Survey* (Colonial Office, 1949).
145. NURKSE, R., *Problems of Capital Formation in Underdeveloped Countries* (1952).
146. PARKINSON, C., Parkinson's Law (Original Statement), *The Economist* (Nov., 1955).
147. PARSONS, T., *The Structure of Social Action* (1937).
148. PENROSE, EDITH, *Theory of the Growth of the Firm* (1959).
149. PIGOU, A. C., *The Economics of Welfare* (1920).
150. PRAIS, J. and HOUTHAKKER, O., *The Analysis of Family Budgets* (1955).
151. PREST, E. J., National Income of the United Kingdom 1870–1946, *E.J.* (March, 1948).
152. RAMANADHAM, V. V., Certain Aspects of the Industrial Structure of India, *J.I.E.* (June, 1958).
153. REDDAWAY, W. B., *The Development of the Indian Economy* (1962).
154. REDDAWAY, W. B., The Economics of Underdeveloped Countries, *E.J.* (March, 1963).
155. RICARDO, D., *Principles of Political Economy and Taxation* (1817).
156. ROBERTS, B. C., *National Wages Policy in War and Peace* (1958).
157. ROBERTSON, SIR D., *The Control of Industry* (1927).
158. ROBERTSON, SIR D., Increasing Returns and the Representative Firm, *E.J.* (March, 1930).
159. ROBINSON, E. A. G., *Structure of Competitive Industry* (1931).
160. ROBINSON, E. A. G., The Changing Structure of the British Economy, *E.J.* (Sept., 1954).
161. ROBINSON, E. A. G. (Ed.), *The Economic Consequences of the Size of Nations* (1961).
162. ROBINSON, JOAN, Imperfect Competition Revisited, *E.J.* (Sept., 1953).
163. ROBINSON, JOAN, *Economic Philosophy* (1962).

164. ROETHLISBURGER, F. J. and DICKSON, W. J., *Management and the Worker* (1939).
165. ROSENBLUTH, G., *Concentration in Canadian Manufacturing Industries* (1957).
166. ROSKILL, O., *Who Owns Whom?* (1959).
167. ROSTOW, W. W., *The Process of Economic Growth* (1953).
168. ROSTOW, W. W., *The Stages of Economic Growth* (1959).
169. RUSSELL, LORD, *The Analysis of Matter* (1927).
170. SARGANT, W. L., *Recent Political Economy* (1867).
171. SAUNDERS, C., Consumption of Raw Materials in the United Kingdom, 1851–1950, *J.R.S.S.* (Part III, 1952).
172. SCHUMPETER, J., *The Theory of Economic Development* (1934).
173. SMITH, A., *Wealth of Nations* (1776).
174. SMYTH, R. L., Economics for the Uninitiated, *The Advancement of Science* (May, 1961).
175. STEINDL, J., *Small and Big Business* (1945).
176. STRACHEY, ALIX, *The Unconscious Motives of War* (1957).
177. STYKOS, J. M., *Family and Fertility in Puerto Rico* (1955).
178. SUKHATME, P. V., The World's Hunger and Future Needs in Food Supplies, *J.R.S.S.* (Part IV, 1961).
179. TAWNEY, R. H., *Equality* (1931).
180. TEW, B. and HENDERSON, R. E., *Studies in Company Finance* (1959).
181. TROUGHTON, F., The Teaching Concerning Cost Functions in Introductory Economics, *J.I.E.* (March, 1963).
182. U.K. CENSUS OF PRODUCTION, *Summary Tables* (1951, unless otherwise stated).
183. UNITED NATIONS, *Demographic Yearbooks*.
184. UNITED NATIONS, *Patterns of Industrial Growth*.
185. UNITED NATIONS, *Statistical Year Books*.
186. U.S. FEDERAL TRADE COMMISSION, Divergence between Plant and Company Concentration (1950).
187. U.S. FEDERAL TRADE COMMISSION, Report on Changes in Concentration (1954).
188. U.S. NATIONAL RESOURCES PLANNING BOARD, *Industrial Location and National Resources* (1943).
189. U.S. PUBLIC HEALTH SERVICE, *Bulletin 106, Comparison of an Eight-hour Plant and a Ten-hour Plant* (1920).
190. U.S.S.R. ECONOMY, *A Statistical Abstract* (1957).
191. VEBLEN, T., *The Theory of the Leisure Class* (1899).
192. VEBLEN, T., *The Theory of Business Enterprise* (1904).
193. VEBLEN, T., *Engineers and the Price System* (1923).
194. VILLARD, H., Some Notes on Population and Living Levels, *Review of Economics and Statistics* (May, 1955).
195. VILLARD, H., *Economic Performance* (1959).
196. WALKER, G., Road and Rail Competition, *E.J.* (June, 1933).
197. WALLAS, G., *Human Nature in Politics* (1916).
198. WEST MIDLAND GROUP, *English County (Herefordshire)* (1943).

199. WEST MIDLAND GROUP, *Conurbation (Birmingham and the Black Country)* (1948).
200. WHEELWRIGHT, E. L., *Ownership and Control of Australian Companies* (1957).
201. WHYTE, W. H., *The Organization Man* (1957).
202. WINSTEN, C. and HALL, MARGARET, The Measurement of Economies of Scale, *J.I.E.* (July, 1961).
203. WOOLF, L., *After the Deluge* (1931).
204. WOOTTON, LADY, *The Social Foundations of Wage Policy* (1954).
205. WRIGHT, N. C., The Current Food Supply Situation and Present Trends, in *Hunger* (British Association, 1961).
206. YOUNG, ALLYN, Increasing Returns and Economic Progress, *E.J.* (Dec., 1928).
207. ZIPF, G. K., *Human Behaviour and the Principle of Least Effort* (1949).

Additional Books for 1960–8, and the Anglo-American Edition

208. ANDREWS, P. W. S., *On Competition in Economic Theory* (1964).
209. BAIN, J. S., *International Differences in Industrial Structure* (1966).
210. BAUMOL, W. J., *Business Behavior, Value and Growth* (1959).
211. BLAIR, J. M., Administered Prices. A Phenomenon in Search of a Theory, *American Economic Review* (May, 1959).
212. CAVE, R., *American Industry, Structure, Conduct, Performance* (1967).
213. EMERY, F. E. and OESER, O. A., *Information, Decision and Action* (1958).
214. FARRELL, M. J., On the Structure of the Capital Market, *E.J.* (Dec., 1962).
215. FLORENCE, P. S., *Visual Analysis Series; Atlas of Economic Structure and Policies* (1969).
216. FUCHS, V., Determinants in the Redistribution of Manufacturing in the U.S. since 1925, *Review of Economics and Statistics* (May, 1962, pp. 167 ff.).
217. GAINSBURGH, M. R., *Economic Growth in the Forces Influencing the American Economy* (1965).
218. GALBRAITH, J. K., The Language of Economics, *The Advancement of Science* (May, 1963).
219. GALBRAITH, J. K., *The New Industrial State* (1967).
220. GORT, M., *Diversification and Integration in American Industry* (1962).
221. GRANICK, D., *The European Executive* (1962).
222. HEFLEBOWER, R., Toward a Theory of Industrial Markets and Prices, in Heflebower and Stocking, *Readings in Industrial Organization and Public Policy* (1958).
223. HIGGINS, B., *Economic Development* (Edition 1968).
224. KAPLAN, A. D. H., DIRLAM, J. B., and LANZILLOTTI, R. F., *Pricing in Big Business* (1967).
225. KISER, C. F. (Ed.), *Research in Family Planning* (1962).

226. LARNER, R., Ownership and Control in the 200 Largest Nonfinancial Corporations 1929 and 1963. *American Economic Review* (September, 1966).
227. LUPTON, T., *On the Shop Floor* (1963).
228. LYON, L. S., WATKINS, M. W. and ABRAMSON, V., *Government and Economic Life* (1939).
229. MARCUS, M., Firms Exit Rates and their Determinants. *J.I.E.* (November, 1967).
230. MARRIS, R., *The Economic Theory of Managerial Capitalism* (1964).
231. MASON, E. S., The Apologetics of Managerialism, *Journal of Business of the University of Chicago* (January, 1958).
232. MYRDAL, G., *Asian Drama* (1968).
233. PARKER, S. R., BROWN, R. V., CHILD, J. and SMITH, M. A., *Sociology of Industry* (1967).
234. SANDS, S. S., Changes in Scale of Production in U.S. Manufacturing Industries, *The Review of Economics and Statistics* (November, 1961).
235. SHEPHERD, W. G., Changes in British Industrial Concentration 1951–58, *Oxford Economic Papers* (March, 1961).
236. *U.S. Census of Manufactures* (1963 unless otherwise stated).
237. *U.S. Enterprise Statistics.*
238. U.S. SENATE, Hearings before the Sub-committee on Monopoly and Anti-Trust, 1964–68.
239. *U.S. Statistical Abstract* (1966, unless otherwise stated).
240. *U.S. Survey of Current Business Input and Output Tables* (November, 1964; October, 1965)
241. U.S. Temporary National Economic Committee.
242. WOODWARD, JOAN, *Industrial Organization, Theory and Practice* (1965).

U

INDEX

NUMBERS in brackets (placed before the page references) refer to the Bibliography, pp. 271–9.
All numbers in the bibliography are indexed, under the authors' names, even though only the
number, not the name, is mentioned in the text.
Particular industries in the manufacturing "sector" are not indexed but whole sectors are, e.g.
agriculture, banking, building, as contrasted with manufacturing.

282
INDEX

Construction, *see* Building
Consumer demand, 45, 102
Consumer expenditure, 165–6, 263–4
Consumer sovereignty, 45–6, 102–3
Consumption function, 235
Contraceptives, 217–20
Control, 134–61
  divorce of ownership from, 148–9
  market, 23–4
  pyramiding of, 142
  span of, 140
Conurbations, 65, 70–3, 75–6, 86–7, 115, 164–5, 228
Co-operative movement, 116, 140, 255,
Co-option, 146
Copeman, G. H., (43), 144
Corporation, *see* Company
Costs, analysis of, 108, 226
Cumper, G. E., (44), 190

Davison, J. P., (45), 48, 127–31
Dean, Joel, (46), 109
Death-rate, 37, 134
  see also Public hygiene
Deciles, 35
Decongestion, 82, 85–6
Delegation of authority, 109, 140
Demand, 45, 102
  income-elasticity of, 46
Democracy, 231–2, 256
  Jeffersonian, 254
Demography, 64, 201, 227
Demonstration effect, 236
Depersonalization, 115–16, 132–3
Deployment, 46
  see also Mobility
Depressed areas, 85–6, 169
Development—
  conflicting forces in, 61–4
  economic trends in, 1–28
  limits to, 199–208
  sociological trends in, 28–34
Dickson, W. J., (164), 122, 243
Directors—
  Board of, 142, 146–51
  guinea-pig, 153
  interlocking, 142, 153
  motives of, 114–15
  shareless, 148–9
Dirlam, J. B., (224), xiii, 135, 156
Discipline, social, 167
Disclosure, rules of, 95,
Diversification, 47–8, 62, 66–7, 82–3, 231
  measures of, 104–6
  see also Integration
Dividends, 138, 152–5
Dodd, D. L., (90), 152
Domestic service, 39, 52
Douglas, P., 240
Drücker, P., 123,
Duncan, J. C., 262
Durability, 156, 265–7, *see also* Perishability

Earnings, 55, 97, 98, 101, 127–8
Ecology, 228, 233–5
Econometrics, xi, 155–61, 194, 197–8, 240
Economic man, x, 54, 123, 126, 149–50, 153–4, 242
Economics, 225–35

Economies—
  capitalist, 3, 22–3, 31–2, 61, 134
  communist, 23, 31, 103, 157–8
  external, 30, 78, 81, 104
  internal, 104, 187
  pull-out, take-back, 191
  self-sustaining, 20
  through-putting, 18–20, 169, 191
Education, 8, 37, 180, 196
  obstacles to, 202–3, 208
Edwards, P. S., (47), 158
Elite, 197, 203, 211, 253
Emery, F. E., (213), 167
Empire building, 16
Employment, full, *see* Unemployment, reduction of,
Engel's Law, 18, 45–6, 165, 240
England and Wales, Census of Population, (48), (49)
Entrepreneur, 12, 15, 138 (def.), 143–4
  motivation of, 112–13, 228
  risk bearing of, 31, 71, 108-10, 112–13, 137
Equilibrium, 144–5, 251
Ergological interpretation, 28, 62, 81, 101, 157, 261
Ergological process, 32, 63, 71, 81, 101, 106, 153, 255
Evely, R., (50), 93–4, 147, 157
Exports, 17, 18, 193

Families, extended, 36, 41
Family budgets, 18, 45
Family business, 143–4
Farmers, independence of, 168, 252
Farming, subsistence, 41, 168, 200, 210
Farrell, M. J., (214), xi
Fashion, 31, 103
Fatigue, 49, 108, 121, 125, 132
Fayol, H., 247
Feasibility, 69–70, 83–5, 192, 198, 221, 228
Feather-bedding, 193
Federations, 175
Fetish, 249
Feudalism, 213
Finance, 72, 73, 100
Financiers, 33, 144
Firms—
  growth of, 2, 63
  motives for expanding, 109–10
  multi-plant, 16, 93–4, 264
  size of, 57, 91, 94–5, 106–7, 116, 265
Firth, R., (51), 234
Fisher, A. G. B., (52), 9
Fisher, G. R., (53), 154
Fisher, R. M., (54), 72, 78
Flew, A., (55), 219
Florence Effect, 78, 80, 103, 241
Florence, Lella S., (56), 220
Florence, P. Sargant, (32), (45), (57–9), (61–8), (70–1), (74–7), (80–2), 6, 40, 48–51, 72–3 78, 84–6, 97, 108, 117–22, 126–31, 169, 179, 209–11, 216, 219, 226, 241, 244, 252–7
  Industry and the State, (73), 32, 49, 210, 212, 252, 256
  Investment, Location and Size of Plant, (69), 10, 14, 25, 67, 88, 97, 240, 261

Logic of British and American Industry, (72), 10, 16, 24, 26, 46, 53, 67, 79, 81, 86, 98–9, 103, 106, 110–14, 144–5, 190, 237, 246
Ownership, Control and Success of Large Companies, (78), 10, 135, 143, 147–53
Post-war Investment, Location and Size of Plant, (79), 67, 80, 90, 91, 97, 102, 240
The Statistical Method in Economics and Political Science, (60), 21, 74, 141, 176, 238, 243–250
Visual Analysis Series: Atlas of Economic Structure and Policies, (215), 48, 67, 70, 125,
Fluctuations, 85, 99, 137, 267
  see also Slump, Trade Cycle
Follett, Mary P., 247
Foods and drug control, 158
Ford Motors, 93
Forecasting, 46, 72
Freud, S., (83), 124, 243
Fuchs, V., (216), 83
Function, use of term, 156, 237
Gainsburgh, M. R., (217), 3
Galbraith, J. K., (84), (218), (219), 46, 251
Gambling instinct, 138, 252
General Electric, 93
General Motors, 93
"Gentleman-ideal", 249
Geography, human, 201
Giffen, R., 241
Giffen Effect, 241
Glaisyer, Janet, (85), 84, 188
Glass, D. V., (86), (87), 57, 214
Golden handshake, 113
Golden rule, 154
Goldmark, Josephine, 125
Goodrich, C., (88), 78
Gordon, R. A., (89), 147, 149, 151
Gort, M.,(220), 104, 105
Government, industrial, 93, 138–46, 232–3, 236, 246–7
Gradability, 21
Graham, B., (90), 152
Granick, D., (221), 145, 247
Grant, A. T. K., 147
Gray, Barbara, (45), 48
Green belt, 66
Green hands, turnover, 117
Gresham's Law, 140
Group behaviour, 123, 130, 134
Groups, non-competing, 56, 228
Growth of industries, 121
  see also Development

Hague, D., (91), 135
Haldane, J. B. S., 87
Hall, Margaret, (202), 245
Hall, R., (92), 135
Haney, L. H., (93), 141
Hawthorne Works, 122, 126, 204, 243
  see also Mayo
Heavy industries, 264
  see also Portability
Heflebower, (222), 30
Henderson, H. D., (94), 138
Henderson, R. F., (180), 147
Herd instinct, 249
Hierarchy—
  bureaucratic, 116
  definition of, 74